THE MAKING OF LUKE-ACTS

Henry J. Cadbury

*With a new introduction
by Paul N. Anderson*

HENDRICKSON
PUBLISHERS

Hendrickson Publishers, Inc.
P. O. Box 3473
Peabody, Massachusetts 01961-3473

The Making of Luke-Acts, second edition
ISBN 1-56563-453-5

This edition is published by the kind permission of the
estate of Henry J. Cadbury. © 1999 Hendrickson
Publishers, Inc. Foreword to the present edition © 1999
Paul N. Anderson.

First edition © 1927
Second edition © 1958 Henry J. Cadbury

Printed in the United States of America

First printing — April 1999

FOREWORD

More than two years ago, as I conducted my research on Henry J. Cadbury in the Haverford community, Howard Clark Kee recalled one of Cadbury's characteristic greetings: "Tell me Howard," Cadbury would say as their paths crossed at Brynn Mawr College, "what have you learned that I ought to know?" Apparently, Professor Kee was not the only one greeted in such a way. Donald Jones recalls being asked a similar question by Cadbury upon their first encounter at Earlham College. Having just completed a Ph.D. on Luke–Acts, Jones appropriately reversed the query back to Professor Cadbury: "I have been asking that question of you, sir, for the last three years."[1]

Of Cadbury's more than one-hundred and sixty published New Testament-related books and essays, and among his more than two hundred fifty reviews of New

[1] See Donald L. Jones, "The Legacy of Henry Joel Cadbury: Or What He Learned that We Ought to Know," in *Cadbury, Knox and Talbert: American Contributors to the Study of Acts* (ed. Mikeal C. Parsons and Joseph B. Tyson; Atlanta: Scholars Press, 1992), 28–36 (esp. 35f.). Margaret Hope Bacon also mentions Cadbury's asking a similar question of Kee in her excellent biography, *Let This Life Speak: The Legacy of Henry Joel Cadbury* (Philadelphia: University of Pennsylvania Press, 1987), 203. I am indebted to her for connecting me with Hendrickson Publishers. The Cadbury family must also be thanked for releasing the rights to this book, as should the Haverford Quaker Library and George Fox University for granting me a Gest Fellowship and sabbatical and summer research grants, respectively.

Testament books,[2] it is fair to say that his most influential contributions lay in the field of Luke–Acts, and among his many contributions in that field the most significant single work is his ground-breaking book, *The Making of Luke–Acts*. Following on the heels of several more technical treatments of Luke and Acts,[3] this work drew together many of Cadbury's views in an exceptional synthesis. Bringing together considerations of underlying sources and their transmission, the distinctive functions of vari-

---

[2] See the bibliographies at the end of the collection of Cadbury's New Testament essays I am gathering (Trinity Press International, forthcoming). Included also are bibliographies of works on Cadbury and reviews of his New Testament works by others.

[3] "Studies in the Style and Literary Method of Luke" (his 1914 Harvard Ph.D. dissertation, later published as *Style and Literary Method of Luke* (Harvard Theological Studies 6; 2 vols. Cambridge, Mass: Harvard University Press, 1920 [repr. New York: Kraus Reprints, 1969]); "A possible Case of Lukan Authorship," *Harvard Theological Review* 10 (1917): 237–44; "Luke—Translator or Author?" *American Journal of Theology* 24 (1920): 436–55; "The Purpose Expressed in Luke's Preface," *The Expositor* 8 (21, 1921): 431–41. Four articles from a single work merit notice: "The Composition and Purpose of Acts: The Greek and Jewish Traditions of Writing History," 7–29 (with the editors), "The Identity of the Editor of Luke and Acts: The Tradition," 209–64, "The Identity of the Editor of Luke and Acts: Subsidiary Points," 349–62 (co-authored with the editors), "Appendix C—Commentary on the Preface of Luke," 489–510, in *Beginnings of Christianity. Part I: The Acts of the Apostles*. Vol. 2 (ed. F. J. Foakes Jackson and Kirsopp Lake; London: Macmillan, 1922); "The Knowledge Claimed in Luke's Preface," *The Expositor* 8 (24, 1922): 401–20; "The Relative Pronouns in Acts and Elsewhere," *Journal of Biblical Literature* 42 (1923): 150–57. Two other text-critical essays in *Beginnings of Christianity* are notable: "Collation of the Peshitto Texts of Acts," 291–375, and "Collation of the Vulgate Text of Acts," 276–90, in *Beginnings of Christianity: Part I: The Acts of the Apostles*. Vol. 3 (ed. James R. Ropes; London: Macmillan, 1926). See also "Lexical Notes on Luke–Acts. I," *Journal of Biblical Literature* 44 (1925): 214–27; "Lexical Notes on Luke–Acts. II, 'Recent Arguments for Medical Language,' " and "Lexical Notes on Luke–Acts. III, Luke's Interest in Lodging," *Journal of Biblical Literature* 45 (1926): 190–209 and 305–22. Many others, of course, appear later.

ous literary forms, parallels with ancient literature, disparate linguistic issues, and factors related to the personality and purpose of the author, Cadbury produced what has become something of a classic in the field. The longevity of the study is suggested by Cadbury's modest but telling reflections on the appearance of the second edition. After the first edition had evoked an entire generation of discussion, he commented in the preface to the second:

> For a book like this to be reprinted after thirty years, and to be reprinted without thorough rewriting, is unusual. The only justification is that such an analysis of the process by which this double unit of the New Testament came into being has continued to seem to myself and others a useful study and that no other work has appeared in the interval covering the same ground. . . . There have been commentaries on Luke and, especially in this decade, on Acts. But all these studies, whether by myself or by others, have given little reason for reversing earlier judgments or resolving earlier uncertainties. Neither the Revised Standard Version nor the Dead Sea Scrolls have suggested any changes!

The same can be said after the next triad of decades. An interesting fact about *The Making of Luke–Acts* is that while the work comes across as less erudite than many of Cadbury's earlier treatments, it seems to have made a more substantial impact than many of his more technical works.[4] Especially if taken together with its sequel, *The*

---

[4] For instance, when the volume appeared, the *London Times* (Literary Supplement, Nov. 24, 1927, p. 850) observed, "The work before us is not primarily designed for scholars. It is addressed to the more general circle of those who are interested in New Testament problems but who have not the equipment to appreciate a more technical treatment. But none will read it with deeper interest than Professor Cadbury's fellow-workers, who will be best able to appraise the labour, skill and originality which he has brought to his task." Nearly fifty years later, Ward Gasque appraises *The Making of Luke–Acts* as "one of the most

Book of Acts in History, The Making of Luke–Acts is undoubtedly Cadbury's most enduring single contribution to
biblical studies. Even at its initial appearance, E. F. Scott
commented about the range of this work's appeal:

> He writes in an interesting manner, and his argument
> at most points can easily be followed by any intelligent
> reader. At times, perhaps, he has been unduly careful to
> make everything clear and simple; but no one who is
> acquainted with the subject can mistake the value of
> the book. There is more genuine scholarship in it than
> in nine-tenths of the ostentatiously learned books that
> are being written today about the New Testament. Its
> outstanding merit is that in every chapter it is the out-
> come of first-hand research.[5]

Several particular contributions of this important work
emerge for the reader. For one, Cadbury analyzes the Gospel
of Luke and Acts as a unified two-volume work—a sound
judgment, which was novel at the time. Regardless of varying ways of seeing the connection between the two books,
Cadbury's judgment has remained largely unchallenged over
the last several decades within Lukan scholarship. A simple
review of the number of recent books and articles on
"Luke–Acts" suggests the validity of this judgment.

The volume likewise contributes to our understanding
of Luke–Acts by demonstrating the value of considering
personal factors of authorial intent and procedure that
are based on linguistic and stylistic phenomena in the text
itself, rather than merely assuming certain qualities could
be attributed to the author. This approach has bothered
some readers because of Cadbury's reluctance to support
traditional views of authorship and to make "definitive

strikingly original studies of the Lucan writings ever conceived" (*A History of the Criticism of the Acts of the Apostles* [Peabody, Mass.:
Hendrickson, 1989], 185, note 65).

[5] E. F. Scott, "The Genesis of Luke–Acts," *Journal of Religion* 8
(1928): 285.

pronouncements."[6] A point here should be clarified. Cadbury, here and elsewhere, does not claim to know who the author was *not*. He simply raises questions about the extent to which the author can be identified and offers a more conservative approach, limiting himself to what can be known reliably from the texts themselves. Claiming the author's identity *cannot be known for certain,* however, is not the same as claiming that the view that Luke authored Luke–Acts is *known not to be true.* On the subtlety of this point, and ones like it, some interpreters on both sides of the issue have foundered. For Cadbury, greater reward is offered through "motive criticism," which analyzes why an author writes. Such attempts to recover an author's motives must concentrate, then, on the stylistic, rhetorical, linguistic, and narrative aspects of the writing itself. While such an approach may require painstaking care, it moves from the philological and linguistic phenomena in the text itself to draw inferences based on the data alone. In that sense, it infers no more, or less, than the text itself suggests.

Cadbury's impressive synthesis of form and source criticism enriches Luke–Acts study in a third way. As one of the first American scholars to introduce European views of form criticism to American biblical studies, Cadbury demonstrated the practical value of this interest by considering the history and function of Luke's material before it came to be used by Luke. Alongside this formal analysis, Cadbury applied form-critical observations to redaction and source analyses by showing how Luke's uses of earlier material were conditioned by the character of their form and function. In that sense, the evangelist was helped by sources, but he was also limited by them. From a broader source-critical perspective, since Cadbury's analysis of Luke's use of Mark and Q, the Two Document Hypothesis (that

---

[6] Ibid.

Matthew and Luke both used at least Mark and another source, Q) has become all the more firmly established in the minds of most New Testament scholars. The many similarities among the Synoptics, as pointed out by Cadbury, make it extremely difficult to explain the literary data any other way.

Finally, Cadbury's comparative work, identifying similarities and differences between Luke and ancient writers, affords the reader many insights into Luke's perspective, context, and historicity. Though comparisons and contrasts with the likes of Josephus raise questions of historicity in both directions, Cadbury lifts the discussion above apologetic interests in one text being "right" at the other's expense. He then relocates the focus on the interpretive and hermeneutical implications of the biblical renderings, which is where biblical interpretation is always most meaningful. In this and other explorations, Cadbury's pervasive fairness comes through. While Cadbury only occasionally engaged other scholars explicitly in his analysis (indeed, he saved that for his massive number of reviews and other essays), he did engage the text in the light of their works. This probably accounts for the long-range value of his work, over and above the life spans of hermeneutical trends and scholarly fashions.

What difference will the renewed accessibility of Cadbury's work have upon New Testament studies in the future? No one can tell for sure. If Cadbury's exceptional analysis of the Greek text, his sobriety of judgment, and his multileveled and interdisciplinary approaches to his material provide any pattern for future scholarship, the effect is certain to be positive. Indeed, Cadbury brings together the often disparate approaches of historical-critical, literary-rhetorical, and theological analyses into an impressive whole; but such is made possible only because of his intensive and extensive treatments of relevant texts and themes elsewhere.

If one were to ask of Henry Cadbury, along with Donald Jones, what he had learned that we ought to know, the answer would certainly begin with a fresh consideration of *The Making of Luke–Acts*. With the availability of this new printing, such is now possible!

PAUL N. ANDERSON

Yale Divinity School
New Year's Day 1999

PREFACE

The third evangelist came to be regarded by tradition as a portrait painter. He has himself been painted by medieval illuminators and artists and he still constitutes an attractive subject for portraiture. The following pages aim to recover some features of his character, to visualize the other factors which went into his noteworthy undertaking, to illustrate from his contemporaries the methods of composition that he employed, and so to give as clear, comprehensive and realistic a picture as possible of the whole literary process that produced Luke and Acts.

Such a purpose differentiates this volume from studies along conventional or more special lines. This is not an introduction, an apology or a commentary. Least of all is it a work of edification, though it is written with the conviction that the religious and moral value of the Scriptures often best becomes effective where an initial interest is awakened in the reality and naturalness of the historical background, whether of the events recorded or, as in this instance, of the creative literary performance.

It has been necessary to raise many of the technical questions of scholarly discussion and to express opinions about their solution (or insolubility), without supplying the fullness of evidence and argument that scholars themselves demand. Occasionally I have been able to refer to fuller presentations elsewhere, either by myself or by others. For the rest I have been content to suggest a general picture of the process of composition, without defending each of the details and without refuting or even mentioning opposite views, which, as I am well aware, exist in various quarters. Much, of course, is uncertain, but instead of dwelling on the debatable points and attempting to discover the slight differences of probability between well-balanced alternatives, I have had the advantage of being able to leave many of them where they belong, still *sub judice.*

This applies particularly to two questions so often in the foreground of controversy: Was the author Luke? Is his record accurate? The present examination bears from time to time on these questions and should help to a proper attitude toward them, as I try to indicate in the last chapter, but it is not marshaled about these interests. It is sufficient here to focus attention merely on the history of the books' origin. Readers familiar with the usual path of approach may find in the difference a relief.

Because realistic description rather than argument was aimed at, profuse bibliographical references have been avoided. In referring to Luke's writings, chapter and verse are not regularly cited; some familiarity with Scripture, on the part of the reader, has been assumed. As scholars will recognize, I am indebted to various modern students of these writings, and I gladly acknowledge here my debt to them, including those with whom I disagree. I have tried to rely, however, mainly on my own prolonged and direct study of Luke and Acts, and to think my way through the problems that these books present. To read and digest all the literature available and constantly appearing on the manifold questions here treated would have left no time for independent study. To cite it in all its detail would have left no room for a continuous and readable exposition of the subject along more general lines.

If the reader should find any merits in this work, I hope he will attribute them to the influence of my colleagues in the theological faculties of Andover Seminary and Harvard University, and to the love of sound learning which, with the greatest variety of high personal achievement, they uniformly inspire. At the close of seven years of happy association this volume is appropriately dedicated to them out of filial and fraternal affection.

HENRY J. CADBURY

Bryn Mawr College,
Pennsylvania,
October, 1926.

PREFACE TO THE SECOND EDITION

For a book like this to be reprinted after thirty years, and to be reprinted without thorough rewriting, is unusual. The only justification is that such an analysis of the process by which this double unit of the New Testament came into being has continued to seem to myself and others a useful study and that no other work has appeared in the interval covering the same ground. Furthermore I have not felt called upon to make revisions or additions. With the correction of a dozen misprints and a few other items this edition is photographically reprinted from the first.

There have of course been since 1926 many studies in parts of the field, studies in the synoptic problem, on form criticism, on the Semitic element in the language of the author, and other matters; but in many areas almost no independent investigations have appeared. Yet those areas have not been protected by any "No Trespassing" sign. There have been commentaries on Luke and, especially in this decade, on Acts. But all these studies, whether by myself or by others, have given little reason for reversing earlier judgments or resolving earlier uncertainties. Neither the Revised Standard Version nor the Dead Sea Scrolls have suggested any changes!

The reader should recognize that to some extent the book is "dated". This is less evident in the views expressed in the text than in the references to "recent" books. The sparing bibliographical notes cite nothing published since the first quarter of the present century. It would have been possible now to refer to more recent valuable essays, such as those by Martin Dibelius on The First Christian Historian and The Speeches in Acts in his *Studies in the Acts of the Apostles*, 1956, previously published separately and also collectively in German, by B. S. Easton on *The Purpose of Acts*, published by S.P.C.K. in 1936 and reprinted with other material in 1954; or on the eschatology of Luke by H. Conzelmann.

It may help the reader place this 1927 publication in past history to remind him how many other books in English since then have taken cognizance of form criticism or have employed the convenient hyphenated expression "Luke-Acts". My purpose and self-limitation in writing it were sufficiently defined above in the original preface. In *The Book of Acts in History*, 1955, I have published a partial sequel or companion.

HENRY J. CADBURY

Haverford,
Pennsylvania.
May, 1958.

CONTENTS

PART III THE PERSONALITY OF THE AUTHOR

PART IV THE PURPOSE OF THE AUTHOR

THE MAKING OF LUKE-ACTS

CHAPTER I

LUKE-ACTS: ITS INTEREST AND UNITY

An attempt to bring fresh light on part of the New Testament requires no apology. Whatever else one may think of that volume, it is at least the most widely distributed of publications. Its circulation in our generation has already reached many million copies per annum. Month after month the New Testament in all its forms, with additions or subtractions, invariably heads all lists of best sellers, fiction or non-fiction. Doubtless it is not always read when received, nor heard when read, nor heeded when heard. It obtains, nevertheless, a vast amount of attention of all kinds throughout Christendom.

The principal contributor to this noteworthy collection is, as probably few people realize, not one of the more familiar names, but the author of Luke and Acts. These two volumes together occupy more than one quarter of the New Testament. Neither the thirteen epistles of Paul nor the five writings which commonly bear the name of John, even if in either case they should be assigned to a single author, amount in bulk to the total of Luke and Acts. In extent of his writings, therefore, as well as for their circulation, the third evangelist must be accounted one of the most important writers in history.

The pages of this writer, whom for convenience we may call by his traditional name Luke, are packed full of interest. The bulk of his writings is not due to mere diffuseness of style, but to the great range of his subject matter. Compared with Justin Martyr, the first Christian writer from whom more extensive writings have come down to us, Luke conveys to us vastly more of both information and thought. Indeed, few contemporary writers of history can compare with this author in variety, rapidity, condensation and wealth of detail. Tacitus perhaps is something like him, but Josephus and Dionysius and Polybius and Livy move more tediously and monotonously. Closest in this respect to Luke are the Gospels of Matthew and Mark, with whom indeed he shares so much of his material. But the loss of neither of them would reduce the amount of our information about Jesus as seriously as would the loss of Luke. This volume contains the largest part of the unique material in the synoptic gospels.

The Book of Acts is even more indispensable. No narratives parallel to it have survived. It is our sole record of the apostolic age. The other New Testament books only indirectly throw light on events in that most significant era. The Book of Acts, written independently of them, forms the background to their understanding, and it alone tells the story behind them. Even the extensive and self-revealing correspondence of Paul would leave his life and setting afloat for us in a sea of ignorance were it not for the succinct outline of his career sketched for us in Acts. The Book of Acts is the keystone linking the two major portions of the New Testament, the "Gospel" and the "Apostle," as the early Christians called them. To change the figure, the Book of Acts is the only bridge we have across the seemingly impassable gulf that separates Jesus from Paul, Christ from Christianity, the gospel of Jesus from the gospel about Jesus. Though the writings of Luke do not answer all the demands that our curiosity makes of them, it is only fair to recognize how much of interest they do supply us.

The present study does not aim to deal as such with the events narrated by this writer, but with an event of greater significance than many which he records—the making of this work itself. This production would be advertised by a modern publishing house as an event of epoch-making importance. And such indeed it was. It may be difficult sometimes to distinguish between the immediate effect of a deed and the effect of the knowledge of a deed. Historic facts work through the minds of those who know them as well as through the unrecorded chain of cause and effect in the unconscious processes of history. One can hardly exaggerate the difference for the history of Christianity caused by the fact that its beginnings were not left unrecorded for many centuries or even many decades. Unless one believes in an inerrant tradition and a supernatural church as organs of transmission, one can hardly suppose that much reliable information about Jesus would have been handed down through generations of unchecked oral repetition or even through the frequent celebration under indubitable apostolic succession of a meal held in remembrance of him. The ancient world perhaps recognized more than we do what the past owes to its recorders. "How many recorders of his deeds," cries Cicero, "does story say the great Alexander had with him. Yet he, when he stood at Sigeum by the tomb of Achilles, said: 'O fortunate youth, that thou hast found in Homer the herald of thy valor.' And truly; for unless that Iliad had been in existence, the same tomb that covered his body would have brought oblivion to his name." [1] One may safely say that many of the events narrated by Luke, if unrecorded, would have had slight and transient influence compared with their continuing effect upon generation

---

[1] Cicero *Pro Archia* x. 24. *Cf.* Harnack, *Acts of the Apostles,* pp. xix, 301: "If these heroes [Peter and Paul] had found no historian, it is highly probable that in spite of Marcion we should have had no New Testament."

after generation of his readers. This is one reason why their historicity is from the point of view of influence of so little importance. Their consequences have been dependent upon their being told more than upon their being true. Thus the writing of Luke-Acts takes rank with the great events of early Christian history.

In like manner the author of this work must be counted a person of importance alongside of his heroes. It is well known to students of history that every historical writing supplies information of two kinds: what the author tells of the past and what he unconsciously reveals of the present. In greater or less degree every writing reveals the writer. Old Testament scholars tell us that the Books of Chronicles give more fresh information of value about the author's age than about the age whereof he writes. Macaulay's *History of England* is perhaps a better history of Macaulay than of England. Who can tell whether the charm and fascination of Carlyle's *French Revolution* is due to the author's vigor or to the inherent dramatic interest of the events narrated?

So, in addition to the indispensable service to the student of Christian origins which Luke's writings render by what they describe, the revelation of the author's own personality and point of view must be reckoned as an historic contribution of the first importance. After this writer lets the curtain fall on Paul with the end of his work, our knowledge of early Christian history becomes almost extinguished for a generation. We have only pious traditions of apostolic martyrdom of uncertain value and post-apostolic writings of uncertain date and authorship. It is safe to say that no figure of this period is much clearer in our knowledge than the surviving biographer of Jesus and Paul. He does not intentionally bring his own personality into his writings; nevertheless it can in part be recovered from them. The method is tentative and the reconstructed portrait is so incomplete that many a modern

Christian will be tempted to say, in the words of the demon to the sons of Scaeva: "Jesus I know and Paul I know, but who are you?" But the more zealous seekers for knowledge will welcome any new light that a careful literary analysis of the writings of Luke can cast upon the obscure period in which they were written and upon their composer.

The inquiry into the origin of these writings is not a new one; indeed it has long been pursued, and recent study has especially devoted itself to these problems. The output of capable and suggestive books on Luke and Acts in the last twenty years only is very great and they have brought much new light and interest. The sources, the method and the personality and viewpoint of the writer are all considered in these studies. A review of the recent literature on the Book of Acts may at this point be instructive.

Of commentaries we have some of recent date which are most voluminous. In Germany two of the best are also quite brief, those of H. H. Wendt in the famous Meyer series (9th ed., 1913), and of Erwin Preuschen in Lietzmann's *Handbuch* (1912). Theodor Zahn, the learned conservative scholar, after a commentary on Luke (1913, 774 pages) and a very full editing of the text of Acts (1916, 400 pages), issued a lengthy commentary at the age of over eighty years (884 pages, 1919-21) at the same time that in France Alfred Loisy, the liberal critic, was publishing one of equal bulk (1920, 963 pages). Of recent monographs we may well begin with the series of Adolf von Harnack issued in German in 1906, 1908 and 1911, which were published in English, each shortly after its appearance, under the titles *Luke the Physician, The Acts of the Apostles,* and *The Date of the Acts and of the Synoptic Gospels,* and have had a wide influence on English scholarship. Harnack's colleagues at Berlin, specialists in other fields, have also brought to the subject their trained skill. Eduard Norden, the philologian, contributed in 1913 the far-reaching discussion called *Agnostos Theos*. Eduard Meyer, the historian, has reviewed the whole beginnings of Christianity, including an analysis of Acts as well as of the gospels (*Ursprung und Anfänge des Christentums, 3* vols., 1921-23). Julius Wellhausen, at Göttingen, the veteran Old Testament scholar, contributed after the manner of his comments on the gospels (including *Das Evangelium Lucae,* 1904) two series of notes on the Book of Acts (1914 and 1917). No less original or incisive in its brevity is the essay of another Semitist, C. C. Torrey of Yale, *The Date and Composition of Acts* (1916). In English there is appearing a kind of international composite work on Acts published in England and edited in America, of even more extensive dimensions. It is entitled *The Beginnings of Christianity* and includes the contributions of scholars of several countries and of differing points of view.[2]

These works and others like them all contribute to our

---

[2] Vols. I and II, Prolegomena, 1920-22, edited by F. J. Foakes Jackson and Kirsopp Lake, 480 and 539 pages. Even since these words were written the material increases in France and America. My colleague, Professor J. H. Ropes, has published a monumental work on the text of Acts (*The Beginnings of Christianity,* Vol. III, 1926, 784 pages). At the same time appeared the French commentary of E. Jacquier, which runs, introduction and notes, to the vast total of 1131 pages. On Luke there has appeared the first critical English commentary in thirty years by B. S. Easton (1926, 407 pages), and Loisy has issued as a companion volume to his Acts a characteristic treatment of the Gospel (1924, 600 pages). Two apologetic works on Acts slightly less recent should also be mentioned: W. M. Ramsay, *The Bearing of Recent Discovery on the Trustworthiness of the New Testament* (1915, 417 pages), mostly on Luke and Acts, and A. Wikenhauser, *Die Apostelgeschichte und ihr Geschichtswert* (1921, 457 pages), a Roman Catholic work noteworthy for its bibliographical completeness.

understanding of the making of Luke-Acts. But their scope is not identical with the present inquiry. Their ultimate interest is not the author and his times, but the subject matter of his history. His own interests are considered merely as they color or adulterate his story. He is someone to be allowed for, eliminated and discounted, not someone to be studied and appreciated for his own sake. His literary methods are examined in order that we may discover the earlier sources behind them, or the facts and personalities lying behind the sources. All this is significant and valuable, but when these studies are completed and even while they are going on there is still place for concurrent studies of the historian himself.

In another way the study of Luke's writings has been affected by the conventions of criticism. They have been usually dealt with as separate books, not as a single work. We may be thankful that the older study of Scripture as a collection of texts is giving way to its treatment as a collection of books. Even in popular study there is a recognition of the book as a proper unit. In the case of Luke-Acts and of some other compilations a further step is necessary—the substitution of the whole work as the unit for consideration and study. Through the conventions of Biblical scholarship, commentaries and introductions are written on each volume separately, and no amount of cross reference quite corrects the sense of isolation.

Professor Eduard Meyer, who complains of this separate treatment of Luke and Acts, says it is as unreasonable as though we treated as separate works the account concerning Tiberius in Tacitus' *Annals* and that concerning Claudius and Nero, or as if we divided the several decades of Livy, or separated the first part of Polybius (Books 1-29), in which he worked over older presentations of the subject, from the latter part (Books 30-40), where he arranged the material for the first time, working independently as one who lived at the time and participated in the events.

In each case the personality and individuality of the writer ought to be made central.   He adds that so far as he knows a treatment of the whole work as a unit—an edition and commentary—has never been undertaken.   It is perhaps significant that Friedrich Schleiermacher, who over a century ago projected a discussion of the writings of Luke, published only the First Part (1817; English Translation, 1825).

In any study of Luke and Acts, their unity is a fundamental and illuminating axiom.   Among all the problems of New Testament authorship no answer is so universally agreed upon as is the common authorship of these two volumes.   Each is addressed in its opening words to the same Theophilus, the second volume refers explicitly to the first, and in innumerable points of style the Greek diction of each shows close identity with the other.   Whatever their difference in subject matter and sources, each volume is in its present form the work of the same ultimate editor. If anything can be proved by linguistic evidence, this fact is proved by it.   The evidence has long been known and accepted.   The recent theory of Norden and Loisy which attributes not Acts but its principal source to the author of the Third Gospel does not square with the phenomena of the language.   Its sponsors apparently have not taken the uniformity of vocabulary sufficiently into account.   The unity belongs to the ultimate editor rather than to his matter.   It is he who has given to divergent materials such homogeneity in diction as is now revealed, in spite of some variations in style, from the beginning of Luke to the end of Acts.   As explaining the variations in style and in viewpoint and the other evidences of redaction which are alleged in support of different editorship for Acts, other solutions are more probable.

Even the recognition of the common authorship of Luke and Acts is not enough.   They are not merely two independent writings from the same pen; they are a single continuous work. Acts is neither an appendix nor an afterthought. It is probably an integral part of the author's original plan and purpose. To the modern English reader its opening words are misleading. The first account (τὸν πρῶτον λόγον) which they mention is not a "former treatise," but simply "volume one." The review of the preceding volume and the renewed address to Theophilus belong to the conventions of ancient writing. The second of Josephus's two books, *Against Apion*—to mention only one example—begins: "In the former book, my most honored Epaphroditus, I have shown our antiquity and confirmed its truth by the writings of the Phoenicians and Chaldeans and Egyptians," etc. The division of long works into rolls, like the modern division into volumes, was a matter of physical convenience and not an evidence of separate origin or publication, and the words which now give the impression of division were intended to mark the close association and continuation. Philo's essay, *That Every Good Person Is Free,* refers to a lost preceding volume: "Our former book, O Theodotus, was on the thesis that every base person is a slave." Occasionally, no doubt, independent works were addressed to the same patron and referred to one another in terms similar to the examples we have ·given, but without specific knowledge to that effect the presumption in such cases is that the two volumes are really a single work. The preface of Luke confirms rather than opposes this presumption.[3]

[3] There are reasons for supposing the preface of Luke specifically contemplates Acts as well as the gospel. See my articles in the *Expositor* for June, 1921, and December, 1922, and *The Beginnings of Christianity,* Vol. II, pp. 491 f. The unity and continuity of Luke and Acts deserve further discussion, since it is so often assumed or dogmatically affirmed that Acts is an afterthought. The arguments that are put forward, such as the slight differences between the vocabulary of the two books and between the farewell scenes of Luke xxiv and Acts i, permit of other explanations and do not seem to counterbalance the probability that we have here the usual two-volume work with a single general preface.

It is easy to understand how the early separation of the volumes took place. The first one corresponded in style and scope to a type of writing which preceded and followed it in the early church. With three other books of this class it came into a position of prominence in the esteem of the church and so passed into the New Testament canon. These four books, whatever their original name, came to be known collectively or individually by the word "gospel" (εὐαγγέλιον), and in varying order were always transmitted as a single group. The companion volume belonged to another category of Christian writings, memorabilia about the apostles. Possibly it was the earliest writing of that class. At any rate, we know of no earlier ones. Under the name of Acts (πράξεις) it had its later imitations or rivals, but this specimen alone was canonized. In the New Testament, therefore, it was severed from its companion volume, and its subsequent textual history as well as its canonical position was determined by other factors. It was oftener copied with the Catholic Epistles than with the gospels. This inherited separation is reinforced by the modern tendencies and misunderstandings to which reference has been made and needs explicit correction. Unfortunately the two writings do not enjoy in our Testaments even the suggestive advantage of juxtaposition, but are divided by the Fourth Gospel.

The two books of Luke need above all a common name. No doubt they once had such a name and were distinguishable as Book I and Book II. What that name was we cannot know; it perhaps contained none of the words "gospel," "acts," "Luke," or "apostles." To rechristen the work now, so as to suit both its contents and the bibliographical terms current to its writer and first readers, would be an interesting task, but the new title could scarcely be expected to supplant the older names. Sometimes when a book or associated books survived without author's name or title their identity or unity was indicated by newly adopted names. In classical literature some works suffered just such vicissitudes. Often the addressee, who was named in the text, was known, but the name of the author or the title or both had been lost, perhaps partly because they were not in the text or superscribed, but written if anywhere on a separate tag or on the back of the roll. In the first case they were known by the title, and an author was sometimes guessed for them, as (Longinus?) "On the Sublime." In the second case they were known by the author and addressee as Theophilus, *Ad Autolycum*. In the last case, which is that of Luke and Acts, though the title and author were sometimes conjectured, they were better designated by the addressee merely, as the *Ad Herennium* attributed to Cornificius and the little Christian apology, *Ad Diognetum*, long circulated with Justin Martyr's writings. Another analogy is suggestive for Luke's writings. Biblical books when divided were numbered, as the books of Samuel and Kings, which were named in the Greek Bible "Kingdoms I," "Kingdoms II," etc. If we applied these methods of nomenclature we should have for Luke and Acts *"Ad Theophilum I"* and *"Ad Theophilum II."* We may observe further among the customs of Biblical study that even entirely independent works were associated under a common name, as the four Books of the Maccabees. Conversely, books which formerly belonged together, but which have acquired separate names have been given a collective designation by modern scholars as the "Octateuch" or "Ezra-Nehemiah." Hyphenated compounds are not typographically beautiful or altogether congenial to the English language, but in order to emphasize the historic unity of the two volumes addressed to Theophilus the expression "Luke-Acts" is perhaps justifiable.

CHAPTER II

FACTORS IN COMPOSITION

"Of making many books," said the Preacher, "there is no end." But the multiplicity of the act, more obvious as it is in our day than it was two thousand years ago, should not conceal from us its complex character. That which is common is not always simple. In animal and plant life the most familiar processes are sometimes the most complicated. "The meanest flower that blows" suggests the most complicated emotions or the most subtle philosophical question, "what God and man is." How much more remarkable are the miracles of ordinary human thought and action! "What a piece of work is man!" And what a mechanism is the human brain in conscious or subconscious action. This is the machine that lies behind every human writing.

The naive appreciation of this miracle was expressed in the ancient world by the doctrine of inspiration. Authorship was a superhuman function. The poet or prophet was a man possessed, inspired by the Muses or the holy Spirit; hence the more than human genius that marked his writing. The modern world has lost much of the childish wonder of the past; it takes books for granted as it takes for granted the wonders of nature and of science. In a blase way it assumes that books write themselves as flowers grow or as watches are turned out by machinery. Instead of adopting either the ancient extreme or the modern one, it is possible for us to examine analytically the human factors of composition.

12

A special psychology of authorship [1] has never yet been written, but it is evident what the principal headings of such a textbook would be. The process of composition falls exclusively in neither the conscious nor the subconscious realm of mind. To some extent the writer determines his own course, but much of it is determined for him by forces beyond his control or definite selection. Without claiming exhaustiveness for the classification we may conveniently refer to four principal factors in composition.

1. In all composition—and particularly in descriptive writing like history and biography—much depends on the *accessible materials*. If the writer is an eyewitness, these materials are limited by the extent of his observation and his powers of memory. If he is not an eyewitness, the written and oral sources at his disposal are his dominant masters. What he can say and what he must omit are from the outset determined by these factors. Whether the writer is an eyewitness or not, the nature of this accessible material is often limited, accidental and arbitrary. What he or others have observed and remembered is not always "the truth, the whole truth, and nothing but the truth." It is colored and sifted and otherwise subconsciously affected by apperceptive factors.

Where the writer is giving not first-hand information but the substance of his written or oral sources, his helplessness and dependence are obvious even to himself. He might like to know much more, but he cannot honestly go much beyond the information at hand. He must tell what his informants tell and in the way they tell it, and must omit what they omit. His own powers of selection, presentation and testing count for little compared with the initial limitations imposed upon him by his material. Anyone who studies to-day the life of Christ or the apostolic age feels this sense of limitation. He cannot go behind the exiguous

[1] I find the phrase now also in Streeter, *The Four Gospels*, p. 379.

records of the evangelists to supplement or test them. The same determining factor was present in the work of Luke, in a degree that was sometimes only slightly less binding. In general this alien control of composition is far more significant than either author or reader usually appreciates.

2. A second factor that determines the ultimate character of a book consists of the *conventional media of thought and expression*. This also is often none of the author's own choosing. The language in which he writes is determined usually by his historic setting. It is the language of himself and his readers. Every language is nothing but a mass of human conventions. There are variations within a given language, often quite conscious selection of words, often quite unconscious personal mannerisms of the speaker and writer; but the bulk of the wording of a literary work is a predetermined factor wherein the individual plays a slight selective function.

Quite as much as grammar and diction other elements in the form and content of a writing are due to the collective habits of his group. Literary writers conform to the *genre* of their particular field of writing. Unliterary writers follow less consciously similar traditions and precedents. Certain ways of speech, certain types of material, certain methods of presentation are usual for certain kinds of writing in certain ages or places. The civilization of one's time and place and social group determines largely whether one uses Latin or French, direct or indirect discourse, literal quotations or paraphrase, religious or literary language, scientific proof or the attestation through miracle. Neither author nor reader may be very much aware of these factors. But for one who belongs to another age and environment a correct appraisal of them is of the utmost importance.

3. A third factor in literary composition is the author's *individuality*. Here at last is something that is the au-

thor's own, not something quite outside him; but even here he exercises little conscious control. It appears in spite of himself. His interests, his tastes, his prejudices, his mannerisms of speech crop out here and there in all his writings, whether he wills it or not. In some writers they are less pronounced than in others or less obvious to the reader, but no writer can entirely obliterate himself. In some degree this factor must be included in the analysis of any piece of composition.

4. Finally among the factors in authorship there is the author's conscious *purpose*. More than all the others this factor is generally recognized, though its influence on the nature of the resultant composition is often relatively slighter. Sometimes a writer seems to himself or his reader to bend all things to his controlling purpose. In argument this is more obvious than in history, but even history may be colored by propaganda, polemic or apologetic. The selection, the proportion and the presentation of incidents are subject to the writer's aim. He may handle his material with the skill of an artist or the strategy of a general. His objects may be various. They may be artistic, religious or practical, and several objects may be combined in the same work, one appearing in one part and one in another. Even the most objective of narratives often conceals beneath it a real purpose. When objectivity is intentional that in itself is an aim—and not always an easy one to fulfill. The mere fact of writing indicates some compelling motive or at least some effective impulses. It is quite possible to overemphasize this factor in composition, to assign to it the most fanciful and exaggerated rôle. We must admit that Biblical study has sometimes erred in this direction. Yet the influence of the author's purpose cannot be entirely omitted from calculation.

Such, then, are some of the chief factors that enter into the complicated mental processes of authorship. Their share in the result is not always easily determined, though we may know that in a general way they have played their part. The product itself is often the only clue we have to its history. Sometimes we know something from outside sources of the material which the author used. Usually we have some knowledge of the habits of speech, of thought and of style of the group to which he belongs. If we know the author through other works, or if we are acquainted with him through biography, or if he is our own contemporary whom we have seen and talked with, our knowledge of his personality is not confined to the writing that we are analyzing. Sometimes the writer himself states his own purpose. But in most cases, as in the writings of Luke, we are left very largely to our own devices. We must draw deductions from the material at hand.

The analytic task precedes the synthetic one. If we would make clear and real the process by which Luke-Acts was written we must first study in turn these four factors that determined, humanly speaking, that process. The results can be only tentative. There is much room for difference of opinion. The classification suggested is neither exclusive nor decisive. Some other divisions might be proposed. It would be possible to regard the destination or intended readers of the writing as a separate category. They constitute an influence that asserts itself partly in the author's conscious purpose and partly in the language, style, and method of presentation which he unconsciously adopts.

There are many features of Luke's writings which permit of more than one classification. Our ignorance, extending in part to all four factors, makes many phenomena ambiguous. Even of his vocabulary we cannot often say whether it is due to the general language of his time, to his own idiom or possibly to his sources. To a much greater extent will doubt surround the character and scope of his material. Is his emphasis due to the proportion of his sources or to his own treatment? Does he make omissions because he does not know, because he does not care or by way of deliberate suppression? Our uncertainty will only partially destroy the value of our investigation, for though our reconstruction may not always be certain and demonstrable the attempt to understand the factors and processes of the original construction will give suggestions of the actual history, even where it fails correctly to recover it. We may be able to claim that the writing could have come into existence in a given way, that it probably did come into existence in that way and that if it did not its actual origin was at least similar to the one proposed, since it must have represented some mixture, though in different proportions, of the same primary factors.

PART I

THE MATERIALS

CHAPTER III

STAGES IN THE HISTORY OF THE MATERIAL

Complicated as is the writing of Luke's works when psychologically analyzed as a single event, it is scarcely more complicated than one of the component factors, that is, the material which he used, when the latter is taken by itself and examined as an historical development. It is necessary so to examine it if we would understand its ultimate form. The material accessible to Luke is determined in content and form by its history. Conversely, its history may be inferred principally by its ultimate form. The study of such matter is like the study of geology; we examine the rocks and soils of the earth to discover their past, and then we write the history of that past as explaining the world that now is. For an understanding, therefore, of the material which was at Luke's disposal when he wrote, we must include at least some examination of its prior formative history. The making of his work, so far as this one of its principal factors is concerned, begins long before "it seemed good to write."

In a sense the writing of Luke-Acts began with the deeds that he records. His heroes are, to use a modern phrase, "the makers of history." [1] We must not forget that

[1] Significant as is the recorder of history (see above, pp. 3 f.), he deserves not the meed of the man of action. Plutarch, in words that remind us of the works of Luke, declares: "Historians are as it were the reporters of acts ($\pi\rho\acute{a}\xi\epsilon\iota s$), men of eloquence who succeed in expression because of the beauty and power of their style. Men who for the first time read or consult their works owe

ultimately events themselves are a kind of first cause; no matter what succeeds them they cannot be overlooked, and since in this essay we must omit the discussion of the events it is well to warn the reader of this most vital omission. In spite of all the other factors there would be no history at all were it not for at least some slender nucleus of actual occurrences. *Ex nihilo nihil fit.* Even the extremists who think Jesus never lived do not deny the existence of early Christianity. Luke's work is not entirely spun out of his own brain or the brains of his predecessors, as the spider-web is spun out of the spider. It has a connection more or less remote or accurate with events in the plane of objective experience. They are events concerning which the Christian church has felt an intense interest and a justified curiosity. Their recovery is the ultimate object of all the vast amount of thought and study which has been applied to Luke's writings. To record the results of this study, to give even in outline the probable course of the underlying facts, would be a long and arduous task. It has been done by others and must be omitted here. But it can never be left out of account in any complete enumeration of the formative factors in the writing of Luke or in the tradition that lies behind him. Luke appears to refer to them in his preface as something definitive, complete and final—"the things fulfilled ($\pi\epsilon\pi\lambda\eta\rho o$-$\varphi o\rho\eta\mu\dot\epsilon\nu\omega\nu$) among us."

Even when we limit our thought to the remainder of the history of Luke's material there spreads before us an interesting though complicated and obscure process. Between the event and the record there is not a simple and automatic connection, mechanically produced as the land-

them a reward for good news ($\epsilon\dot\nu\alpha\gamma\gamma\dot\epsilon\lambda\iota o\nu$). Of course they are also highly praised, being remembered and read because of the men who have done successful deeds. For the records ($\lambda\dot o\gamma o\iota$) do not accomplish the acts, but because of the acts they are thought worthy of a hearing" (*De gloria Atheniensium* 3, p. 347ɛ).

scape is produced on the photographic plate. History, we need to remember, does not write itself, or tell itself orally, or even think itself in the mind of the eyewitness. There enters in one or more stages of human transmission, and we know that humanity is rarely mechanical. Like the original facts these stages also are named in Luke's preface. There is (1) the first-hand impression on spectators and participants ("eyewitnesses and ministers of the word"); there is (2) the transmission, in part at least oral and collective ("they delivered unto us"); there is (3) the attempt to arrange and record ("many have taken in hand to draw up a narrative"). All this lies behind Luke, though it is possible that for different parts of his narrative he intercepts the stream at each of these three stages of its course. All this is exactly what we should naturally expect to be the history of the material, as it is the history of all ancient tradition. There are three steps between Luke and the events fulfilled.

1. There are other passages in Luke's writings and elsewhere in the New Testament which confirm the view of the history of the material that suggests itself from the words of the preface and from the intrinsic probability of the situation. We often read of the impressions on the eyewitnesses and participants. They wondered, or they rejoiced and praised God, or took courage, and later they remembered or told. They recollected how their hearts burned within them, they recognized that Peter and John had been with Jesus, they reminded one another of the words of the Lord Jesus Christ. They kept things in their hearts, even if they were silent at the time or failed to understand. Indeed their silence and their failure to understand are definitely mentioned. Luke says in one passage, "But they understood not this saying, and it was concealed from them, that they should not perceive it; and they were afraid to ask him about this saying."

We are told also the reactions of Jesus' enemies and the

outsiders. They understood not the parables, or else they understood that they were spoken against them. They were filled with anger or hatred or remorse. So toward Jesus' followers all kinds of unfavorable attitudes are re-corded—they mocked or gnashed with the teeth, they were "sawn through" as well as pricked in their hearts. Prob-ably the enemies of Christianity had little to do with the ultimate record of the movement. Their immediate reac-tions, even if like Paul they were subsequently converted, do not determine the later tradition. The story was handed down through sympathetic channels.

Nor can one lay stress even on the recorded effect on Jesus' followers themselves, for many if not all of the passages which speak of their appreciation or lack of ap-preciation may be secondary, due to the motives of tradi-tion rather than to the memory of actual feelings. But these notices must be recognized as having verisimilitude, and they at least suggest what in the nature of the case would have happened anyhow. It is inconceivable that Jesus failed to create attention, and attention is the pre-condition of observation and memory. There is a sense in which, after all, events do "make an impression," as we say, as light makes an impression on the photographer's plate or sound records itself on the phonographic disc. But the transmission is partial and inaccurate. Recent psy-chology has warned us against exaggerated confidence in the evidence of the eyewitness. Its incompleteness at least everyone will acknowledge. Of what happens we observe only a part, of what we observe we attend to only a part, of what we attend to we recall only a part. All through this limited series, confined as it is to the eye-witness, there is a factor of selection if not of error. Our perception is affected by our apperception, our atten-tion by our interest, our memory by our subsequent ex-perience. In so far as our material comes from eyewit-nesses at all, if those eyewitnesses expected a Messiah before Jesus came and still expected one, if early or late they identified him with that Messiah and counted his followers as a true Messianic movement, these factors—to mention no others—have had their effect on the record which we owe to them. Matthew Arnold once spoke of Jesus as "over the heads of his disciples and reporters." We may say of Jesus and Paul, and of every historical character, that he is apart by at least one remove from his reporters.

2. For the oral transmission of the material we may also appeal to various references in the New Testament itself and to the intrinsic probability of the situation. That which was done was bruited abroad. This we are told and this we know is human nature. Luke himself repeatedly reminds us of this fact, though his object is not to explain the history of his material so much as to underscore its significance. While Mary, we are told, "kept all these sayings, pondering them in her heart," the shepherds "made known concerning the saying which was spoken to them about this child." At the birth of John, not only was there loosed the tongue of Zacharias, his father, but "all these sayings were noised abroad throughout all the hill country of Judaea." Three times in the early chapters on Jesus' ministry Luke says in effect, "a fame went out concerning him through all the region round about." The whole Book of Acts is a long narrative of such transmission, "how they carried the good news from Jerusalem to Rome." The other evangelists speak at least predictively of the gospel's being preached to the whole world or to all nations.

We need, however, to be reminded that the gospel thus mentioned is not necessarily identical with the material contained in Luke's writings, not even with the material in his first volume, though we now call it a gospel. Certainly gospel or good news suggests historic fact, but scarcely bare history. The impression we get both from Paul's letters and from the sample outlines of apostolic preaching provided in the speeches of Acts is that the narrative of events was a minor element in the vocal expression of Christian thought. Acts, it is true, sometimes summarizes the career of Jesus. The speeches of Paul at Antioch of Pisidia and of Peter at Caesarea mention the two termini of that career—the baptism of John and the death on the cross—and even that he "went about doing good, and healing all that were oppressed of the devil." But the interest is not in the anecdotes of Jesus' life nor even in his teaching; it is in the fulfilment of Scripture by his death and resurrection and in the "word of salvation," "good tidings of peace," preached in his name.

Even more is this the case with Paul, so far as our evidence goes. Whatever he knew of the petty details of Jesus' career or of his teaching, and whatever he taught about it orally, his letters reveal a minimum of such knowledge and information. There is no need here to discuss at length the acute problem presented by Paul's relation to Jesus' historic career; nor should we label it ignorance and indifference, on the one hand, or try to excuse and deny the omission of connection in his letters with the Jesus of history, on the other. In more than one sense Paul could say that he knew Christ no longer after the flesh and "the gospel which was preached by me . . . is not after man. For neither did I receive it from man, nor was I taught it." The gospel preached by Paul was not a collection of anecdotes and maxims like our gospels. Indeed, apart from these narrative books themselves there is very little in any Christian literature before Justin Martyr, either in the New Testament (Epistles and Revelation) or outside of it, to suggest the existence of any considerable quantity of such tradition in oral memory or in written record. Such simple records as we have in the gospels are unexpected, an extraneous, one might almost say a gratuitous, addendum to the main line of Christian thought in the first century.

It might perhaps be supposed that this isolation of the narrative material guarantees in part its authenticity. If it was unimportant in the eyes of the early Christians, why should it be affected by their prejudices? Unfortunately this advantage cannot be wholly claimed for it. The more alien pure recollection was to their main line of interest, the more surely the selection and presentation of the material were due to their religious motives. The evidential value of the past was paramount—to prove that Jesus was the Messiah, that "never man so spake," that he "was a prophet mighty in deed and word before God and all the people." This was the form that the oral tradition took. Even that which is recorded in Acts had been already molded and affected by pragmatic motives. We are told in Acts that Paul himself reported his missionary work as "done by God through his hands," a viewpoint agreeing in thought, if not in wording, with many references in his letters to the grace or stewardship given to him.

The early Christians' interest in the present and future not only decreased the interest in the past, but also modified it. Such teachings of Jesus or experiences of Paul as were useful or edifying in the present, whether as precept or example, would unconsciously come to the fore. Can we not imagine the value to a Christian in the circumstances in which First Peter was written, of the words reported of Jesus assuring his followers of protection in persecution and of ultimate divine intervention? The defiant boldness of the apostles as portrayed in Acts would fortify the confessor who read it to "obey God rather than men."

There were few places or periods through which the oral tradition circulated that did not have these or other interests. They would be creative and controlling factors in the history of the material. The period of circulation was a period of great change in Christian experience and standards. The gospel was transferred not only from Aramaic to Greek—but from Palestine to Europe, and from Jews

to Gentiles. This involved a change in linguistic, geographical, racial and cultural background; in addition to
which there were the religious changes within Christianity,
more rapid, more divergent and more momentous in this
formative period than in any other generation of Christian
history. The more vividly one pictures to himself the
probable channels through which the historical traditions of
Christian origins must have passed, the more significant
must seem this factor in conforming fluid memories to ever
more various interests and aims.

3. As regards the written transmission of the Christian
historical tradition, the New Testament gives no explicit
confirmation of Luke's reference to many predecessors.
The Gospel of John in a note at its close says much could
be written on this theme, but it does not say much had been
written. The same evidence which we have quoted as
showing how remote was the oral tradition behind our
evangelists from the major Christian interests would indicate the improbability of written record. It is usual to
point out in this connection that Jesus is nowhere recorded
to have written anything except perhaps once upon the
ground and that Peter and John are described as "unlet-
tered" men, a word which is used in contemporary records of
persons who cannot write even a receipt or sign their name.
Luke once shows us that Jesus could read. Paul could at
least sign his own letters and he wrote voluminously by
means of an amanuensis. But his correspondence mentions
events in his own life and in Jesus' life only by way of
reminder or explanation. It deals with the present and
was never intended for record. For all early Christians,
as for the author of Revelation, the time was at hand, and
there was no use in sealing up or even in writing books for
posterity. More than a full century after Jesus' death
Papias still expected his return, and for knowledge of
the past he relied on what he could learn second or third
hand orally, thinking, he says, "that what was to be got

from books would not profit me as much as what came from the living and abiding voice." [2]

This evidence—much of it, to be sure, evidence from silence—suggests that Luke's reference to many who had tried to compile records must be taken with a grain of salt. The "many," after all, may be but a convention of frontispiece rhetoric. In this case the written like the oral transmission of the events is a peculiar, unexpected, not to say a providential surprise, unaccountable from the situation itself. Our gratitude, however we divide it between men and God, must accordingly be all the greater to those who inspired, wrote and preserved the five books that stand first in our New Testament. Instead of complaining that we are offered so little, and that additional records were either lost, as were Q, the ending of Mark and the sources of Acts (and the sequel to Acts, if it ever existed), or never written at all, we should be thankful that we have what we have. Some would even regard the existence of these books a greater miracle than anything they record.

Several modern tendencies seem to be moving opinion away from this extreme toward its opposite. As for the general improbability of early record of what Jesus and the apostles did, we have been reminded that illiteracy was not universal in the Roman Empire and that in Egypt hundreds of autograph letters have been recovered from men who were as humble socially and culturally as the Christians whom God used at Corinth to confound the noble, wise and mighty. Even the mighty and noble may well have taken cognizance of the story. "It was not done in a corner." The apocalyptic outlook of the first Christians probably did not have either the ethical or the practical results one would logically expect of it. It is not only the heedless and the unbelieving who buy and sell and

[2] Quoted in Eusebius *H. E.* iii. 39, 4. It is unhappily not clear just what Papias meant by this contrast.

B*

eat and drink and marry and give in marriage and write
contemporary history. To-day even those who theologi-
cally expect the world to end soon remember and record
current events from their own viewpoint. The apocalyptic
hope was not the only factor in the first Christian generation's outlook, and even if it belongs to the dominant
factors we have reason to suppose that the gospel material survived in spite of these factors. The scarcity of
reference to the life of Jesus in Paul's letters may be due to
their special purpose or to sheer accident.

The gospels themselves are inescapable evidence that
the writing of gospels did occur. If their existence is
really intrinsically unlikely, then we shall conclude that
some people did just the intrinsically unlikely thing. We
have four of them, not altogether independent, to be sure,
but sufficiently different to indicate a fairly wide and varied
interest. Is there any other movement or person in ancient
history of whom are preserved records more numerous or
more independent, or more promptly compiled? There
were great men and great deeds in Greece and in Rome,
where one would expect more publicity. There are some
two or three accounts of Alexander the Great and of Julius
Caesar and of the Second Punic War. Some of the writers
were as near their subject as were the evangelists to Jesus,
but they are not more numerous or more independent.

Beside the four gospels, other gospels now lost were
written. We know the names and have fragments of several that were probably only a little later in date than
the latest canonical gospel. As we shall see, the literary
analysis of our gospels suggests also a prior literary activity. At least two Greek documents can be assumed as lying
behind Luke's gospel. This assured outcome has encouraged scholars to seek for further evidences of written
sources, and many of them are convinced that the phenomena in Mark, John and Acts, as well as in Matthew
and Luke, justify the hypothesis of written Greek sources.

Even more recent is the wave of opinion—for even contemporary Biblical scholarship has its successive fashions —which would carry this literary activity back of our Greek books and their Greek sources into Aramaic writings. A whole lost Aramaic literature is postulated, of which our canon represents a partial translation. C. C. Torrey is sure that Acts i. 1-xv. 35 is a literal translation of a single Aramaic source, and that all four gospels are translations from the Aramaic, excepting apparently only Luke i. 5-ii. 52, which he derives from the Hebrew. C. F. Burney's *The Aramaic Origin of the Fourth Gospel* is only a little less positive. Other scholars grant the probability if not the certainty of such theories. If they should be ultimately accepted, this would add a whole new factor in our scheme of transmission of gospel history—a layer of Aramaic writings. It would mean that the transfer from Aramaic to Greek occurred not in the oral stage as we used to think, but in the literary stage.

New chronological judgments contribute to this increased emphasis on the written factor in our gospel material. For many years the dating of New Testament books has been getting earlier. Harnack, to mention one example, dated Acts in the second century in 1887, between 78 and 93 in 1897, about the year 80 in 1906 and before 64 in 1910.[3] An early dating of Acts carries with it an early date for Luke, if it was written before Acts, and for Mark, which was written before Luke. Another principal source of Luke's writings, that is commonly called Q, Ramsay thinks was written before Jesus' death.[4] Wherever Aramaic documents preceded our Greek ones, still

---

[3] Harnack, *Expositor,* Third Series, Vol. V, May, 1887, p. 334 note; *Geschichte der altchristlichen Litteratur bis Eusebius,* ii, *Die Chronologie,* 1, pp. 246-250, 718; *The Acts of the Apostles,* pp. xiii, 290-297; *The Date of the Acts and of the Synoptic Gospels,* pp. 90-125.

[4] W. M. Ramsay, *Luke the Physician,* 1908, p. 89.

earlier dates are required. For example, Torrey dates his Aramaic source of Acts in the year 49-50.[5]

Early dating of sources does not actually increase the amount of writing that enters into our reconstruction of the history of Luke's material, but it at least gives more room for that increase. Evidently we must not exclude anywhere in his writings the possibility that written material underlies the story, no matter how early we date his work. Perhaps even his sources had sources. The popular notion that our evangelists sat down with nothing but a blank roll of papyrus before them and wrote what they remembered of what they had seen and heard must give place to a process that is complicated by the influence of written record. On the other hand, we must never exclude from our attempt at the understanding of the gospels the influential factor of oral tradition, whether in the final or semi-final stages of composition. How far it was the oral and how far it was the written method of transmission that determined the character of the materials as they came to the evangelists, and what effects each method had, are questions on which their work itself gives some illuminating data.

[5] Torrey, *The Composition and Date of Acts*, 1916, p. 68. For the completed Greek Acts he gives the date 64 A.D. (*ibid.*, p. 67). Believing that Mark xiii reflects the threatened sacrilege at Jerusalem under Caligula, Torrey dates the whole gospel of Mark (I suppose he means in Aramaic) in the year 40 A.D. See B. W. Bacon, *The Gospel of Mark: Its Composition and Date*, 1925, pp. 54 ff. See also J. Moffatt, *Introduction to the Literature of the New Testament*, 3d ed., 1918, p. 625.

CHAPTER IV

MOTIVES IN THE TRANSMISSION OF THE MATERIAL

For the history of the material used by Luke we are fortunately not dependent exclusively on what is told us in his writings or on what we can infer as historically probable. The material itself reveals something of its own past. As surely as the excavator's spade yields to the trained archeologist reliable information on extinct civilizations, so does the analysis of the written record disclose the forces at work in its transmission. The "aetiological" study [1] of the gospels and Acts is therefore an essential element in the understanding of their present contents.

The first impression made by such a study is one of multiplicity of motives, forms and methods. Unlike the stratified mounds of Mesopotamia or Egypt, the successive stages in the narrative transmission do not exactly retain

[1] I owe this term to Professor B. W. Bacon. Compare his words in *The Beginnings of Gospel Story*, 1909, p. ix: "The key to all genuinely scientific appreciation of biblical narrative, whether in Old Testament or New, is the recognition of motive. The motive of the biblical writers in reporting the tradition current around them is never strictly historical, but always aetiological, and frequently apologetic. In other words, their report is not framed to satisfy the curiosity of the critical historian, but, as they frankly acknowledge, to confirm the faith of believers 'in the things wherein they have been instructed,' to convince the unconverted, or to refute the unbeliever. The evangelic tradition consists of so and so many anecdotes, told and retold *for the purpose of explaining or defending beliefs and practices of the contemporary Church*."

their chronological sequence. Indeed, no chronological sequence can be absolutely established for the few decades that lie betwen the life of Jesus and the written records. Various motives worked at different times and places, and their influences paralleled, crossed and neutralized each other in many ways. The brevity of the period does not preclude the utmost pliability and diversity in the surviving material. As we know from experience, determining motives in the transmission of tradition arise and change with surprising rapidity, and they express themselves in several forms. Their process is to select, emphasize, transform, omit and add in accordance with their own tendency. But their process is largely subconscious and collective, rarely attributable to a single individual with a conscious aim. As the writing of Luke's works was said to require a knowledge of the individual psychology of authorship, so the history of his material should be interpreted by the social psychology of tradition.

Among the determining motives in the transmission of history should be mentioned first and foremost the inherent interest of the event. At the very start tales are told for their own sake, and things uninteresting tend to be forgotten. Here is a drastic selective process automatically working in the earliest stage of transmission. Even Boswell does not tell us everything about Johnson, and Jesus and Peter and Paul had no Boswells. The same motive goes even further. It is not satisfied with its tyrannical exclusion of the commonplace; it even determines how the interesting things shall be told. They are told with a view to their interest. Unessential details tend to be omitted promptly, so much so that they cause remark when, as occasionally in Mark's gospel, they are retained. The place, the person, the time, in so far as they are not bound up with the point of the incident, tend to disappear. The material is more often satisfied with "a certain man," "a woman," "once upon a time," etc. The settings of Jesus' sayings were early lost if the saying was memorable and complete in itself. A careful analysis of the records we have shows how drastically that which does not contribute to the primary interest of the recorded item has been sloughed off.

Only a little less obvious is the influence of the primary interest in the direction of emphasis and even exaggeration. There are several ways of emphasizing the interest of an incident. To describe the surprise and wonder of the spectators is one of them, for the hearer or reader tends to catch the same reaction. This is common in the evangelist's material. The same effect is produced by the spectator's failure to appreciate or understand. Though the narrator makes clear his meaning, the incidents by themselves are too striking to be understood. Oftentimes the text of our gospels sums up a whole controversy, in which credulity and incredulity have been engaged, with the triumph of the former. The failure of those who saw him to recognize or believe in the risen Jesus is used thus in Luke and John to assure the reader of the resurrection.[2]

The cures are among the characteristic incidents of Luke's material that illustrate this interest and its expression. The wonder of the spectators evinces the interest of the event. The case is often described, but the description is not a diagnosis for the purpose of therapy: it is to indicate how serious the disease was. Its duration is told; it is either congenital or chronic. Its symptoms are never slight or trivial, they are high fever, or violent insanity, or incurable hemorrhage, or extreme deformity. The certainty of the disease (or death) is sometimes emphasized

---

[2] *Cf.* Acts xii. 9, 11, 13-16; John ix. 8-9, 18-21. Sometimes similar scenes may represent actual controversy, or at least perplexity, on the part of Christians and thus embody the remnants of a long series of assertion, objection, rebuttal, doubt, denial, attempted explanation, reflection and inference, *e.g.,* Matt. i. 18-25; iii. 14-15; xxvii. 62-66; xxviii. 11-15.

as much as the certainty of the cure, and indeed the identity of the patient before and after curing is sometimes
mentioned in order to mark the contrast. The lame man
not only walks but leaps, or carries his pallet. The change
from sorrow to joy is another confirming item. The swift-
ness of the cure is noted usually, even when it is done at a
distance, a circumstance which in itself is mentioned as
remarkable. The means of the cure are never difficult or
elaborate, at most a word or a touch, and in one or two
instances a little saliva. Even the clothes or the shadow
of the hero can cure.

The striking element in wonders of other kinds is similarly underscored. Only bad storms at sea are mentioned,
only close escapes or impressive conversions, and the details given show how bad or close or impressive they were.
Premonitions of danger or escape make the event significant, and when there is a definite oracle or prediction fulfilled the significance is all the greater.

When we pass from the striking event to the striking
person, the same influences are at work. His career as a
whole now can be emphasized by the accumulation of
noteworthy events connected with it. He has not one but
many escapes. Providence thus intervenes regularly for
him. This is shown by the stars and by earthquakes.
Especially about his birth and death cluster such striking
evidences.

These formative influences in the molding of Luke's
material are not peculiar or unique. They occur in John as
well as in the synoptic matter, in the Old Testament as
well as in the New, and in pagan tradition of all races,
civilized or uncivilized. They are not even limited to religious literature; they are universal. Their prevalence and
agreement have long puzzled mankind, and even to-day it
is too generally supposed that they are borrowed or imitated from one case to another, or derived from a common
source, or due to some subtle human psychoanalytic com-

plexes. They are indeed due to a universal psychological law, but it is the simple law of interest and the natural ways of its expression.

There were, however, religious and specifically Christian *motifs* in the transmission of Christian story. They agree in part with the *motif* of simple interest; in part they diverge or conflict with it. The more general religious motives include a belief in the supernatural, moral evaluation of conduct and an interest in the future life. The specifically Christian ones imply a special interest in the Christian movement and in the problems connected with its actual development in the first generation.

To the quite secular interest in the coincidence of outcome with anticipation was added the religious interest in the divine control of history as evidenced by the agreement of prophecy with fulfilment. It is beyond doubt that the record of Jesus' life was selected and perhaps otherwise influenced by the idea that it fulfilled the Old Testament. Conversely, his words were selected and perhaps otherwise influenced by the idea that they were in turn fulfilled by his death, his resurrection, the experiences of his followers in persecution or in preaching, and other contemporary events prior to his return.

The vindication of Christ and the Christian movement is a pragmatic motive frequently visible, especially in the Acts of the Apostles. The story is told as of a movement which constantly enjoys every manner of divine guidance and approval. At every turn its partisans are triumphant and its enemies, whether Jew or Gentile, confounded. Even when its enemies seem to succeed, persecuting to the death, God's justice is ultimately vindicated by their conversion or gruesome fate. Hence we are told the death of Judas and Herod Agrippa I, the discomfiture of the Jews before Pilate or Gallio, and the conversion of Paul. Angels and Asiarchs, dreams and earthquakes, come to the assistance of the endangered or distressed. Even death

is escaped at Nazareth and Lystra, or triumphed over by
resurrection. The more the movement is oppressed or
suppressed, the more powerful grows its headway.

These motives did not work only as unconscious prejudice. In some stages at least they represent also the conscious purposes of winning or holding the allegiance of men
to the movement. The latest of the evangelists states at
the close of his work that his aim is "that ye may believe
that Jesus is the Christ, the Son of God; and that believing
ye may have life in his name." A like purpose affected
no doubt all those who had written or told the story before
him. It is doubtful whether the material as we now have
it was intended so much for non-Christians as for Christians. It represents the pastoral rather than the missionary element in Christian teaching. But whether it was
meant to create or to confirm belief its form and contents
would be much the same, and it still serves both purposes.
In estimating the material which Luke adopted for his use
we must never forget that it had already been sifted and
censored before him for the purpose of apologetic and
propaganda, edification and confirmation. Like other Scriptures it had been not only written but orally circulated and
transformed "for teaching, for reproof, for correction, for
instruction which is in righteousness." It was told of
Christians, by Christians, for Christians. Removed as it is
from much intentional bias, it is equally removed from the
categories of unadulterated tradition on the one hand and
of myth fabricated out of the whole cloth on the other.

But even this does not conclude our enumeration of the
variation of motives during the short period of the pre-
canonical history of the record. For within the early community there were differences of opinion, sometimes violent,
and divergences of interest and developments. To discover the exact interests and uses of the material now
in our gospels is a difficult and sometimes dangerous task.
Those who have sought a single clue have mostly gone

wrong. Above all things the multiplicity of interests must be emphasized. In controversial matters the material in the gospels, even in one gospel, does not all point one way. Concerning the problem of the relation of Judaism and Christianity made so prominent to us in the records of Paul, we can no longer say with Baur and his followers that Matthew is Jewish-Christian and Luke Pauline, though some of the material in each confirms that simple classification. On the other hand, Matthew's gospel contains references to world-wide evangelization and the severest criticisms of Judaism, while Luke's contains a long list of traits showing friendliness to the Jews. Judaism presented to the Christians more than one aspect, and the attitude toward it of a single individual at a given time cannot be subsumed under the simple rubrics pro and con; and much less can the attitude of the groups through which the gospel tradition was transmitted for some decades. The same may be said of the question of eschatology, which also looms large in the deposits of Christ's teaching as transmitted to the evangelists. The differences of view among early Christians and between Christians and others were not simply that they either did or did not believe in the Lord's return; the time and the manner and the moral significance of that event were questions of interest as well.

Already the figure of Jesus is the center of many different lines of interest which became explicit in the traditions about him. Various aspects of his significance are distinctly reflected in our records, as the white rays of the sun are divided into many colors when passing through a prism. His identification as the Messiah is sometimes asserted and sometimes corrected. It is attested by fulfilment of Scripture, by voices from heaven and by the witness of demons and of men. A literal anointing is told, whether in water or in the Spirit, in tears or in spikenard. The miracles that he wrought and those that accompanied

his birth and resurrection were valued as evidences. To
predict what subsequently came to pass, to control Nature,
to triumph over disease, especially over demons and death,
were confirmations of his Messianic office. The same
evidences served to ratify also other synonymous or similar titles, as Son of God, son of David, prophet, Savior
or Lord. For some of them, however, other more literal
evidences were more appropriate, as physical descent from
David or from God. Behind other synoptic passages lies
the question of the relation of Davidic sonship, Lordship
and Messiahship, and the identification of the expected
forerunner Elijah with the actual forerunner John. Interests like these were doubtless an uninterrupted *motif* in
the re-telling of his life. His death also had to be accounted for. Before it was converted into an asset it was
at least a liability, a stumbling-block to be explained. The
motif of Scripture fulfilment is more prominent in the passion narratives than elsewhere.

Even the more practical or formal interests of the church
have left their mark on the gospel material. How in the
cities of Israel the early bands went forth to preach, village
by village, with the simplest equipment, trusting in God
and human hospitality; how they were abused and accused
and how they rejoiced in persecution; how when on trial
they relied for defense on the inspiration of their faith;
how they were tempted by false cries and false Christs, by
the uncertainty and the excitements of their times, but
still patiently endured the delay of the Lord—all these experiences of the early decades are faithfully reflected not
merely in Acts, but in both of the earliest recoverable collections of the transmitted sayings of Jesus. The more
these sayings seem to lose their value as uncolored records
of the Lord, the more they gain in value as sources for
the early apostolic age.

How far the organization—the leadership and services
of the church as we now call it—enters into our gospels

may be a doubtful question.[3]   The apostles' names and the rebuke of their ambitions, John the Baptist and his baptism, and the feeding of the multitudes and the Last Supper, would scarcely have been so prominent in the synoptic gospels if the church had not already an interest in its leaders and its simple ritual.   The ecclesiastical interests behind the Fourth Gospel are as unmistakable, even if they are quite different.   In the current text of Matthew we find two references to the church by name, a definite command to make and baptize disciples, and many less explicit allusions that fit the "church-consciousness" of the author or his predecessors.   It is inconceivable that the author of Acts could tell all that "Jesus began both to do and to teach" without feeling in the telling some of the interest in the church which his second volume exhibits.

This long list of pragmatic motives—and it makes no claim to completeness—did not all work at once in the history of the material, but the gospels themselves indicate that they have each been at work at some stage.   A motive which worked on some of the material did not affect other parts of it, and when one censoring and selecting interest tended to exclude or retain a theme or trait, another may have canceled it by inversely retaining or excluding.   Some of the material may have survived merely on the basis of its inherent general interest, and the scope of the more special or partial interests, the theological or controversial, can easily be exaggerated.   On the other hand, only a subordinate place can be given to what is often thought of as the chief motive of history—a simple antiquarian curiosity.   However much the modern man may think he can inquire into Christian origins with a dispassionate spirit of scientific inquiry, he cannot assume that much if any of the material in the gospels survived or

[3] This view is emphasized, for example, by Loisy, *L'Evangile selon Luc*, 1924, and the articles there cited, p. 23.   Compare G. Bertram, *Die Leidengeschichte Jesu und der Christuskult*, 1922.

was sought out in any stage of its history for corresponding purposes.

This is not the place to appraise the relative influence of each motive or to estimate how far its effect was to transform, idealize and invent as well as to emphasize, select and omit. Such questions belong to the discussion of the individual item and can be answered in general only after an examination in detail. Our present aim is to discover the character of the material out of which the third evangelist wrote and to realize how that character was determined by the motives which controlled its transmission. For the sake of concreteness it may be well to illustrate this control by a single example—the treatment of John the Baptist.

In one sense John is not part of the Christian story. He is not one of Luke's principal figures; yet no person receives more attention in all four gospels in the sayings of Jesus and, aside from Jesus himself, in the narrative. Whatever the actual prominence and permanent influence of John in Jewish history, his place in the gospels was determined by the interest felt in him by Christian tradition. Josephus also mentions him, and the way he is treated by that writer makes an instructive comparison with the evangelic material. We need not suppose that Josephus himself is uninfluenced by other motives which explain in part his comparative brevity and his different description, or that his account is more accurate than the Christian version. There is no real contradiction between the two and, by their substantial agreement in representing John as preaching and baptizing and gaining considerable influence with the people until he is first imprisoned and then executed by Herod Antipas, they mutually confirm the truth of their common picture. Josephus writes of John as follows:

> John was a good man who bade the Jews first cultivate virtue by justice towards each other and piety

towards God, and so to come to baptism; for immersion, he said, would only appear acceptable to God if practiced not as an expiation for specific offences, but for the purification of the body, when the soul had been already thoroughly cleansed by righteousness.

Now when all men listened to his words with the greatest delight and flocked to him, Herod feared that the powerful influence which he exercised over men's minds—for they seemed ready for any action which he advised—might lead to some form of revolt. He therefore decided to put him to death before any revolution arose through him. To forestall events appeared far better policy than a belated repentance when plunged in the turmoil of an insurrection. And so, through Herod's suspicions, John was sent as a prisoner to Machaerus, the fortress already mentioned, and there put to death. The Jews supposed that the destruction of Herod's army was the penalty expressly inflicted upon him by God to avenge John.[4]

Josephus's mention of John, "surnamed the Baptist," is quite incidental. Like the single reference to Christ this passage is only an illustration of the political history of the Jews. Josephus is at pains to show throughout the hostility between the Jews and their Herodian or Roman masters. Herod feared the people. The people liked John and disliked Herod and, with the kind of motive from which Christian writers were not free, they connected Herod's defeat with his execution of John. This is the material and the motive which Josephus transmits without comment of his own. John's baptism is explained rationally to suit Western readers, in the way in which Josephus throughout handles the ritual of the Jews. John's teaching is translated into simple Gentile ethics, just as Josephus translates the messages of Old Testament prophets.[5]

[4] *Antiquities* xviii. 5, 2 §§ 117-119, Thackeray's translation.
[5] For an example see pp. 153 f.

The Christian tradition, on the other hand, has other motives. It does not associate John with the downfall of Herod or with the constant friction between Jews and Romans. It treats John as a part not of Jewish history, but of Christianity. With him the two oldest records seem to begin their memorabilia, and repeatedly in Luke's writing is he named as the beginning. Though Luke and Matthew insert birth stories before John's ministry, Luke consistently with the tradition still retains John's priority by relating his birth before that of Jesus.

The career of John is assimilated to that of Jesus, not only in the parallel birth stories just mentioned, but elsewhere. In birth, in ministry and in martyrdom he is the complete forerunner of Jesus. No doubt they were men more alike than modern Christians realize, and tradition was interested in the likeness. According to the Fourth Gospel Jesus or his disciples also baptized. The evangelists, especially Matthew, borrow phrases from one for the other. If John used the expression, "Ye offspring of vipers," Jesus repeated it; if Jesus' message was "Repent ye, for the kingdom of heaven is at hand," John anticipated him in it. John's teaching was preserved in a collection of sayings of Jesus, and their teaching is similar. With both it was a combination of social ethics and apocalypse. Jesus meets the question about his authority by an appeal to John's authority. Twice the suggestion is made that Jesus is John *redivivus.* Herod, who executed John, plays with the thought, and in Luke's gospel is said to have desired both to see Jesus and to kill him. According to the same evangelist Jesus is even tried by Herod, though not condemned. Luke omits, however, Mark's account of the execution of John. In the gospels where it is told, it is told quite as incidentally as in Josephus, although the occasion is not to explain Herod's political misadventure, but his superstitious interest in Jesus.

To the Christian tradition the conflict is not, as to Josephus, of John and the common people against Herod and Rome, but of John and the common people against the chief priests and the scribes and the elders of the Jews. His enemies were the enemies of Jesus, and his friends Jesus' friends. Here again John appears in just the rôle of the Jesus of tradition, arraigning the Pharisees as needing fruits meet for repentance, rejected by the Pharisees and the lawyers but accepted by the publicans and harlots, regarded by the people as a prophet so that their leaders hesitated to belittle him; for in his case as in that of Jesus, "they feared the people."

The Messianic element has played a large part in the Christian interpretation of John, in both the canonical and pre-canonical stages. He was identified with the expected forerunner of the Messiah as Jesus was identified with the Messiah. The Scripture on which that expectation was based is Malachi, especially iii. 1-3 and iv. 5-6. The former passage, from which the Jews named the book "My Messenger," is quoted in Mark and apparently in the non-Marcan synoptic source, which describes also the teaching of John about "the coming one" in terms of fire akin to Malachi iii. 2; iv. 1. The second passage, echoed now in Luke i.17, identifies the forerunner with Elijah. Besides the echo in Luke, Mark and Matthew both make the identification, the latter explicitly and repeatedly; and evidently this *motif* has affected earlier stages of the tradition as well. John is an ascetic figure, a Nazarite, a hermit of the desert like Elijah. Though such men sometimes entered kings' houses they did not wear soft raiment. John's raiment of hair and his girdle of leather correspond precisely with the description by which Elijah the Tishbite was known (2 Kings i. 8). How far the latter's penchant for anointing and how far the etymology of Messiah affected the story of John's baptism, and especially his baptism of Jesus, cannot now be known. It is possible also that Mark's account of John and Herodias comes from a stage of tradition in which the parallel with Elijah and Jezebel was in the mind of the Christian interpreter. That in its present form the New Testament narrative gives the apparent triumph to the wicked princess rather than to the outspoken prophet would not interfere with the parallel, for Jezebel shed the innocent blood of many prophets, and Herodias and her consort came to an unhappy end. Besides, Elijah did not die, but was carried to heaven to return later. His subsequent death and resurrection may already have been part of the Jewish myth of the Messiah's forerunner, as Revelation xi. 11 suggests. The gospels hint the possibility of John the Baptist's reincarnation.

The motive of Messianic fulfilment is even more completely expressed in John's relation to Jesus as the Christian tradition conceived it. His ministry does actually precede and prepare for that of Jesus. The latter begins only when John was cast into prison. So at least Mark tells us, while the Fourth Gospel, for reasons of its own contradicting Mark, makes their work more nearly alike and contemporaneous. Even more closely is John brought in touch with Jesus. He it is who actually anoints him— an event which by the outward rite, by the visible descending of the Spirit and by the audible divine voice attests Jesus as the real Messiah. In the Gospel of John, the Baptist not only predicts the coming one, but explicitly identifies him with Jesus. According to this author John "came to bear witness of the Light," "that he should be made manifest to Israel." "Saying unto the people that they should believe on him that should come after him, that is, on Jesus"—this, according to Acts, and the fact that "John baptized with the baptism of repentance," were the two things that Paul had to say of him at Ephesus.

The practice of water baptism in the Christian community not only perpetuated the memory of the forerunner, but guaranteed for him in the tradition a peculiar place of interest. The same custom emphasized the baptism of Jesus and represented it in accordance with the practice and theory of Christian baptism. It was an inward grace for Jesus, and an outward sign for the spectators. Matthew justifies the tradition that even Jesus condescended to the rite. Luke mentions the bodily form of the dove as he mentions the tongues of fire and the other outward phenomena in the receipt of the Spirit in the early church. Tradition soon added a fire to the scene at the Jordan. The fourth evangelist leaves of the incident only its evidential value to the Baptist.

These motives in Christian tradition were met by other motives which though equally natural give the resultant material a certain complexity. There was a tendency not only to explain John as Christ's predecessor and the real starting-point of Christianity, but to exalt Christ at John's expense. He was the foil and contrast to Jesus. Great as he was, more than prophet, the greatest among them that are born of women, nevertheless he that is least in the kingdom of God is greater than he. He is the end of the old order quite as much as the beginning of the new. Twice it is noted that, unlike Jesus and his disciples, John and his disciples fasted. Much stronger are John's own words oft repeated in varying wording. He is unworthy to unlatch the shoes of the more mighty one. His baptism is only with water, not with spirit or fire. Even in Acts it is repeatedly pointed out that John's baptism is not enough. A "second experience" mediated by apostles will bring the holy Spirit.

The Fourth Gospel, it has been thought, wishes deliberately to counter an exaggerated view of John. It adds such explicit phrases as "He must increase, but I must decrease." John's priority is no superiority: "After me cometh a man who is become before me: for he was before me." Even before John's imprisonment Jesus (or his disciples) made and baptized more disciples than John. In other ways this evangelist follows a different line from the others. The title of Elijah is explicitly rejected by John. But concerning Jesus there is none of the doubt suggested by the synoptists' message of John from prison, "Art thou he that should come or look we for another?" with the ominous reply of Jesus, "Blessed is he who shall find no occasion of stumbling in me." Jesus counts John not merely a prophet but a God-sent witness to himself, and John relies on divine proof for his testimony, disclaiming all human authority: "And I knew him not: but he that sent me to baptize in water, he said unto me, Upon whomsoever thou shalt see the Spirit descending, and abiding upon him, the same is he that baptizeth in the Holy Spirit. And I have seen, and have borne witness that this is the Son of God."

The gospel records concerning "John the baptizer" illustrate from a single and limited theme the influence of motive as it affected the transmission of all the New Testament history. Here we recognize *in parvo* both the variety of motives operative in the course of tradition and the way in which they could determine the character of the material long before it came to the hands or ears of Luke. Motive is not so much a creative as a molding force. But the extensive part it played in the selection and presentation of what in the first instance was intrusted by history to the vicissitudes of an oral transmission would perhaps surprise us if we knew all the facts, both because of its scope and because of its various and unsuspected forms.

CHAPTER V

FORMS IN THE TRANSMISSION OF THE MATERIAL

The forms in which Luke's material was transmitted before him depended on the motives for transmission, and since the motives were various the forms were various too. Naturally a study of the one goes hand in hand with the other; recent German criticism has devoted itself successively to these two phases—*"religionsgeschichtliche"* and *"formgeschichtliche,"* as they call them.

An exact classification of the material is not to be expected and no convenient set of formal rubrics is available. Perhaps that is an advantage, since the forms into which the material shaped itself were entirely spontaneous. Other material has had similar history, and those who have classified the Christian material have borrowed some of the terms from Greek literary forms. This nomenclature is convenient for scholars, but it does not suggest to the ordinary reader of the New Testament the simple phenomena which he has found there. It suggests that alien existing forms have played some part in fashioning the Christian tradition. This is scarcely ever the case. Those who told or wrote about Jesus and the apostles were not imitating literary models, but were following the natural trend of motives and purposes which influenced the material.

It must be obvious to anyone who examines the narratives of the New Testament that the material there given consists of many separate units now gathered together. That they had an original connection we need not doubt.

49

They were once the acts and words of one person or of a group of persons, severally connected in time and place and common interests, but they have passed from their original connection to their present connection through an intermediate stage of reduction to single units. Each item has been told separately in such a way as to make it complete in itself. They are detached scenes or episodes. In transmission they have acquired the kind of finish that goes with complete units. They have rounded themselves out, as drops of oil stand off under surface tension. They have their own well-defined edges, their own beginning and ending. Their setting and detail tend toward a minimum. The study and classification of the individual units constitute the first step in an understanding of the material.

For the gospel material a simple and ancient division already exists. It consists of two types—what Jesus did and what he said. Luke himself describes his gospel as an "account of all that Jesus began both to do and to teach," and he adopts the classical pair, word and deed, to summarize the Master's powers. The combination is possibly older than Luke. In Mark the astonished countrymen of Jesus ask, "What is the wisdom that is given unto this man, and what mean such mighty works wrought by his hands?" Both elements enter into the material of Mark's gospel, and in varying degree into later records, for the proportion was not always constant. The earliest reference to Mark (in Papias) calls attention to the twofold character of its contents—"either things said or things done by Christ." The Book of Acts with its abundance of speeches continues the impression of double activity. It is not merely "the acts." Indeed, as early as Mark vi. 30 the report of the apostolic mission is described as including "all things, whatsoever they had done, and whatsoever they had taught."

The units in the gospel material as we find them justify us in differentiating these two large classes, but suggest further classification also. Of the mainly narrative type we have the miracle story. It illustrates well the complete and self-sufficient character of the unit. It is a single, self-explanatory paragraph. The circumstances are briefly told—the event and the effect. All that is unnecessary falls away. After repeated re-telling even the names of the persons and places disappear. Most of Jesus' patients are now anonymous; they are simply a leper or a blind man. Their ailment is of course an essential part of the story. The time also is mentioned only if it has something to do with the story, e.g., the sabbath for controversy with Pharisees, night for terrifying storms, etc.

Partly narrative also is the controversy. There are the two disputants, their contest, the dialogue and usually the outcome. Both the gospels and Acts are largely strewn with this material. Sometimes a miracle is combined, as when Elymas the sorcerer is struck blind, or when the Christian representative escapes a lynching. Often the effect on the opponent or the bystanders concludes the scene. At other times the sayings of Jesus or a speech of the apostle reduces the narrative element to still smaller proportions.

Similarly, we may distinguish the scenes so common in the gospels where a striking saying of Jesus is the real nucleus and a narrative framework has been retained to explain it. His comment is to a specific question or situation. The saying and the setting are usually both reduced to the simplest terms. The former is crisp, epigrammatic and final, requiring no sequel, usually not even the effect on the interlocutor or bystanders. The setting is as brief as possible and includes no irrelevant details of time or place or person. Here are some examples from Luke:

> A certain man said unto him, I will follow thee whithersoever thou goest. And Jesus said unto him, The foxes have holes, and the birds of the heaven have

nests; but the Son of man hath not where to lay his head.

And one of the multitude said unto him, Master, bid my brother divide the inheritance with me. But he said unto him, Man, who made me a judge or a divider over you? And he said unto them, Take heed, and keep yourselves from all covetousness: for a man's life consisteth not in the abundance of the things which he possesseth.

A certain woman out of the multitude lifted up her voice and said unto him, Blessed is the womb that bare thee and the breasts which thou didst suck. But he said, Yea rather, blessed are they that hear the word of God, and keep it.

And the apostles said unto the Lord, Increase our faith. And the Lord said: If ye had faith as a grain of mustard seed, ye would say unto this sycamine tree, Be thou rooted up and be thou planted in the sea; and it would obey you.

In this form of tradition the actors are almost never named; the interlocutors are "someone," "they," "the apostles." Only because the story required distinguishing names may we suppose that Mary and Martha are mentioned in the scene introducing Jesus' comment upon them. Often a class name appropriate to the question is sufficient: "some woman" pronounces the beatitude on Jesus' mother, "a rich man" is told to sell all, "a poor widow" casts in two mites, "some of the Pharisees" rebuke Jesus' disciples. The name of the centurion whose faith exceeded that found in Israel is not preserved. That he was a man possessed of authority is part of the dialogue and explains why we are told so much as his profession and rank. Nor are other notable beneficiaries of Jesus' power usually named. That one was a foreigner, a Greek woman, Syrophoenician

(Mark), or Canaanitish (Matthew), was a detail more or less necessary for the story, as was the information that others were a royal courtier (John), a ruler of a synagogue, or simply a ruler (Matthew). The name Jairus for the last of these was perhaps originally added by Luke. Only one patient of Jesus is named by Mark, Bartimaeus, the blind beggar at Jericho. His name is not retained in the parallel gospels.

Similarly, of persons interviewed few are mentioned by name, especially in the older Palestinian stories. Inference could be responsible for the view that words of Jesus about treasure in heaven (compare Q) were addressed to a rich (Mark) young (Matthew, for Mark's "from my youth") ruler (Luke). But not even the Gospel according to the Hebrews in re-telling the story added his name. At Jericho Luke names Zacchaeus, a chief tax collector; at Caesarea, Cornelius, a centurion of the Italian cohort; and as he proceeds, several Roman officials and some magicians. The evangelists who record Jesus' praise for a woman's expensive gift of nard do not record her name. "Wheresoever the gospel shall be preached throughout the whole world, that also which this woman hath done shall be spoken of for a memorial of her." It is her "beautiful deed" with Jesus' word upon it that in tradition outlives even this woman's name.

In the incident just mentioned the place is given exactly by Mark and Matthew, "in Bethany in the house of Simon the leper." Even Luke's variant account contains the name Simon, a Pharisee, though he implies that his house was in "a city" of Galilee. John retains Bethany and identifies the woman as Mary the sister of Martha and Lazarus. As to the time, they show little agreement. But usually the place is not more essential to this form of material than the person or the time. Fishermen, of course, are called by the seaside, as a publican is at the place of toll; but in Luke, Mary and Martha are in a certain village, and other

c

scenes occur "in one of the synagogues," "in a certain place," "in the house," or "on the road."

This form of tradition is especially characteristic of the gospels, and it was this which gave them their special likeness to the Greek *memorabilia* (ἀπομνημονεύματα), best known to us in Xenophon's work on Socrates. But an even simpler unit is made by one further step, reducing the narrative until it disappears altogether. The isolated saying also has its classical equivalent in the sentences (*sententiae*) or apothegms (ἀποφθέγματα) of the philosophers, but it existed in Semitic literature also in the sayings of prophets, sages and rabbis, and in Christian literature it was a natural result of tradition.

The separate sayings of Christ tend to a gnomic form, and under easy mnemonic devices they were remembered and passed on. No setting was needed for their explanation. They stand on their own merit. But they permit wide and varied application. Many of them are in couplets:

> The sabbath was made for man, not man for the sabbath.

Often they are paradoxical:

> Many last shall be first and the first last.

Or they are hyperbolic:

> Ye strain out the gnat and swallow the camel.

Their picturesque and metaphoric language helped their survival:

> Wheresoever the carcase is there will the eagles be gathered together.

> If the blind lead the blind, both shall fall into the pit.

Certainly no unit of tradition was so well calculated to defy the sponge of oblivion as such striking sentences.

Another type of teaching with power of longevity in tradition as well as immediate pedagogical value is the parable. To this form Greek literature offers no real parallel, but the rabbis of Jesus' day used identical forms and even identical subjects. Like the narratives of Jesus' life these illustrations present the simplest and most essential elements of the story. Unnecessary detail is retained only in so far as it makes the scene vivid. In fact, these parables are usually artistically superior to the narrative of events. Thus it is the habit of fiction to surpass history.

The reduction of tradition to units and the process of selection and attrition which accompanied it are readily imagined from the evidence which the material now presents. But this stage was succeeded by other processes which worked in opposite directions—collecting, connecting, arranging, with a view to the higher unity of the whole picture.

The sayings of Jesus were early brought into written, perhaps into oral, collections. The arrangement was sometimes on the basis of literary form, such as the grouping of parables; sometimes on the basis of subject matter, such as the grouping of beatitudes or woes or words about the future; sometimes by the simple law of association of ideas, as when one saying follows another because a catchword supplies the cue: "the fire is not quenched . . . everyone shall be salted with fire . . . salt is good," etc.

Similarly, the incidents of Jesus' life were collected. It has been thought that one of the oldest complexes is what we now call the passion narrative, beginning with the night that Jesus was betrayed and ending with a series of resurrection appearances. Paul in passages of 1 Corinthians gives hints of the first and last parts of this series. The gospels supply a fuller though somewhat varying out-

line. Whether it was a kind of ritual celebration in the
church in memory of these events, or the strong emphasis
laid upon Jesus' death and resurrection, which caused the
creation of this fuller narrative of the circumstances connected with the passion we cannot now tell. It permitted
at least a more continuous arrangement in chronological
order than the more miscellaneous incidents or memorabilia. The latter, like the sayings, were arranged by catch-
words or by similarity of subject matter, as the passages
on community of goods in Acts iv. 32-v. 11, or they merely
followed one another without any real or imagined link.

The combination of narrative and of sayings was another
editorial process at work. It may be that the characteristic
evangelic unit—a pointed saying of Jesus in a narrative
framework—facilitated the association of the purely narrative with the purely didactic material, and even led to
the assimilation of one to the other. Sayings came to be
added to miracle stories, and sayings without setting had a
setting provided them. In our present gospels it is possible
to see these processes at work, the former especially in
Matthew, the latter in Luke. In Matthew also we get the
creation of long discourses by the accretion of congenial
discourse material.

Another type of collection, it has been suggested, underlies the same gospel—a collection of proof-texts from the
Old Testament. Such collections existed in the time of
Cyprian under the name *testimonia,* and Rendel Harris has
detected with great ingenuity earlier evidences of their
existence. In the absence of concordances, numbered chapters and verses, one-volume Bibles and other modern conveniences, they would certainly be very useful. Matthew's
Scripture quotations are particularly numerous. Their
recurring formula, "that it might be fulfilled which was
spoken through —— the prophet, saying," and their frequent divergences from the Greek version of the Old Testament used elsewhere by both this evangelist and the others,

have been thought to confirm this hypothesis. Large supplies of proof-texts often exist in a well-stored mind, as
they do in special collections—as Justin Martyr reminds
us, to mention no more modern example. An hypothesis it
must remain, yet we must not forget that in one form or
another the Old Testament is one of the contributory influences in creating the material of Luke.

While the units of tradition were circulated orally, the
processes of collection must have been mainly written; or
at least the collection secured permanency only when crystallized in writing. But the writing of tradition had other
results than mere association and arrangement. It permitted the introduction of biographical motives, of summaries and of new connections. The last-named process
is especially interesting. One who wrote down successively
the units of tradition could hardly be satisfied with bare
juxtaposition. There was a tendency to mark them off
by introductory formulas. A new saying is introduced
by the words: "And he said," "Verily I say unto you";
a new incident by "and again," "and immediately," or
simply "and." These are the cæsuras in Mark. The
other evangelists have their own connectives also, as Luke's
"and it came to pass" and "in one of the days," and Matthew's favorite "then," "at that time (hour, day)," "from
there," "and it came to pass when Jesus had finished these
words (parables)."

These phrases serve a double purpose; they both connect and separate the units. To create a smooth narrative
with the appearance of geographical and chronological sequence was a natural tendency to which the evangelist
Matthew obviously has yielded. Luke's phrases in part
emphasize the indefiniteness of the setting. On the other
hand, the circumstances of the setting seem to be more fully
elaborated by Luke, so that the units with him are more
intelligible as wholes. In a still later stage, perhaps in
connection with the public reading of the gospels in peri-

copes, the same process may be seen at work in the textual variants. This editorial freedom with the opening words and sometimes with the closing words is one of the important facts with regard to the transmission of the material, and we may conjecture that it existed in the stages behind those which we can now control by comparison of extant gospels and manuscripts.[1]

The summaries may be regarded as merely an enlargement of the same process. They serve a double purpose—to divide and to connect. They give continuity and historical perspective, but they are also of a later vintage than the single episodes. They belong to the stage of collection, representing an editorial need and even an historical interest which cannot be satisfied only with episodes. They are associated with the adjacent incidents which they generalize. They are often merely the conclusion of a single incident expanded. They indicate that the material is typical, that the action was continued, that the effect was general. They fill in the lacunae. Like the first and last of the three colophons of John's gospel they suggest that there was plenty more material of the same kind. They are simple and obvious deductions from single details or collections. Jesus' ministry in Mark begins at Capernaum, with preaching in the synagogue, where he also casts out a demon. There follows a cure of fever, then the cure of many invalids and demoniacs, and finally the typical summary:

> And he went into their synagogues throughout all Galilee, preaching and casting out demons.

So Luke, after narrating the teaching of the Baptist, adds:

> With many other exhortations therefore preached he good tidings unto the people;

[1] See K. L. Schmidt, *Der Rahmen der Geschichte Jesu*, 1919, p. 276; C. H. Turner, *Journal of Theological Studies*, xxvi, 1924-5, pp. 228 ff.

or after Peter's speech at Pentecost:

> And with many other words he testified and exhorted them.

Simple deductions from collections of detail, they come into existence the moment those collections pass in the least degree out of the most amorphous stage, and they serve a useful literary purpose. Later stages of transmission tend to multiply them. Both Luke and Matthew use two or three times the summaries which they find in their source. Any modern life of Christ illustrates in later stages the incurable tendency to generalize from episodes.

Such, then, are the literary forms of our gospels, and conjecturally such are the processes by which their material came into these molds. For much of the Acts, and indeed for many other writings sacred and profane, identical developments occurred. The Book of Acts has its rounded episodes, collected often quite miscellaneously into groups and bound together by mortising the joints or by utilizing summaries as both conjunctive and disjunctive interludes. The miracles in Acts stand on all fours with those of the gospels, though the names of some of the patients, e.g., Eutychus, Aeneas and Dorcas, and of the places, may indicate that the process of simplification had not proceeded so far when they came to be written.

At the same time we should recall that meeting the current toward elimination of names is the counter current of late development, which localized legend and gave to simplified matter the verisimilitude of proper names like Malchus (John), Veronica, the centurions Longinus at the cross and Petronius (Gospel of Peter) at the tomb, and the names of the malefactors crucified with Jesus,[2] and the

---

[2] The Old Latin Codex Colbertinus (at both Mark xv. 27 and Matt. xxvii. 38) represents only one of several attempts to name the penitent and the impenitent thief. Ropes calls attention in

names and number of the wise men at Jesus' birth.

There are, however, two elements in the Book of Acts which require special classification. One is the series of detailed itineraries given for parts of Paul's journeys, the other the speeches in Acts. Each of these deserves more extensive discussion. But from the standpoint of form they may be noted here as somewhat unique. The first raises many questions. The question whether the longer episodes included in the narrative, as the incidents at Philippi and Ephesus, belong to the original outline, or are episodes derived from separate transmission but inserted into it, and the presence of the "we" in parts (but by no means all) of the itinerary, are only two of these problems. Evidently this material is not merely a collection of episodes, but a continuous geographical outline such as to suggest the crystallization of information in an early stage and with real biographical (autobiographical?) interest. It is convenient also in that it provides an editor with a ready-made plan and sequence. Such a form has its parallels in contemporary literature, both serious and fictitious. They range all the way from the *periplus* of the admiral and the *anabasis* of the general to the *True History* of Lucian and the romances of other ancient Gullivers. The journal style is also occasionally undertaken as an editorial framework for episodes, a thread for stringing, like beads, detached incidents, as in the wilderness

his textual commentary on Acts xvi. 27 to the noteworthy reading, "The jailer the faithful Stephanas." This is doubtless due to a scribe who with more cleverness than knowledge of history regarded Macedonia as part of Achaia, and the "house" of the Philippian jailer as Paul's first (male) converts there and hence identical with "the house of Stephanas . . . the first-fruits of Achaia" (1 Cor. xvi. 15). This identification had currency also among commentators and catenists. A different and more modern example of the same penchant for combination between the Acts and the epistles is Zahn's christening of the jailer, his wife and Lydia with the names of Phil. iv. 2 f.

wanderings of the Israelites and in Luke's travel narrative of Jesus. The itinerary in Acts, no matter how discontinuous it may be, is at least of a different *genre* from any of the other material.

The speeches, on the other hand, are probably as much later in their origin as the itinerary is earlier. They are not collections of transmitted sayings, as are the so-called sermons of Matthew, but each is a unit in itself purporting to outline a continuous address on a definite formal or critical occasion. Unless it be in Luke iv. 16-30, these speeches have no parallel in the synoptic gospels. The addresses in John, however, have something in common with them. More will be said of their character in a subsequent chapter.

c*

CHAPTER VI

IMMEDIATE WRITTEN SOURCES

The characteristics of Luke's material discussed in the preceding chapters are its most important features. They are the kind of features that prevail in such material in any language and in any form of transmission. We know that this material, or at least much of it, has passed through two other processes—transfer from oral to written form, translation from Aramaic to Greek—and it becomes a matter of no little interest, though of secondary importance, to inquire whether those processes had already taken place when Luke gathered the material. Were Luke's sources oral or written, Aramaic or Greek, when they reached him?

Both these questions have engaged the attention of scholars, almost overshadowing the study of the earlier and more significant history of the material. They deal with only the last stage in the history of Luke's matter—the immediate form in which he found it. They are, however, questions of considerable interest and must be raised even if they cannot be decisively answered. The ordinary reader of the gospels scarcely thinks of them. It rarely occurs to him that the gospels were written neither in the language of Jesus and of the Palestinian missionaries nor in his own modern tongue, but in Greek. As for a quite close and continuous use of written sources, that suggestion hardly occurs to him. He naïvely thinks of the gospels as books written out of their own information by men who know the story, that is, from first-hand knowledge or oral transmission. He may even suppose the evangelists rested, as we seem to do, on knowledge derived from a general Christian nurture and on the memory of the story of Christ as read or told them long ago. This simple theory of oral sources for the gospels was long held also by scholars and more reflecting readers, and cannot be decisively disproved for the whole of the narrative material in the New Testament, but some of the reasons by which it is assumed or defended are far from valid, and there are other reasons which *a priori* make the theory of written sources more generally probable.

The evangelists never state that they are using written material, but this is no evidence that their immediate sources were oral. They do not allude to sources of either kind as their own proximate predecessors. Nor when they wrote was there the same literary convention which obtains with us requiring that authors acknowledge their sources, if the latter are in writing and are being followed rather closely. Footnote references and quotation marks were devices then unknown, and the literary habits which necessitate them were equally alien. Of course, everything that is finally written in our records was first written by somebody, and in some passages one of our evangelists may have been the first to set the account on paper, but in many cases he may be taking over material already in written form. Luke in his preface alludes explicitly to many writing predecessors as well as to eyewitnesses and oral transmitters. There is good reason to suppose he had read and used these earlier writings. He does not say he used them, but if we may judge from other prefaces to allude to predecessors whom one followed without stating that one followed them was not unusual in antiquity. Nor was it regarded in the least dishonest by contemporary standards. Written records were not copyrighted; they were public property. To employ them was easier and often safer than to discard them in the search for more

fluid oral tradition.   To acknowledge one's use of them
was unnecessary.

This presumption of the use of written sources by the
evangelists is practically proved in part by the resemblances
which obtain between them.   The first three gospels
contain likenesses in subject matter, order and wording
which seem to require as their explanation some literary
relationship.   Though they often differ from each other in
much the same way as independent recorders of oral tradition might be expected to do, they agree in other cases so
closely that in the judgment of most critics some written
dependence seems a certainty.   Whether one evangelist used
the other, or whether they independently used a common
source, the method of transcribing written material is shown
to be their method.   An ancient prejudice in favor of the
independence of the evangelists has survived even to our
own day and has been buttressed by arguments both plausible and far-fetched.   The long debate need not be here
rehearsed.   Perhaps it is not yet closed.   But a century of
synoptic research seems to the present writer to have
demonstrated, at least as a conclusion of the highest probability, that there was a large amount of literary dependence in the composition of the gospels.

Indeed, the same process of research has achieved more
definite results with regard to the literary relationship of
the gospels—results whose probability is also very high,
though on a descending scale.   The synoptic problem is a
complicated one; it becomes more complicated the more
one studies it, and no solution can claim to be complete in
its scope or to be any more certain than is that particular
hypothesis which is more probable than the alternatives.
Two concurrent theses explaining two groups of literary
relationships have thus emerged from testing and retest-
ing every possible combination and have secured the suffrage of an increasing number of scholars.   They serve as
a working basis for an understanding of the phenomena,

and the phenomena when independently investigated tend to confirm them. Alternative theories are in some respects equally possible and are constantly being revived and effectively presented. But when compared with the solutions mentioned they fall somewhat short of the same probability, and must accordingly be tentatively rejected.

In brief—for the full fascinating story of the problem and the evidence which led to its solution may be left to others to tell—the twofold explanation of the literary relationship is this:

1. Mark or a book substantially identical with it was used by the writers of Matthew and Luke.
2. Other matter found in both Matthew and Luke and not in Mark also goes back to a common written source or sources.

For Luke, then (as for Matthew), at least two written sources may be postulated as a probable basis, one of them our Gospel according to Mark, which we can read and compare throughout with the parts of the later gospel dependent upon it, the other some unknown written material (hence best designated by a neutral symbol Q) whose existence is proved and whose content is in part known to us through its independent use by Matthew and Luke where (aside from their borrowings from Mark) they overlap.

Here, therefore, the material of Luke seems to us a tangible reality, underlying written records that he has transferred to his own pages. The *a priori* hypothesis of written sources is thus confirmed by this very probable solution of part of the synoptic problem.[1] For large sec-

---

[1] This solution is commonly called the Two Document Hypothesis. Streeter, *The Four Gospels,* pp. 227 ff., objects to this name as tending to misunderstanding and false assumptions. The Two Document Hypothesis pertains only to parallel passages in the synoptic gospels. It does not of course attempt to explain unparalleled sections of Luke or Matthew or to exclude the possi-

tions of his first volume—altogether nearly half of it—
we have good reason adduced from the existence of parallel
records to assert the author's reliance on earlier writings.
What shall be said of the remaining passages in the
gospel and of Acts? The probability that they depend on
written sources is none the less because parallel passages
are not extant. The means of demonstration are less available, but the probability is still very great. It is no wonder
that scholars are alert to inquire whether some internal
proofs do not still indicate the facts, and to assume on quite
slender evidence underlying sources for the parts of Luke
not found in Matthew and Mark, and for various parts of
Acts. Their several hypotheses may be discussed in detail
more appropriately in commentaries, but it is well here to
recognize the difference between the probability of their
assumption and the fallibility of their alleged evidence.
The assumption is altogether reasonable. Large sections of
Luke's writings have in them no clue that makes the probability of final written or oral sources either less or greater
than in the passages which come from Mark or Q. In fact,
internally considered all the material is entirely ambiguous.
If it carries signs of oral transmission, that does not preclude for it one or more stages of written transmission
after its oral circulation and before it reached Luke. If
it carries signs of written record, that does not exclude the
possibility that when it came to Luke it was oral in form
and that the earmarks of editorial arrangement were first
introduced by Luke himself, who thus becomes both the
first and the final redactor. In the main the material,
whether written or oral, did not differ in its characteristics.
The earliest records are written much as their contents were

bility of further important documentary material as sources for
them. In June, 1912, a report of the Papal Biblical Commission
officially and explicitly condemned the Two Document Hypothesis.
Their decision asserting the unity of Acts, its accuracy and its
Lucan authorship was promulgated the following year.

told. It cannot be too strongly emphasized that, judged solely by themselves (without reference to the parallels), the passages in Luke derived from Mark and Q give us no clear evidence that they had been copied from earlier writings, nor do they suggest what the extent and distinctive traits of those writings had been. Where, therefore, parallels do not exist to Luke's writings, while the assumption of written sources is always a probability, internal evidence of written sources need not be expected. Where such evidence, or evidence of the reverse is claimed, the claims rest on most unreliable foundations.

Sometimes, for example, theories of written sources rely on the evidence of vocabulary. Certain passages, it is argued, reveal a special style unlike Luke's and therefore can be attributed to a written source. But where Luke paraphrases Mark no such alien style betrays his process. There are no peculiarities of Mark's vocabulary that conspicuously distinguish the passages derived from him. On the other hand, it is claimed that certain passages are so similar to the pervading style of the whole work that they cannot be the paraphrase of a written source. Again, Luke's use of Mark suggests caution, for observation shows that where he is using written material from Mark or Q the final editor recasts the language into his own style. His own style is more obvious at some times than at others, but it is never so totally wanting as to prove alien origin for a passage, and it is never so pervasive as to exclude the possibility that a written source existed, although the source be no longer capable of detection by any residual difference of style.[2] Unlike the process of composition attributed by modern scholars to the writing of the Penta-

---

[2] See *Beginnings of Christianity*, Vol. II, pp. 161-166. This negative conclusion was criticized by V. H. Stanton, *Journal of Theological Studies*, xxiv, 1923, pp. 361 ff., but relying on more thorough examination of the problem than I have published I do not hesitate to adhere to my former conclusion.

teuch, by which older writings are woven together in truly Semitic fashion without altering the distinctive language of the originals, Luke's method was to recast his material, paraphrasing into his own style. This habit, which he shares with Greek and Latin writers generally, prevents the determination of his sources by the criterion of vocabulary.

Other suggestions of evidence of written sources are based on the content of Luke's record rather than on its style. The evidence of doublets, i.e., parallel accounts of the same event, has a striking vindication in the analysis of the Pentateuch, and New Testament critics are not slow to use the same arguments here and there in Luke's writings. Various passages permit of being understood as different versions of the same event, either interwoven into one (as the story of the Flood in Genesis) or told one after the other (as in the two accounts of Creation). Even where the events narrated are not parallel, different written sources are thought to be indicated by their different viewpoints—in relation to history, to theology, to the supernatural. Sometimes this contrast in viewpoint is understood to be due to two written sources, sometimes to the difference between the editor and a single written source. Editorial arrangement is found where a smooth context (the source) is interrupted by alien matter (the editor), or where a narrative is left in the air, or where an explanation or conclusion is given that seems to be at variance with the main body of the story. Again, sections with common viewpoint or common interests are taken by the modern critic to imply identity of written source; resumptions of narrative are thought to indicate resumption of a written document; repetition of thought and phrase to indicate repeated use of the same written passage, or at least the use of a document whose continuity is indicated by the consistency of its terminology and tendency.

All these criteria are the recognized tools of source

criticism in literature both Biblical and profane. In the hands of experts they yield interesting and sometimes convincing results. Luke's writings, because of their presumption of literary dependence, make such conjectural analysis especially tempting. The phenomena appealed to as evidencing written background may really require the explanation attributed to them. But in all fairness it must be admitted that the evidence is thoroughly ambiguous and the analysis highly speculative. The miscellaneous character of the material and its polychrome oral history on the one hand, and on the other the editorial habits of the ultimate redactor, constantly suggest other explanations as equally probable. Variations of standpoint existed in the gospel material before it was reduced to writing at all, so that a single continuous written source displays conflicting standpoints, repetitions and other phenomena such as are attributed to the conflation of two or more documents. Likewise, redactorial treatment of oral material resembles the treatment of documents. Breaks, interruptions, repetitions, incompleted narrative may be due to the ultimate editor alone working on fragmentary oral information. Even inconsistency and contrast may be merely the final editor's impress. It is absurd to look upon these as traits always attributable to multiplicity of documents rather than as due to the complexity of the oral material, or to the absence of unity in the editor's viewpoint. Much that critics assign to the tendency of Luke's source may be due to Luke alone. Conversely, as we shall see from a study of Mark, a single written source may be in itself heterogeneous, representing still earlier stages of oral or written conflation. For these reasons the attempt to establish and distinguish written Greek sources for the passages recorded only by Luke seems doomed to prove unsatisfactory and largely subjective. It may be said of these literary criteria, as it was said of the linguistic evidence, that they never would have disclosed Luke's use of Mark and Q. Possibly some of

Luke's sources in Acts left more obvious traces than did
the sources of the gospel, but no analysis of either volume
into sources can hope to approach in probability either the
evidence for Mark and Q as definite sources, or even the
general presumption for the remainder of Luke's writings
that some sources were used.

The second question raised concerning Luke's sources
unfortunately also must fail of a conclusive answer,
namely, the question of their language. It has recently
been urged for all the gospels and for at least the first half
of Acts that they are literal translations of continuous
writings in the Aramaic tongue. The novelty of this suggestion (it is not really new but quite old), its implication
of primitiveness and the cleverness and assurance with
which it is supported, give it an attractiveness quite in excess of its own inherent probability. It has not yet had the
advantage of full publication and of long and thorough discussion among scholars, so that any judgment upon it
whether favorable or unfavorable must be offered with re-
serve. The linguistic evidence to which it appeals requires
great delicacy of judgment and a balance of expert knowledge concerning the idioms of two languages such as
scarcely any single individual may claim. Until an agreement is reached in which both Semitists and Hellenists
generally can concur, the matter must be counted *sub
judice.*

It may be assumed without hesitation, however, that at
some stage in their history parts of Luke's material have
undergone such translation. In so far as his story had
circulated among Semites of Palestine, it must have been
in their familiar language. That language appears to have
been the Semitic dialect akin to Old Testament Hebrew,
which was called by the early Christians Hebrew, in later
times Chaldean, but is now known as Aramaic. Aramaic
was probably the language in which Jesus and his disciples

usually spoke in Galilee or in Judea, in public or in private. Even Paul, though he wrote to his churches abroad in a natural Greek idiom, was, he says, not only an Israelite, but a Hebrew from Hebrew parents. He doubtless spoke Aramaic at home in Tarsus and as boy or man among the Pharisees of Jerusalem. If he rehearsed his missionary labors in the ears of the "mother church," that also may well have been done in the Aramaic tongue. Bilingualism such as that attributed to Paul must have been common, and there is nothing intrinsically unlikely in the supposition that our evangelists knew both Aramaic and Greek and could translate from one language into the other.

The tradition of the early Christians about the history of the gospels is on the surface not unfavorable to the theory of Aramaic originals. Papias evidently assumed that Matthew wrote "in Hebrew," while everyone translated (or interpreted)[3] as best he could. He speaks of Mark as "the interpreter of Peter," as if in this case the first writing was in Greek, though the material was oral and Semitic, namely, the preaching of Peter. Later Fathers refer to Matthew and to other gospels as written in Hebrew.

[3] Unfortunately the verb ἑρμηνεύω used by Papias means either translate from one language to another or interpret the sense of something in the same language. The same ambiguity occurs even in English in the noun interpreter. It seems probable that linguistic translation is what he refers to as required by both Matthew's writings and Peter's sermons. On the other hand, Papias refers to his own "Expositions of the Lord's Logia" as "interpretations" (ἑρμηνεῖαι). All these passages of Papias are to be found in Eusebius *H. E.* iii. 39. I may suggest that, living at Hierapolis in Phrygia, Papias was as likely to suppose that Italians could not understand Greek as to suppose that a Galilean apostle could not speak Greek, and he may have thought that Mark interpreted for Peter into Latin. Colophons of the first three gospels in MSS. of the Ferrar group say that they were written in Hebrew, Latin and Greek respectively. This pleasing conceit not only suited the names of the evangelists which belong to those three languages, but matched the catholicity of the trilingual inscription on the cross.

Clement of Alexandria, Hegesippus, Origen and Jerome profess to know one such Semitic book, the *Gospel according to the Hebrews,* as extant in their own times. No fragment, however, of any gospel in a primitive Semitic form is known to survive.

Neither the tradition of the church nor the inherent possibilities of the case really prove or even make probable the theory of Semitic originals for the works of Luke and for the other gospels. What relation the Hebrew book by Matthew which Papias mentioned had to our Greek gospel of the same reputed authorship is uncertain. It may be argued that the Semitic gospels referred to in the second century are really later than our first century Greek products and that the dependence, if there was any, was in the opposite direction. The first transfer from Aramaic to Greek may have occurred entirely in the oral stage of the material's history, or it may have occurred simultaneously with the transfer from the oral to the written form. Even if it occurred wholly in the written stage it may have occurred before Luke took over the material; that is, his predecessors rather than he himself may have been the translators.

The linguistic evidence to which those appeal who count Luke himself the translator of written Semitic sources does not escape the ambiguity which the other alternatives suggest. It consists of two parts—the general Semitic coloring of his language, and a number of passages where a difficulty in the Greek is thought to be attributable to what may be called either mistranslations or over-literal translation.

The first of these evidences relies indeed on unquestionable facts. In his writings—in some parts more than in others, but quite generally throughout—Luke's Greek has been influenced by Semitic idiom. Some of these Semitisms are recognizable even in the secondary stage of English translation: "he was added to his fathers," "it came to

pass," "the feet of . . . are at the door," "his face was
going," "by the hand of" or "mouth of," "on the face of
the earth," "by the mouth of the sword." These phrases
are no more native to the Greek idiom than to the Anglo-
Saxon. They are Semitic, whether found in the Old Testament or in the New.

Other expressions of Luke are "possible" Greek, but
they occur in such numbers in his writings that their
frequency also suggests some form of Semitic influence.
These are largely minutiæ of grammar which can hardly
be explained here without technical reference to the Greek
and Semitic idioms. Frequently it is doubtful whether a
given phrase in Luke's writings claimed as a Semitism is
really alien to Greek, on the one hand, or congenial to
the Semitic languages, on the other. An increasing knowledge of vernacular Greek in the age of the New Testament
has brought to light among the developments of the language some striking parallels to Semitic idiom where no
Semitic influence can be suspected.

The second form of proof is admitted to be very pre-
carious by those who use it. To those who watch them its
employment, no matter how brilliant and ingenious, seems
arbitrary and unconvincing. The Greek text has undoubted
difficulties as it stands. What considerable Greek text has
not? One wonders whether the difficulties in Paul and
Hebrews, and in other writings not suspected of Semitic
translation, would not yield the same results if the same
panacea were applied with equal cleverness. Until one
single example of assured mistranslation has secured general approval, it is necessary to avoid referring to such conjectures as evidence.

But even the instances of Semitic idiom in Luke and
Acts which remain after all doubtful cases are omitted do
not require the particular solution proposed. To be sure,
we must give up the old idea that there was a fixed dialect
of Greek spoken by the Jews and that this with its marked

Semitic idiom was employed by the evangelists and other
early Greek-speaking Christians.   The Greek of Paul
probably represents more nearly the way a Christian wrote
and spoke Greek when uninfluenced by Semitic sources and
models.   In so far as the diction of the evangelists is
more Semitic than Paul's it may be due to the Aramaic
wording of their material.   But such peculiarities may
have been transferred either (1) directly from the oral
tradition, or (2) indirectly from Greek sources based upon
it, or (3) by a translation from Aramaic writings to Greek
writings prior to our evangelists' own work.   These three
additional alternatives must always be borne in mind when
immediate written Aramaic sources for our evangelists are
proposed.   And (4) quite apart from these Aramaic influences in his material the evangelist's own native tongue
together with his imperfect acclimatization in Greek may
have reinforced the Semitic element.   We are often aware
that in ourselves and in others incomplete bilingualism
produces a transfer of idiom since we are speaking in one
language and thinking in another.

Which of all these alternatives explains the Semitisms
in Luke cannot be decisively determined.   It will be necessary to raise this question in connection with his style,
and the further alternative of (5) imitative Semitism or
Biblicism will then be suggested.   For the moment some
negative conclusions will suffice.   Several of the alternatives
are improbable.   The Semitic element in Luke is not due
to his imperfect command of Greek.   He could write good
Greek and could think in Greek when he wrote in it.   Nor
is the Semitic element often taken over from earlier Greek
sources.   Luke's method of paraphrase was too thorough
to leave much alien style.   The Hebraisms found in Luke's
revision of Mark are not often derived from the Semitic
idioms of the Greek Mark, as we can see by comparing the
two gospels.

Finally, the theory of direct translation of Semitic documents—and that is the alternative which particularly concerns us now—seems to the present writer at least improbable. That Luke's quotations from the Old Testament accord generally with the Greek translation suggests that his writings were composed in Greek rather than translated and then conformed to the current Greek version. His resemblances to Mark and Matthew are also matters of Greek wording rather than of independent translation. The current solution of the synoptic problem points explicitly to Luke's work as compiled in Greek on the basis of Greek sources. Even if this particular solution be challenged the phenomena on which it is based can escape the hypothesis of some literary relationship between the gospels in Greek only by substituting a complicated and improbable alternative involving both Aramaic and Greek interdependence.

In the main, therefore, we must be content to rest ignorant of the scope and of the language of each of the sources from which Luke drew. That they were largely written and written in Greek is the safest conjecture—though only a conjecture. It is possible that some of them were written in Aramaic, and that some of them were not written at all. For many other ancient writings we are equally at sea in the matter of sources, and we should rather congratulate ourselves that for part of his material we have the control which is brought by such parallel narratives as either are his actual source or independently represent it. His treatment of Mark and Q must be the first basis for any deductions as to his way of using sources. They are not equally tangible, but they each deserve some further discussion.

CHAPTER VII

THE GOSPEL OF MARK

To discuss fully the Gospel according to Mark, as one of Luke's sources is now called, would require more space than the size and proportion of the present volume warrant. It might seem to need no discussion. It lies before the reader in his Bible and he can examine it for himself. It is already familiar to him, trebly familiar from the fact that most of it reappears in the Gospels of Matthew and Luke. Familiarity, however, often obscures the nature of a book. Much is taken for granted about Mark, derived from current usage or ancient tradition, that is not well founded, while much that is most obvious about it is often overlooked. Its own individuality is blurred by confusion with its parallels. For an understanding of its parallels it is of primary importance. It was perhaps the longest single source for Luke's writings; it is certainly the best known. It provides substantial blocks of material in his first volume and may have influenced him where he was not actually incorporating it. It furnishes the modern student the parallel by which to discover and test the literary methods of the third evangelist. The questions of Mark's origin illustrate by being raised at an earlier stage the kind of questions that beset the study of the making of Luke-Acts. For these reasons, some consideration of the Gospel of Mark is justified.

The Gospel of Mark began with the baptizing ministry of John the Baptist. The caption which precedes this, "The beginning of the gospel of Jesus Christ [the Son

of God]," is a headline or *incipit* rather than part of the
text. The conclusions found in various forms in late MSS.,
including the one printed in most Bibles as Mark xvi. 9-20,
are not part of the original gospel, which evidently once
told of the appearance of Jesus in Galilee to "his disciples
and Peter," though it now breaks off with the women
fleeing from the tomb dumb with fear. The last hours
of Jesus are described in the previous section—his eating
of the passover, preceded by the plot to kill Jesus ("after
two days was the passover and the unleavened bread")
and followed by the consummation of the plot. The rest
of the gospel is without any reference to day or season
or temporal relation of events, except for controversial
scenes on the sabbath and for references to morning
(twice) or evening (five times), which are also usually im-
plicit in the narrative. Once we read "after six days";
once "on the morrow." The evangelist has also phrases
like "straightway," "from thence," "on that day," "in
those days," "again," "after some days," or simply "and,"
all of which suggest sequence. Frequently there is no
implication of sequence at all, and where it is implied
there is good reason to look upon it as editorial rather than
as part of the original material.

The material itself presents every appearance of having
existed once in the form already referred to as detached
units. Each scene is complete in itself, undatable except
by its contents and usually equally devoid of allusion to
place. Just as certain scenes could never have been told
without reference to the sabbath or the night, others inevitably retained their reference to mountain or sea or
temple. There are three references to Capernaum, references to crossing the lake to the country of the Gerasenes,
to Bethsaida, to Gennesaret or the parts of Dalmanutha,
and there are land journeys to "his own country" (whatever that means) and generally "about Galilee," and outside "to the borders of Tyre and Sidon," "from the border

of Tyre, through Sidon unto the sea of Galilee through the midst of the borders of Decapolis," "into the villages of Caesarea Philippi," "into the borders of Judaea and beyond the Jordan," to Jericho, and to Jerusalem. These scenes outside the environs of the lake of Galilee are grouped by the evangelist in general after those in Galilee and lead up to a series of events, several of which—the triumphal entry, the cleansing of the temple, the scene at the treasury, the comments on the temple, and of course the whole passion series—were obviously at Jerusalem. This arrangement by place naturally suggests a corresponding chronological sequence. The latter is not impossible, though by no means inevitable.

A third determinative of Mark's order appears to have been logical association. This was not systematically, perhaps not consciously, carried through. It shows itself in the series of controversies (ii.1-iii.6) and of hard questions (xi.27-xii.37). The purely discourse material yields more readily to this classifying principle, as the groups of parables [1] or of predictions (xiii.1-37) attest.

The artificial character of the arrangement of these primitive units of tradition is shown by cases where a single unit has been injected into an otherwise continuous context. The most obvious cases are the Beelzebul section inserted in the incident of the intervention of Jesus' family and the anointing at Bethany as it is now enveloped by the plans for Jesus' arrest.[2] Similar, though perhaps older, is the interruption in the episode of Jairus. The Gospel of Mark betrays clearly the dissociated nature of the units of tradition and the beginnings of an editorial

[1] iv. 1-34. These parables are connected by their identical subject as well as by their form. All three have to do with seed and its growth, whether uneven, "automatic" or extensive. In the series of sayings of iv. 21-25 and ix. 33-50, the connection is loose, largely *ad vocem* (*cf.* above, p. 55), and more psychological than logical.

[2] Mark iii. 20-21 + 31-35; xiv. 1-2 + 10-11.

method of association. To the same editorial stage probably are to be referred the summaries of Jesus' activity
distilled out of the individual incidents. They generalize
even the Jerusalem ministry into a routine,[3] for Mark's
Judean material, although it is collected into a single block,
does not suggest that we are limited to the diary of less
than a week.

On the other hand, editorial treatment of a theological
kind, with a subjective interpretation of the incidents or
teaching, is conspicuous by its absence. A few editorial
phrases occur: "for they were fishers," "for it was not the
season of figs," and at more length concerning the ritual
washings of "the Pharisees and all the Jews." Aramaic
words are defined in Greek.[4] Otherwise it is difficult tô
tell whether the evangelist himself or his material is responsible for the characteristics of his gospel. The stories
are told with an objectivity and with a vividness of detail
which suggest primitiveness quite as much as they suggest
an editor's naïveté. In its earlier stages the material in
Mark may have been affected by a variety of the subtler
motifs, of which mention was made in a previous chapter;
the present compiler does not betray any subjectiveness of
his own. We may assume that he regarded Jesus highly,
for he quotes those who do so. His wonder stories suggest
that he found significance in Jesus' power over bodily and
especially over mental affliction as well as over wind and
wave and fruitless trees. Much that we think of as early
Christology may well lie behind his records, even though it

[3] Mark xi. 19; *cf.* xiv. 49.
[4] Mark iii. 17; v. 41; vii. 11, 34; xv. 22, 35. The same ὄ ἐστιν is
used thrice to explain Greek words. In each case, strangely
enough, the explanatory word is really less Hellenic, viz., two
mites or local coppers are worth a standard *quadrans* (xii. 42, *cf.*
p. 89 *note* 15); the courtyard where the soldiers took Jesus is
the *prætorium* (xv. 16); "Preparation" (Friday) is the προσάββατον
(xv. 42).

is not explicit in them. But there is scarcely any thorough-going theological theory that permeates the whole narrative, and many things remain that a single unified theory would hardly have selected or left unexpurgated. The material was already miscellaneous, and Mark tried as little to bring it into theological as into biographical articulation.

There is one pervasive *motif* that may be editorial—the sense of mystery. The objectivity with which Jesus is presented is noteworthy. He is not interpreted to the reader, except perchance by the veil of secrecy with which the editor surrounds him. This desire to remain hid, this private teaching to a group, this injunction of silence about cures, these mysterious arrangements for a colt or for a dining room, these repeated predictions of suffering and other things not understood, the silence before Pilate —all these may of course be historical; they may be earlier than Mark. But their presence in Mark is scarcely acci-dental. They are not unique to this writer, but they are very likely congenial to his own tendency. The longer discourses are esoteric, regularly in contrast with some public utterance.[5] The parables are explained as intend-ing to conceal, the word "mystery," or "secret," being used of them. "He that hath ears to hear, let him hear." "Let him that readeth understand." This cryptic utterance, this failure to perceive or to understand, along with the apoca-lyptic tensity of predicting what will soon be known or seen quite well, gives Mark's story an indefinable weird-ness, a sense of mystery and tragedy which, though not characteristic of conscious art or intention, produces an individual coloration and editorial effect upon the *disjecta membra* of a miscellaneous and polychrome tradition.

The shadow of the cross, the shadow of Christian per-secutions, the shadow of rejection and misunderstandings —these darkening rays unrelieved by the grim expectancy

[5] Note the transitions at iv. 10; vii. 17; xiii. 3; *cf.* iv. 34; ix. 28; x. 10.

of the final resurrection or return—have left their traces upon Mark's record, almost from its earliest pages to the end.[6] It is difficult to see how such a record as it stands, a record of conflict and martyrdom, of warning and rejection, could have won the name of "good news." There is a seriousness about Jesus' words, and even about his cures, that makes this gospel no idyll but an ominous cryptogram. Only Matthew outdoes Mark in somber coloring. Eduard Meyer, who rightly regards Mark's passion narrative one of the greatest creations of all prose literature, finds it only the more gripping because of its quiet objectivity.

It is commonly said that Mark was interested in the deeds, not the words of Jesus, because his gospel has less teaching material than has Matthew, Luke, or John, and we are invited to associate him with Paul, whose emphasis on the cosmic meaning of Jesus' career, and especially on his death and resurrection, and whose silence about Jesus' teaching are counted as significant. But such simple classifications correspond neither to the evidence of Mark's gospel nor to any probable exclusive divisions of early Christian traditions. Mark's picture of Jesus was of a teacher. He mentions his teaching and could quote him at length on controversial or apocalyptic topics. Parables and detached sayings were in the material accessible to Mark. It has been calculated that one-third of the gospel is sayings rather than narrative. Since a favorite form of unit was the anecdote which combined both saying and setting, the discrimination is not easy. That the miracles loom large is due rather to evidential value than to a penchant for narrative, and the account of Jesus' death, if we dissociate it from the Jerusalem material with much

[6] It is not impossible that a contemporary interest of the author or of his material finds expression precisely in this emphasis upon persecution and martyrdom, experienced by Jesus and predicted for his followers. See the original and suggestive article by D. W. Riddle, "The Martyr Motif in the Gospel according to Mark," *The Journal of Religion,* iv, 1924, pp. 397-410.

of which it has in Mark no hint of causal or chronological association, is not so extended as to suggest that Mark made it the central act of a redemptive drama.[7]   It must be repeatedly borne in mind that Mark's material is miscellaneous rather than selected by a single prejudice.   Unfortunately we do not know what was the extent or character of his supply.   We are ignorant, therefore, as to how much material or what sort of material he omitted.

There is a temptation to discover in Mark one or more subtle threads of development, whether of Jesus' self-consciousness, of his method of work and change of plan, of opposition against him, or of recognition of Messiahship. Scholars have succumbed to these temptations.   The unclassified contents yield such results to those who seek them, but they are too miscellaneous and too incomplete to make such deductions probable rather than merely possible.   The evangelist himself is certainly not arranging his gospel by such preconceptions.   Perhaps no distinct biographical or theological motives can be attributed to him. He seems sometimes more simple and naïve than his predecessors who shaped his material.   If he shared with them some special interests he does not plainly reveal that fact. The mystery which he draws over the inner intent of his hero veils also his own inner purposes or prejudices, if he had any.

The style of Mark's Greek corresponds in simplicity to such artlessness of mind.   It is colloquial, repetitious, often rough and ungrammatical, picturesque and direct. It does not have distinctive mannerisms, unless the use of "and" in place of more varied conjunctions or constructions, or of vivid locutions like "exceedingly" or "straightway," and of the historical present, and a fondness for

---

[7] See, however, the preceding note for a possible "martyrological" interest of Mark in the death of Jesus.   He gives a detailed account also of the Baptist's end.

redundancies and short relative clauses,[8] constitute mannerisms. His language, whatever its cultural status, is
clear, his negatives emphatic by repetition, his adverbs re-
dundant, his verbs perhaps over-picturesque. Possibly the
colloquial usage of these verbs had, as often happens,
already weakened the piquancy of this style more than
appears to us. Its emphasis seems natural rather than
assumed. Other traits of his style have been noticed by
students, some of them difficult to evaluate precisely. His
"began to" and his "that" with direct discourse, as well as
his "and" and many less characteristic details, have been
called Semitic; his Latin words are somewhat numerous,
as are diminutives. But none of these things are incompatible with authorship by a simple and uncultivated native
Greek.

The simplicity and objectivity of the author give the
gospel an appearance of primitiveness. Some traits of the
subsequent evangelists bring this feature into relief by the
contrast of their parallels, and the nature of his material
has other confirming characteristics. Mark is the foundation for all lists of Jesus' brothers, or disciples or women
associates. His geographical data are relatively extensive.
It is customary to note in his narrative many picturesque
details which the other evangelists omit, like the cushion
in the boat where Jesus slept, the "green" grass where the
five thousand were fed and their arrangement like garden
plots or drinking companies. The cures are narrated with
circumstance. Several Aramaic transliterations occur in
Mark which Matthew and Luke omit. He alone gives the
nickname of some or all the twelve, "Boanerges." All
these things and others are listed in the commentaries and
are justly cited as confirming Mark's priority to Matthew

[8] J. A. Robinson, *The Study of the Gospels*, 1902, p. 46, counts
190 short relative clauses; Sir J. C. Hawkins, *Horæ Synopticæ*,
2d ed., 1909, pp. 125 f., lists over a hundred "context-supple-
ments" in Mark.

and Luke. But the primitiveness they attest is only relative, not absolute, and not inconsistent with the secondary
character which we have inferred from the literary traits
of the material. The unnecessary details of time and place
and person have already been largely eliminated, in spite of
a few picturesque remains. The geographical data are not
always reassuring, at least in our present state of knowledge. We are not sure that Gerasa belongs on the shore
east of the Sea of Galilee (v.1), or Bethsaida west of it
with Gennesaret (vi.45), as Mark's outline now suggests,
nor do we understand routes described as "from the borders
of Tyre via Sidon to the sea of Galilee, through the midst
of the borders of Decapolis." The combinations, "the borders of Judea [and] beyond the Jordan" (x.1) and "unto
Jerusalem, [and] unto [Bethphage and] Bethany" (xi.1),
are difficult. The manuscript variants in both these passages and at v.1 may suggest that the difficulty was felt
early; the changes in Matthew suggest that it was felt
earlier. The evangelist employs Palestinian place names
rather abundantly. Is he really at home with them? And
is his obscurity in using them merely awkwardness of style?

The Aramaic translations also sometimes rouse the suspicion of Aramaic scholars, while the transliterations are
of such a kind as to suggest not the unconscious continu-
ance of impressive words in tradition, but a kind of ritual
or even magical interest in the efficacious *verba ipsissima*
of Jesus when engaged in exorcism or prayer.

Recently, as in the case of Luke-Acts, stress has been
laid on the Aramaic character of Mark's Greek.[9] The philological questions involved are complicated like those
which we have discussed in the preceding chapter. If Mark

---

[9] See F. Blass, *Philology of the Gospels*, 1898, Chap. XI; J.
Wellhausen, *Das Evangelium Marci*, 1903; A. J. Maclean in
Hastings, *Dictionary of Christ and the Gospels*, Vol. II, 1908,
pp. 129-131, and the articles there mentioned; B. W. Bacon, *The
Gospel of Mark: Its Date and Composition*, 1925, Chap. XVI.

is translated direct from a single Semitic writing, or is
based on Semitic sources more fragmentary and indirect, or
is written by one who wrote in Greek while knowing the
tradition in Aramaic, as the transliterations and translations
together with the tradition of Mark as Peter's "interpreter"
suggest, primitiveness of origin is not a necessary corollary.
Behind Mark, as behind Luke's writings, lies a complicated history.   As an American scholar has said, the composition of Mark was a process

> at least something more than the simple casting into
> written form of a single narrative, the unified product
> of an individual mind. . . . The Gospel was not
> written *aus einem Guss,* but has strata of successive
> periods, seams and faultings, overlappings and dupli-
> cations, like the other compositions of its type.   It has
> a *past,* whose record, difficult though it may be to
> decipher, often perplexing to the most patient scrutiny,
> is written in the phenomena of its structure, and
> will reveal something of the history of the work to
> him who patiently analyzes and compares.[10]

This verdict we must recognize as sound even if we
are not so optimistic about the possibility of recovering
Mark's history.   Its origin raises many questions similar
in kind and in difficulty to the questions of our own ultimate
quest—the origins of Luke and Acts.   By declaring certain
parts of Luke to be derived from Mark, we have only
pushed the questions back a single stage.   There remain
the questions when, where, by whom and on what basis
Mark itself was composed.

To all these questions the Christian readers of the
second century had given attention and answers.   The
author was named Mark.   He wrote in Rome.   His information came from Peter.   But what is the value and origin

[10] B. W. Bacon, *The Gospel of Mark: Its Date and Composition,*
p. 204.

D

of this opinion, which can be traced with some variation back as far as Papias and some of it possibly earlier to an elder whom he quotes? That is a different question on which doctors disagree, and naturally. For the opinion of Christians on such matters was derived partly from historical information and partly from inference based on the text of the New Testament books and upon other presuppositions. The value of the opinion all depends on how much is due to one ingredient, how much to another. And that is very difficult to decide. Evidently inference and conjecture played some part, perhaps a large part. The name Mark is not easily attributable to conjecture, but the apostolic authority of the books ultimately canonized was an early presupposition. Given the mere name Mark and the presupposition that such books came only from apostles, the rest is simple to explain, with the help of a concluding sentence of I Peter: "She that is in Babylon, elect together with you, saluteth you; and so does Mark my son." If the writer is Simon Peter, and if Babylon is Rome, Peter and Mark are both in Rome. Mark is Peter's junior and assistant. This Mark, then, is identified with the Mark of the Second Gospel and with John Mark of Acts, for no matter how common the name (and Marcus is the commonest Latin name), Christian tradition tended to bring into coalescence all persons mentioned in the New Testament under one name. Thus perhaps arose the so-called tradition found in Papias and later Fathers. The author's name is probably historical kernel,[11]

---

[11] Streeter, *The Four Gospels*, p. 562, has stated admirably the principle which the early demand in the church for apostolicity establishes for our judgment about traditions of gospel authorship: "The burden of proof is on those who would assert the traditional authorship of Matthew and John and on those who would deny it in the case of Mark and Luke." But of course "the burden of proof" is not always an intolerable burden when full knowledge of the facts can be acquired, nor is it equivalent to disproof when the facts are irrevocably forgotten.

for no Mark was an apostle in the strict sense or prominent enough in Scripture to have a purely anonymous writing assigned him. The subsequent growth of tradition is due to conjecture and combination. We can see the variation of the latter process in the variation of opinion recorded as to the exact relation of the gospel to Peter. Papias said Mark wrote from memory what Peter had narrated. Irenaeus says much the same. It is not certain, though quite likely, that both of them thought of the writing of Mark as taking place after the death of Peter, but the desire for closer relationship with the autoptic source led other Fathers to the definite dating of the composition as prior to Peter's death. Its composition was said at first to be without Peter's sanction (Clement of Alexandria), then with his approval (Eusebius), finally at his direct dictation (Jerome).[12]

Those who believe that the early church tradition has a larger mixture of authentic knowledge than of inference undertake to verify its statements about this gospel by the contents of the volume. They appeal to its vividness and verisimilitude as indicating first-hand information; to its Aramaic coloring and actual Aramaic quotations as confirming the view that the author was a translator, as Mark is said to have been; to the scenes in which Peter is prominent as confirming the view that he was the author's informant; to the Latin words as indicating Roman provenience; to the prediction of the fall of Jerusalem as agreeing with a date just before or after the traditional martyrdom of Peter under Nero. They repeat the combinations made by the early church. They regard as identical the three Marks—the evangelist, the associate of Paul and Barnabas, the associate of Peter. They accept the First Epistle of Peter as genuine and date it in Rome in the reign of Nero. They often go further than the earlier tradition.

---

[12] *Cf. Beginnings of Christianity*, Vol. II, pp. 253 f.; Streeter, *The Four Gospels*, pp. 561 f.

In the gospel they find evidences of the author's association with Paul and with Jesus as well as with Peter.
Its theology, they say, is Pauline and confirms the author's
companionship with Paul, while though Papias infers that
the author was no eyewitness, modern students find the incident of a close escape from arrest in Gethsemane intelligible if the young man there mentioned was the author
himself.[13]   If so, they think he lived in the house whence
they had come out after the last supper, and that this
house became naturally the one where the church gathered
later, which was none other than "the house of Mary the
mother of John whose surname was Mark." *Quod erat
demonstrandum.*

It is unnecessary to discuss these interesting and possible
combinations.   None of them is demonstrable; some of them
are improbable.   For the vividness and verisimilitude and
for the Aramaic elements other reasons than sheer primitiveness have been suggested above.   It is difficult to make
sure that Peter lies behind the stories, even those where
he is prominent.   Other evangelists give him a prominence
that is often both more extensive and more favorable.
Careful inquiries into the alleged Paulinism of the gospel
have produced quite negative results.   Direct influence of
Paul is perhaps to be excluded.[14]   The Latin words *census,
centurio, denarius, legio,* etc., are precisely those which
would be adopted outside of Italy in any of the Greek-speak-

[13] Mark xiv. 51 f.   Surely we may as well add, then, that no
other than the unnamed author is intended by his curious reference to a man carrying a jar of water into that house (xiv. 13 f.),
and that no other than the same fortunate fugitive is to be found
in the vague "a certain one of the bystanders," who, at the arrest
of Jesus, "drew his sword and smote the servant of the high
priest, and struck off his ear" (xiv. 47).   But the incidents at
Gethsemane may be merely another illustration of the way in
which "the peculiar and the incongruous clings in the mind of
man."

[14] See M. Werner, *Der Einfluss paulinischer Theologie im Mar-
kusevangelium,* 1923; Bacon, *The Gospel of Mark,* Part IV.

ing provinces of the Roman Empire.[15]   Mark's prediction
of the fall of Jerusalem could have been written after the
year 70 or many years before it, and nothing else in the
gospel has decisive bearing on this question of date.   That
Simon of Cyrene is introduced as father of Alexander and
Rufus, and one of the Marys at the cross and at the tomb
as mother of James the less and of Joses, suggests that
Jesus' contemporaries were now best known through their
children and that the tradition had reached the next
generation.[16]

On the other hand, the literary structure of the book and
the apparent history of its materials suggest that processes of gestation and development have been at work.
This is compatible with the retention of primitive elements,
but not compatible with a theory of the primitiveness of
the whole.   As a literary work the gospel is as late as its
latest factor.   The difference between primary and secondary is not readily estimated in years, no matter how obvious
in quality and priority; and the only assurance we can

[15] The other Latin words in Mark are *modius*, *prœtorium*, *quadrans* (κοδράντης), *sextarius* (ξέστης), *speculator* and perhaps *flagel-
lum* (φραγελλόω).   That these words do not localize Mark in Italy
is shown by a glance at the Greek index to S. Krauss, *Griechische
und lateinische Lehnwörter in Talmud, Midrasch und Targum*,
Vol. II, 1899, where every single one occurs and is attested as
being widely distributed in the Aramaic or late Hebrew sources.
It is evident from the Semitic transliterations that the Latin words
were naturalized in Palestine through the Greek.   For one of
Mark's equations, the "widow's mite" (λεπτόν, Heb. *pĕrûṭāh*) =
½ *quadrans* (xii. 42), Krauss (p. 500) happens to quote an exact
parallel in a second century Palestinian *baraitha*.   That Mark's
Latinisms are of such a kind tells perhaps more against than for
that gospel's Roman provenience, while the comparative absence
of such words in Luke shows a difference of taste, not of place.

[16] Mark xv. 21, 40, 47; xvi. 1.   In like manner another Mary is
introduced to readers of Acts (xii. 12), not by the name of her
father or her husband, but as the mother of John, whose surname
was Mark.

have about Mark's date is that, as it is earlier than Matthew and Luke, so it is later than some preceding stages of tradition. Whether one of these preceding stages was written or not makes little difference. The efforts of scholars to identify indications of written sources whether Greek or Aramaic have not met with general approval. The clues from doublets like the two accounts of feeding the multitude, from interpolations like the Beelzebul passage and the anointing at Bethany, are, like the alleged evidence of translation, not incompatible with a writer's use of oral material. But that Mark expanded existing written collections as the other synoptic evangelists afterward expanded his own is an entirely credible, if not demonstrable, supposition.

Though the origin of Mark's gospel may not be exactly known, its character is clear from its contents. Even if we cannot accept all the ancient traditions and modern theories about its authorship and authority, we must acknowledge that it has a place of supreme interest and importance in any effort to reconstruct the historical career with which it deals. This is recognized on all sides, as in the following statement:

> The change of sentiment which has taken place on the subject of the Second Gospel is indeed one of the most notable facts in the history of New Testament studies in our day. In ancient times little was made of this Gospel in comparison with its longer and fuller companions. Its genius was not sufficiently understood. Its special value was not adequately recognized. Thus Augustine could speak of Mark as only the "follower and abbreviator of Matthew," and while many minds occupied themselves with continuous exposition of its fellows, few seem to have done the like for this shortest of the Gospels. Now, however, all this is changed. It is seen to have quite a

distinct character, and to stand in a remarkable relation to the other Gospels.[17]

This appreciation of Mark's value is partly absolute but
mainly relative. On the face of it Mark is evidently an
ingenuous tale based on older information of a simple and
artless character. The preceding quotation continues: "Its
simplicity, the plain objective view which it gives of events,
the vivid way in which it tells its story, the things in it
which bespeak for it a very early date, make it a narrative,
it is perceived, of singular interest and very special
worth." [18] Its very shortcomings in such artificial matters
as conspicuous plan and purpose, its undogmatic viewpoint,
and even its contradiction of the conventional portrait of
Jesus, commend it to the discriminating judge and distinguish it from the "cunningly devised fables" which are to
be expected of deliberate fiction. It is no aspersion on the
historical value of Mark, but rather the contrary, when
Wellhausen says: "The single pieces are often presented
in a lifelike style without unessential or merely rhetorical
devices, but they stand for the most part like a series of
disconnected anecdotes, *rari nantes in gurgite vasto.*" [19]
That is just the way we expect genuine history to look. Indeed the few unessential additions of Mark, that is, such
irrelevant details as occasionally puzzle the commentator,
only further commend it. It has a realism about its descriptions, a human naturalness about the actors, a Palestinian nativeness about its scenes and subjects which suggest that we may trust it for verisimilitude, and perhaps
for veracity.

The same authenticating traits, however, cannot be denied

[17] *Century Bible, St. Mark,* pp. 3 f., new and enlarged edition,
1922, by J. Vernon Bartlet on the basis of the earlier edition by
S. D. F. Salmond.

[18] *Ibid.,* 1st ed., 1902, p. 4.

[19] Wellhausen, *Einleitung in die drei ersten Evangelien,* 1905,
p. 51.

of the other gospels.   To a large degree they are as artless, vivid and untheological as Mark, both where they are parallel to his account and where they are independent.   The great favor which Mark receives in modern study is due in fact to its relative primitiveness.   The scientific theory of history prefers the earlier source, and Mark's priority at once gives it a kind of right of way whenever Matthew or Luke or John parts company with it.   From us, who have nothing else to compare it with, Mark naturally deserves this *a priori* regard.   It is *our* oldest gospel, if not *the* oldest.   We note its comparative simplicity and primitiveness—primitiveness not only as a matter of date, but as a matter of religious standpoint when the other gospels are taken into account.   For example, the cases where Matthew and Luke omit or tone down Mark's suggestions of Jesus' limitation of knowledge or power set Mark before us in relief as a record of unexpurgated naïveté.   Yet much of this superiority of Mark can never be expressed in absolute terms.   Mark's claim to regard is due to our lack of any better standards.   It may not tell all that we wish to know, or with the certainty with which we wish to know it, but we admit that here if anywhere we come closest to any considerable body of reliable data about the life of Jesus.   Burkitt believes that in the matter of order Mark may be trusted to give in the later chapters not merely a grouping of detached scenes as he does up to viii. 27, but the actual succession of events.   But the most that he can really feel sure of is that "nothing that is to be found in any other of the gospels has any better claim to give the true sequence." [20]   Their differences are due not to superior chronological information but to editorial combination and rearrangement of sources.

Our regard for Mark is thus negative as well as positive. His story is effective and convincing in itself.   His com-

[20] F. C. Burkitt, *The Earliest Sources for the Life of Jesus*, 1910, p. 84.

panions show us where he has not suppressed or improved the apostolic tradition that came to him as they have done. We need not infer that he has suppressed or improved nothing himself, or that the apostolic tradition had not felt the effect of its own tendencies and interests in selecting and shaping the material. Mark gives us this process in an early stage. We intercept in him the developing thought of the church. We see the reflection of Jesus' life and words as they were used and valued perhaps a generation after his death in at least one Christian community, or as recorded by one Christian teacher. We may perhaps sum up this phase of our discussion of Mark by quoting with Bartlet some sentences from Johannes Weiss.

The significance of the oldest gospel for the church's history lies before all things in this, that it has fashioned once for all, with vivid touches serving as a model for all who came after, a picture of Jesus on earth which has impressed itself indissolubly on the imagination of the community. In it one can recognize what significance for the Christian mission the "historical" Jesus possessed. Mission preaching, as we have seen, could not dispense with a certain amount of information touching the life of Jesus. . . . The Gospel of Mark, then, teaches us that the need of a living, concrete picture was far greater than has generally been supposed. Fresh converts desired a fuller knowledge touching Jesus, of whom they were told that he is the Son of God: the communities needed for worship and individual piety a living presentation of him who had died for their sakes. Besides there was, no doubt, already arising a certain historical interest: in particular, as the eyewitnesses of Jesus' life were dying out, the necessity became clear of maintaining what they had given as tradition. The oldest gospel, therefore, is only to be understood and rightly estimated, if it is read on the one hand as expressing the conceptions and convictions of the evangelist, and on the other as a collection of older

D*

traditions, which in part grew out of quite other conceptions.[21]

In this way the Gospel of Mark not only interests us as an actual source for Luke; it shows us the character of the situation in which the later evangelist found himself and of the task and materials which lay before him.

When we turn from our own consideration of the Gospel of Mark to inquire what Luke thought about it, we must realize that many of the questions and interests which have been in our minds would have been absent from his. It is possible that he knew from more immediate knowledge the answers to such questions as author's name, date or sources of information, while we rely on a later, perhaps a different tradition and on our modern methods of verification or alternative conjecture. If he knew the answers to these questions, or thought he knew them as facts, that knowledge must have satisfied all curiosity about Mark's origin. It is perhaps more likely that he did not much concern himself with such questions, but that like many readers of Mark since his day he took the book for the inherent worth of its contents more than for any external credentials. Nor would Luke apply to the contents of the book the same kinds of criticism and criteria that we apply. Some of the very things that commend it to us were not attractive to him, as he shows by his omission of them. He would scarcely apply our abstract tests of primitiveness. He had other sources of information—he refers to many writings —and they may have seemed much like Mark in general character and value.

Yet Luke's use of Mark shows that for the period of which it deals he depended extensively and confidently upon it. For convenience, if for no other reason, he left its order of scenes largely intact. He copied Mark in

[21] Bartlet, *op. cit.*, pp. 48 f., quoting J. Weiss, *Das Urchristentum,* 1917, p. 544.

blocks and interspersed other material in blocks also. His principal omissions from Mark form also a continuous block.[22] It is possible that his copy of Mark had already lost or had not yet received this passage, and there are other shorter passages or phrases in Mark in which we are not sure that our text is identical with the document that was in Luke's hands. In particular we do not know how the Gospel of Mark continued after the point where it is now abruptly mutilated with the resurrection and appearances of Jesus announced but not yet related, or how far it continued into the events following the resurrection as Luke records them in Acts. Burkitt has suggested that it continued as far as the escape of Peter from Agrippa's imprisonment. In that case Mark's record would have included near the end a reference to John Mark himself, its reputed author, for we are told that it was to his house that Peter escaped. But if like the other gospels it closed with resurrection appearances of Jesus, we may be sure from Mark's anticipations [23] that these were located in Galilee, and that Luke did not use them.

Here as well as in the preceding passion narrative Luke is evidently not dependent on Mark alone, and since this other information dealt with the identical events—farewell conversations, arrest, trial scenes, crucifixion and resurrection appearances—he interwove or used alternatively the data from Mark with the parallel matter. In a few earlier passages Luke transposes and transforms incidents of Mark to such an extent that he appears to be combining Mark with other information, or substituting another narrative for that of Mark altogether. Thus he depends on a second source for his record of John's teaching and of Jesus' temptation. He presents quite independently of Mark, both in contents and in position, Jesus' visit to Nazareth, the call of the fishermen, an anoint-

[22] Mark vi. 47-vii. 26.
[23] Mark xiv. 28; xvi. 7.

ing by a woman and the conversation about exorcism by Beelzebul.[24]

But even when Luke varies considerably from Mark he is often nevertheless using him—merely paraphrasing more freely or elaborating out of his own imagination rather than abandoning Mark for some parallel account. Thus in the story of the transfiguration Mark does not tell us that Jesus went up the mountain "to pray," that they descended only "next day," and that the disciples were "heavy with sleep," but Luke may simply have inferred all these things from Mark's account or from Gethsemane and fitted them into his favorite scheme of Jesus' all-night vigils for prayer in the open. He might well have assumed that Moses and Elijah would also appear in glory and, like the written law and the prophets [25] which they respectively represented, would speak in advance of Jesus' "decease which he was about to accomplish at Jerusalem." Why he changed Mark's "after six days" to "about eight days after these sayings" I do not know.

Here as elsewhere he is following Mark's sequence of events. Where he inverts two sections within a series or anticipates a sentence which Mark brings in at the close of a scene, his motive is usually logical and can be reasonably guessed. This fidelity to Mark's order was doubtless, as I have said, out of convenience, for he does not hesitate to leave Mark on one side in order to insert whole series of incidents, only to pick him up again near the point where he had dropped him. Luke almost seems to avoid the inference that Mark's sequence means chronological connection, since he prefaces scenes from Mark with indefinite phrases like "it came to pass" or "on one of those days."

[24] Luke iv. 16-30; *cf.* Mark vi. 1-6; Luke v. 1-11, *cf.* Mark i. 16-20; Luke vii. 36-39, *cf.* Mark xiv. 3-9; Luke xi. 14-23, *cf.* Mark iii. 22-27.

[25] Luke xxiv. 25-27, 44-46.

On the whole, then, we may conclude that Luke had at hand in writing to Theophilus a Greek manuscript substantially the same as our Gospel of Mark and that he found in it an extensive, congenial and usable source. "Beginning from the baptism of John," it told "the story that occurred throughout all Palestine—namely of Jesus of Nazareth beginning after the baptism which John preached,—how God anointed him with the holy Spirit and with power, who went about doing good and healing all that were oppressed of the devil, for God was with him." [26] It agreed, therefore, with Luke's own idea of the ministry of Jesus. It also agreed in the main with his views of Christ's character and of the circumstances of his death. Its details Luke had little reason to question, its order he had no wish drastically to revise. Following the customs of his time he exercised little criticism upon its contents, while he dealt very freely with its wording. With slight exceptions his modifications or omissions of Mark were due more to following his own ideas or the information and sequence of some other source than to any conscious weighing and rejecting of what Mark offered. And so the main bulk of Mark he readily fitted after and between other materials, and he continued to use it at least about as far as to its present abrupt ending.

[26] Acts i. 22; x. 37 f.

CHAPTER VIII

Q

Second only in probability to the hypothesis that Luke and Matthew derived part of their contents from Mark is the corollary that other parts of their contents depend upon other common written record. The evidence for this corollary is the body of similar matter found in the two later gospels, but not found in Mark. The agreements of wording in these passages between Matthew and Luke are sufficient evidence of literary relationship of some kind. That either evangelist copied from the other is less probable than the only other alternative, that a common source lies behind both. Like that which they derive from Mark, this material already lay in writing before the two evangelists. For this material scholars are wont to use the symbol Q, though the "logia," the "second source," the "apostolic source" and other terms are still in vogue in some quarters. To this matter we must now turn in the consideration of Luke's sources.

Our knowledge of this source and of its history is not so extensive as our knowledge of Mark. It may seem that we know so little about it that its very existence is equally problematical. That is not the case. As often happens in literary criticism the existence of a common written source can be asserted with a good deal of assurance, when its scope and origin must remain unknown. In spite of our ignorance of detail the modern discovery of this stage in the transmission of the gospel is a significant and almost romantic event.

A firm foundation for the study of this now lost predecessor of Matthew and Luke can be laid by careful self-limitation. Where Matthew and Luke agree they provide sufficient evidence of their common origin; where they differ we rely on conjecture, not on evidence, and we must never obscure this distinction.

Our situation may be compared to what we should have known of Mark if Mark itself had in like fashion been completely lost. We should then have had in Matthew and Luke large remains of the lost Mark. By their agreements we could have reconstructed much of its contents, order and wording, but where only one evangelist retained the original material we should have been dependent on doubtful conjecture; where neither evangelist represented the original we should have been helpless. We should never have known how much of the common material belonged previously to a single writing; we might have conjectured too many or too few sources, either including the Q matter with the Marcan matter in a single lost document, or subdividing the Marcan matter into two or more documents. Two ancient expressions may be adapted as warning maxims for this study. (1) One is the Jewish law of corroborative testimony: "At the mouth of two witnesses shall every word be established." Only the agreements of Matthew and Luke merit general confidence in the reconstruction of their lost source. (2) The other is the old English prayerbook phrase, reprinted thus: "Read Mark, learn, and inwardly digest." Luke's relation to his best-known source must never be forgotten in our conjectures about Q and other sources less known.

The passages common to Matthew and Luke not derived from Mark—for this is what in its narrowest sense Q means—have frequently been listed, and while there is room for difference of opinion as to whether certain passages are alike enough to warrant such classification the listings usually agree. They include the cure at a distance

worked for the centurion at Capernaum and references to
other mighty works, the parables of the Lost Sheep, the
Mote and the Beam, and other shorter illustrations, and
perhaps the longer and less similar parables of the Talents (or Pounds) entrusted to servants and of the guests
invited to a Marriage Feast (or Great Supper). Most of
the material is, however, sayings of Jesus in picturesque
and epigrammatic language rather than extended parable
or historical narrative. Among its more familiar passages
are (in quite variant form) the Beatitudes and the Lord's
Prayer,[1] and (in more near agreement) Jesus' teaching
about worry, non-resistance, prayer, faith and courage
under persecution. There are woes against the Pharisees,
predictions and warnings about impending doom, and a
striking passage on John the Baptist. This last mentioned
discourse and several other sayings contain brief narrative introductions. The unframed saying has not in this
material entirely excluded the characteristic evangelical
unit of saying-in-setting.

Beside the parallel passages in Matthew and Luke which
have no resemblance to Mark several other parallels should
undoubtedly be included in Q, where, though Mark deals
with the same subject, the agreement of wording of Matthew and Luke against Mark makes it plain that the first
and third gospels are here derived not from the second,
but from some other written source. The introductory sections on John's preaching and on Jesus' temptation indicate that Q contained a much fuller version of these items
than Mark did. The same is true of the woes against the
Pharisees. The discussion on casting out demons by Beelzebul, the parable of the Mustard Seed and a few additional
passages show by their wording that Matthew and Luke

---

[1] I let this passage stand, and without argument, though Streeter
thinks some of these items, *e.g.*, the parable of the Lost Sheep,
the Beatitudes, and the Lord's Prayer, are derived from independent but overlapping sources.

are quoting in common a version of these sections that overlaps Mark in substance, but differs from Mark in expression.

The passages found in both Matthew and Luke and attributable to Q amount in bulk to roughly two hundred verses, or one-sixth of each gospel that includes them. No doubt other material now contained in one gospel or the other originally lay before both evangelists, as well as some matter which neither retained. Except for the birth and resurrection stories, nearly anything found only in Matthew or only in Luke, especially sayings or parables, can be looked on as an illustration of Q material which one has taken and the other left. Motives for omission may be conjectured and serve as evidence of original attachment to Q material, but in cases where one witness alone exists it seems hopeless to try to decide whether or not the items came from Q. For example, Matthew and Luke have four beatitudes in common, Matthew alone four other beatitudes, Luke alone four woes. If the common material belonged to Q, it is possible that either one of these evangelists omitted four verses which the other retained. But it is equally possible that the additional material in either case was not derived from the common source at all. Similar questions arise when we consider whether Luke's parable of the Lost Coin came from Q, as did the adjacent one of the Lost Sheep, or whether Matthew's saying of the second mile is from the same source as the adjacent Q passage on the other cheek. It is well to put such questions to one side for the moment, while one first considers the origin of Luke's matter.

For the wording and order of Q the same general principle holds in any attempt at reconstruction. Where Matthew and Luke agree we have little doubt; where they disagree we have little confidence. We may appeal to their habits in dealing with Mark. But their divergence from each other's order in Mark is less than in Q, and we are not sure that the same reasons hold for supposing that Luke's gospel represents very closely the original order of this material as it does in his treatment of Mark. The character of the material and its history may be different. As it stands in the two gospels there is much confusion in sequence as well as such striking agreements as the series: John's preaching, Jesus' temptation, the Beatitudes, retaliation, judging others, the Two Builders, the centurion of Capernaum. It is quite reasonable to suppose that this was the order of these units in the original, but shall we include between the Beatitudes and the Two Builders the sayings on salt, on lamps, on the jot or tittle and on conciliation, the Lord's Prayer, treasure in heaven, the single or evil eye, etc., as Matthew does in his Sermon on the Mount; or does Luke more accurately represent the original order of these sayings when he places them in a different order and later position in his gospel? [2]

Equally puzzling are the questions that arise about the original wording of Q. Sometimes the differences are slight and insignificant, and the extensive identical text of the two gospels may be confidently accepted as the text of their common source, as in the following passage:

Matthew xii. 43-45	Luke xi. 24-26
But the unclean spirit, when he is gone out of the man, passeth through waterless places, seeking rest, and findeth it not. Then he saith, I will return into my house whence I came out; and when he is come, he findeth it empty, swept, and garnished. Then goeth he, and taketh with himself seven other spirits more evil than himself, and they enter in and dwell there: and the last state of that man becometh worse than the first.	The unclean spirit when he is gone out of the man, passeth through waterless places, seeking rest, and finding none, he saith, I will turn back unto my house whence I came out. And when he is come, he findeth it swept and garnished. Then goeth he, and taketh seven other spirits more evil than himself; and they enter in and dwell there: and the last state of that man becometh worse than the first.

[2] Chapters xiv, xi, xvi. xii, xvi, xi, xii, xi, etc., respectively.

Sometimes the differences are considerable, as in the Lord's Prayer, where the agreements in order of clauses and in wording (notably the rare Greek word ἐπιούσιος) show literary relationship, while the differences of wording—"to-day" *vs.* "every day," "debts" *vs.* "sins," and the absence from Luke of several clauses—make the wording of the original source doubtful.

Matthew vi. 9-13	Luke xi. 2-4
Our Father which art in heaven, Hallowed be thy name. Thy kingdom come. Thy will be done, as in heaven, so on earth. Give us this day our daily bread. And forgive us our debts, as we also have forgiven our debtors. And bring us not into temptation, but deliver us from the evil one.	Father, Hallowed be thy name. Thy kingdom come. Give us day by day our daily bread. And forgive us our sins; for we ourselves also forgive every one that is indebted to us. And bring us not into temptation.

Sometimes the habits of the evangelists in general and in their use of Mark make their own changes quite obvious, as in the first passage Matthew's addition of "then," Luke's choice of "return"; in the second passage Matthew's addition of "who art in heaven," Luke's "every." These are characteristic of the respective writers, and almost certainly are due to them and not derived from Q. Usually, however, the divergences between the canonical texts give us less certainty even of such a negative kind about the precanonical wording.

It is customary to deal with Q as though like Mark it was a single work and lay before the later evangelists in the same form. That is possible, but there are other possibilities which need to be remembered. The unity of Q can hardly be proved or disproved from its present descendants. It contains miscellaneous material, or characteristic gospel units, especially sayings of Jesus, such as two or more collectors might have provided independently. Moreover, it is possible that what these gospels have in common rep-

resents an older nucleus already included in two different later works, which each of our evangelists severally
employed still later.

For example, it may be conjectured that prior to Luke's
writing of the gospel these two hundred verses had already
been expanded by addition and combination into a much
longer work, including the bulk of Luke's peculiar material,
and that Luke took them over already interwoven with the
material which Matthew does not share. The joining and
expanding of older collections is the method of Luke himself and it was natural for his predecessors. The non-
Marcan, like the Marcan material in the central part of
Luke, occurs mostly in two long blocks—Luke vi.20-viii.3
and ix.51-xviii.14. It is possible that like Mark it lay
before Luke in a single consecutive collection, including
both what Matthew shows us ought to be designated as Q
matter and what source analysts are wont to attribute to
a special Lucan source.[3]

It is possible, on the other hand, as the Chicago school
of critics held, that these two blocks represent two different
sources first brought together by Luke. In that case the
Q material which they contain also goes back to two separate sources. Thus while the unity and identity of the
source from which Matthew and Luke derive is often assumed, and while this assumption perhaps has the advantage of being simpler than any other, it must be admitted
that the phenomena prove nothing more than ultimate common derivation and do not preclude intermediate redactorial stages or a plurality of common sources.

These alternatives make more difficult than is usually
recognized the questions of Q's origin, which are difficult

[3] This source is often called L. B. Weiss, B. S. Easton, B. H.
Streeter and others who have attempted to identify it believe that
even its original characteristic vocabulary and viewpoint can still
be detected in spite of Luke's version. Streeter's *Proto-Luke*
(see below, p. 109 *note* 6) = L + Q.

questions at best. An hypothesis of Schleiermacher which identifies this rediscovered material with Matthew's collection of the Lord's *logia* mentioned by Papias has had an undeserved vogue, especially in England, and has led to unfortunate assumptions where confessions of ignorance would be more in place. The agreements between the Q of modern reconstruction and the description by Papias of the work of Matthew are not striking. Papias either is propounding theories concerning our Gospel of Matthew as a whole or is speaking of some book that is beyond our ken, perhaps beyond his own. To adopt his word *logia* for our Q material implies more knowledge of that word and of that material than we actually possess. For of Q are known only some things that it contained, chiefly sayings; it is not known that it omitted narratives; while *logia* is a quite general term, and "logia of the Lord" may mean the oracles of God in the Old Testament. Papias seems to say that Matthew did and Mark did not collect *logia,* but our Gospel of Mark, while it shows a smaller proportion of discourse to narrative (ratio about 1 to 2) than either Matthew or Q (as far as we know the latter) contained, is hardly to be divided from them by such absolute words as Papias uses.

Papias further says that the *logia* were written in Hebrew (or Aramaic), but the Q which lies behind Matthew and Luke was in Greek, for it is by its verbatim agreements in Greek that its existence is vindicated. To be sure, an earlier Aramaic original is possible for Q, as it is for all other Greek gospel documents, but the language does not require it, either when the gospels agree or when they disagree. The identification of a document known to us in no Semitic form but only by coincident Greek quotations with a document described by Papias as having existed in a single Aramaic form and in a diversity of Greek translations, can hardly rank as more than a most hazardous conjecture. For the same reason it will be safer to dismiss the idea that Q was Matthew's work. The association of Matthew everywhere else in tradition is with our first gospel, which he is said to have written in Hebrew; and if, as is likely, this tradition is mistaken, it is more probably based on the change of Levi (Mark ii. 14) to Matthew (Matt. ix. 9, *cf.* the corresponding addition of "publican" to "Matthew" in x. 3), than on the apostle's authorship in Hebrew of some other smaller writing like Q, which the first evangelist is not alone in employing.[4]

The date of Q is fixed, like that of Mark, only in that it is prior to Matthew and Luke. No inner data or outer traditions suggest other limits. Its apparent silence about the death of Jesus has led some to the extravagant view that it was composed in Jesus' lifetime. But the argument from silence is even more futile than elsewhere in the case of material of which we know only the partial contents. The material looks like reminiscence rather than contemporary record. It has some marks of the processes of oral transmission. On the other hand, it may have been separated from the later gospels by some intervening written stages of editorial enlargement.

Its relation to Mark both in date and in viewpoint is a natural subject of inquiry. As the two discoverable sources

[4] I should like here to register a protest against the habit, which seems to have undeserved currency, and not only among conservative critics, of explaining traditions of authorship by the convenient but unlikely hypothesis that the reputed author of a book was the author of one of its sources. Thus we are told that the apostle Matthew really wrote Q or some other source used by the first gospel, which was accordingly named as a whole for him; that Luke the physician wrote the "diary" of Acts, or Proto-Luke, or the unmutilated original of the gospel that now bears his name; that John was the oral informant or writer upon whom the Gospel of John in part depends, etc. This fancy of a kind of literary synecdoche is hardly more worthy of serious critics than were the ancient inferences of non-apostolic editors, translators or secretaries for writings whose apostolic origin could not be easily otherwise defended.

of Matthew and Luke and the two oldest definite documents of the synoptic family, Mark and Q invite contrast, while the passages where they deal with similar subjects provide grounds for comparison and raise the questions of dependence and priority. These parallel passages are more numerous than is often realized. Some of them have been already mentioned. It seems strange that so many subjects of Jesus' teaching recur in the two sources if they were entirely independent, and that several passages are identical in thought if not in wording. These doubly attested sayings [5] present one of the most interesting and complicated of the minor problems of synoptic study. When literary dependence is thought of, the priority is usually attributed to Q. Q then must be redefined, not as the source from which Matthew and Luke derive in common what they do not derive from Mark, but as the source from which they derive *directly* what they do not derive from Mark. For Mark itself may derive from Q much if not all its teaching matter. In this case Q gains even greater significance—as the oldest of all the family and the ancestor not of two but of three gospels—contributing independently to each and also indirectly through Mark to the other two.

The literary dependence of Mark upon Q rests, however, on very much slighter verbal evidence than do the two main hypotheses of literary relationship in the synoptic problem. The verbal likeness between Mark and Q is never greater than would be likely for two independent streams of oral transmission, and Wellhausen has argued that the viewpoint of Mark seems sometimes by comparison more primitive than that of Q. Unfortunately for our settling of this question—but fortunately for our knowledge of Jesus—a viewpoint dominating the whole of Q

[5] See F. C. Burkitt, *The Gospel History and its Transmission*, 1907, Chapter V; Wellhausen, *Einleitung in die drei ersten Evangelien*, § 6.

is no more obvious than is one for Mark. Except for the preponderance of teaching in contrast to narrative, the extant evidence concerning this lost body of material suggests the disorganizing process of natural tradition rather than the organizing influence of a single mind or of an all-controlling purpose. The sayings are crisp and epigrammatic, arranged (so far as we can get behind our gospels to the order of the source) by subject matter or association of ideas rather than by chronology. They seem to presuppose in the reader a knowledge of Jesus, who he was and what he did. They represent an interest in what he taught, an interest characteristic of a Christian feeling that attributed value to his advice. They deal with questions of character and conduct, with the greatness of John, with the faults of the Pharisees, with Christian faith and insight and fidelity, with Jewish unbelief and hostility, and with the day of the Son of man when appropriate reward and punishment are to be expected. All this at least the Q material contained and this viewpoint it presented. But how much more it contained and especially what it did not contain when Luke came upon it are questions that cannot be answered.

What it means to us to possess in part alongside of Mark this early store of evangelic record has been convincingly stated by Harnack in his *Sayings of Jesus.* But what did Q mean to Luke? He was as innocent of knowing that name as are most Christians to-day, nor did the material that scholars thus designate by a kind of algebraic formula stand apart for him any more than it stands apart in our gospels. Some matter found only in Luke was certainly part of the original Q. According to an attractive hypothesis recently urged in England all this Q matter, with most other parts of Luke's gospel that were not derived from Mark, may well be supposed to have existed already before Luke wrote to Theophilus, as an extensive and continuous source, one of the earlier narratives to which his preface refers.[6] Such a document Luke could have welcomed and used much as he did Mark. Where it dealt with subjects found in Mark he may have combined, suppressed or substituted its version. Elsewhere he could simply take it over in long alternating blocks. If the sayings now found in both Luke and Matthew were already incorporated in this longer "Proto-Luke," we may suppose that they had already been given much their present order and setting, matters in which they so widely differ from Matthew's parallels. But their wording manifestly has often been left almost untouched by the two or more editorial hands through which they have passed. Being largely sayings of Jesus they were exempted from the more drastic paraphrase which the narratives experienced. This difference of treatment we meet generally in testing the editorial use of the gospel sources. But Luke also partly recasts the sayings into his own style, and thus nearly obliterates any individuality of style in his source.

The unity of this pre-canonical source for Luke is scarcely demonstrable, and if his non-Marcan material came from two or three sources its distribution between them can be guessed with no assurance. Neither Matthew nor Mark gives us much help here. Very likely both Q in the strict sense and the MS. or MSS. before Luke which embodied what we thus designate differed little from Mark or other sources in simplicity of diction, in primitiveness of theology and in discontinuity of subject matter. Our evangelist found the non-Marcan material no less congenial to his purpose and used it without hesitation. All this material

[6] The source is called "Proto-Luke." The term and the elaboration of the theory are due to B. H. Streeter, *Hibbert Journal*, October, 1921, and *The Four Gospels*, Chapter VIII. The more detailed testing of the hypothesis has been already begun by B. S. Easton in his commentary and by Vincent Taylor (*Behind the Third Gospel: a Study of the Proto-Luke Hypothesis*, 1926) with results that seem to the investigators favorable.

exceeded Mark in amount of definite ethical teaching and in variety of parables. The latter Luke seems to have enjoyed with an aesthetic as well as a religious appreciation; the former he regarded as "words of our Lord Jesus Christ" to be "remembered" for present warning and guidance. And so he set down perhaps most of them that were supplied him, though he knew without including in the gospel at least a few other sayings of Jesus, as the quotation of one such *agraphon* in Paul's speech at Miletus shows us. Unlike Mark, this material when once incorporated into Luke finally lost any separate circulation. This is unfortunate. But its preservation in Luke (and partly in Matthew) was a most fortunate occurrence.

Altogether Mark and (in the strict sense) Q account for only half of one of Luke's two volumes. Three-quarters of his whole work remains without identified sources. Without repeating what we have already said or venturing further into the fascinating speculation about oral informants and written documents, we may conclude our discussion of this first factor in the making of Luke-Acts by saying that, whatever their origin, scope and contents, the traditions and information in all parts of his work represent materials which had had a varied and complicated history, which they only partly now reveal. It need not be supposed that Luke knew all that history himself, but he diligently and carefully embodied what thus came to him into a new comprehensive publication, editing it in accordance with the conventions of his time, adapting it to his purpose and in part stamping it with his own personality. The sources he used are after all only the under writing of a palimpsest and are not often clear and legible. As a factor determining the character of his final production they had a most profound influence, which even if they are not known to us must not be forgotten as we turn our attention to the three other formative factors just mentioned.

PART II

THE COMMON METHODS

CHAPTER IX

THE COMMON LANGUAGE

We are the creatures of habit and convention. Few writers and fewer of their readers realize how much the composition of books is determined by group habits. No writing is the result of free and untrammeled choice. It is a process hemmed in with the compulsions of convention. To think of any author, whether sacred or profane, as sitting down and taking up his pen to write in any way he pleases is as fictitious a picture as the crudest theories of mechanical inspiration. No more can the writer himself than the divine afflatus within him really dictate his own wording verbatim, literatim and punctatim. His viewpoint, his use and presentation of his materials, his method of composition, and his style and diction are only slightly matters of free will or conscious decision. The very language in which he will write was determined before his birth. When the writer is one of our own group, we who read him take these things for granted. In so far as his idiom, his punctuation, the format of his text and his attitude agree with what is familiar to us, we scarcely notice them, but as soon as we move out of our own cultural background into alien or ancient literature we need careful orientation in order that we may recognize the different conventions. The literary habits which Luke thus derived from his environment need for the modern reader some fairly extensive discussion.

All language is social convention, an arbitrary medium of exchange, related to ideas much as money is related

to the commodities it helps to transfer. But since the
memory of man began varieties have existed in language
corresponding to different human groups. The phenomena
described of the Tower of Babel are still with us. We all
have, as Acts tells us, "our own language in which we were
born," whether "Parthians, Medes and Elamites," British,
French or German. To describe and place exactly the
language of the author of Acts is our present difficulty. To
say that it is Greek is not sufficient, for that ancient language has differed at every stage of development for at
least thirty centuries.

Luke's Greek is neither classical Greek nor modern
Greek. It is Hellenistic Greek, sometimes called Koine,—
the Greek that was employed in the first century when
Luke wrote. It differed from the classical Greek in many
ways that are obvious to the classical scholar and annoy-
ing to the purist, but natural to the development of language and unconsidered by any of Luke's contemporaries
except the pedant. But it also differed within itself.
Spoken as Greek then was in a wider area than ever before,
it had supplanted the older dialects of its narrow Aegean
days with new variations. Some of these were doubtless
local, though probably more obvious in spoken than in written Greek, as is the case with variations in the English-
speaking world to-day. Local variations at any rate are
not now within our knowledge, and Luke's language does
not reveal any criteria of locality.

More significant were the variations of culture, and
cultural tests are more feasible in Luke's style, though
exact classification must be a delicate if not impossible
task for late-born barbarians like ourselves, unable to ac-
quire for Greek that spontaneous sensing of differences
of style that we feel for a native tongue. From extremes
of style Luke may certainly be excluded. He is not of
the lowest cultural grade on the one hand, nor on the
other does he belong with the Atticists of the time, who by

rigid rules and conscious imitation attempted to write in a style comparable to that of the classical masters of Greek prose. Between these extremes there were many grades of culture and many other linguistic groupings. Can Luke be placed here? It is customary, for example, to distinguish the style of the writers of literature who precede the Atticist movement from the spoken Greek of the age. The line is arbitrary and obscure. It would be useful if it could be established. Certainly Luke falls neither on one side nor on the other. Even when he is free from Semiticism he shows affinities with both popular and literary Greek.

The details of his style, when analyzed one by one, as can only be done by those who have read widely in all grades of contemporary Greek and have striven for judicious sense of valuation, lead to conclusions that are only tentative and partial. In the use of the optative he is more conservative than some of the respectable Greek writers of his age. In vocabulary, though at times he agrees with the rules of the Atticists, he frequently violates other of their rules. He had not read their books, and his language would seem to their critical taste commonplace, uncultivated and quite vernacular, like the rest of the New Testament. Among New Testament writers he stands high, from the cultural viewpoint excelling not only the other evangelists but even Paul, who wrote a vigorous and natural Greek free from the errors of ignorance. His vocabulary has much in common with Paul's, but in the Greek Bible the books nearest in style are Second Maccabees and the letter to the Hebrews.

Such likenesses and differences do not suggest any distinct grouping, and it is natural to inquire what affiliations of the author determined his style. To students of the New Testament in the eighteenth century acquainted with profane literature, that whole volume, and indeed the Sep-

tuagint and other Jewish Greek writings as well, seemed to
represent a distinct dialect of Greek.   The differences between the sacred writers were less than those which existed
between all of them taken together and pagan Greek,
whether the latter was judged by the older masters or
whether, as was less commonly done, a comparison was
instituted with contemporary Greek prose literature.
Hence Luke and the rest were thought to have written in a
special style of their own, sometimes extravagantly called
"the language of the Holy Ghost," at other times assumed
to be a special Jewish dialect of Greek.   In the one case
its peculiarity was due to divine inspiration. in the other
to the racial idiom of all the authors.

Neither of these explanations is probably correct.   Certainly there is no evidence that Jews spoke a Greek that
differed extensively and uniformly from the language of
other nationals.   Except as subject matter requires, the
Greek of Philo and Josephus is not Jewish.   Nevertheless
there is some community of style among Biblical writers
that must be explained.   Many of them have some genuine
Semitic characteristics, some of these due to the translation of Semitic originals, others to the influence of the
Aramaic in which the authors thought or received their
information orally, and others to the Septuagint itself,
which in quotations and elsewhere affected the Christian
writers.   The most obvious kinship between New Testament writers is in religious vocabulary, and some of this
may certainly be due to their Jewish or Christian membership.   The major part, however, of the unclassical elements
of language which they have in common is traceable neither
to Semitic nor to religious antecedents, but to their common
use of the vernacular speech of their time.   For Biblical
study the greatest result of the discovery in Egypt and
publication in Europe of great numbers of letters and
memoranda surviving on the original papyrus leaves is the
demonstration of this fact.   The New Testament language,

whatever narrower classification it still permits, is found now to belong to a wider category—the language "understanded of the people," used not merely by the Hellenistic Jews, but by contemporary Egyptians, Macedonians, Anatolians and Italians.

With this new knowledge of vernacular Greek and a renewed study of the more formal language of the time the style of Luke comes into clear perspective, and the meaning and connotations of his words can be more accurately estimated. Many words that formerly were not known to be used before Luke and were hence supposed to be coined by him may now be put to the account of the current idiom, and many more words and meanings which he shared with other Jewish or Christian writers must likewise be removed from the category of "Biblical" or "Sacred Greek," while the words employed only in his writings among the New Testament books are often found so generally in Greek literature as to lose the distinctive value often assigned to them as characteristic of Luke. They show neither personal traits nor even the effect of special influences, but rather Luke's membership in a wide fellowship of all sorts and conditions of men throughout the world.

In the light of these suggestive discoveries we must apply some caution to many cherished theories of New Testament criticism. The uniqueness of a word in Luke's writings is not proved by its absence elsewhere from the New Testament, for the New Testament is linguistically a purely accidental collection; nor is it proved by its rarity in secular Greek literature which we possess, a still more accidental limitation. Discovery constantly turns up such words in new places. Thus we are reminded that, where we in our ignorance diligently examine a word or expression of Luke's, remark its peculiarity, compare his use with the few other occurrences known to us, and draw inferences from its etymology, the author himself had set it

E

down on his paper naturally and simply, without any special attention to what he was doing, since it was an inevitable way for him or his readers to express the idea. The choice of words, be it repeated, is rarely a conscious choice and often carries no special association with it.

Frequently associations with certain writings or groups of writings have been imagined in Luke's vocabulary which more general consideration would have easily refuted. With Josephus, with the Greek medical writings and with special but far-fetched Old Testament parallels, Luke has been found to have much community of vocabulary, and literary influence or professional association has been hastily inferred when a slight reading in other literature would have shown that the agreements in vocabulary were not striking but commonplace. The argument from language for Luke's medical knowledge has had especial vogue. It rests on the same fallacy as has led modern scholars to argue the Baconian authorship of Shakespeare's plays from alleged legal terminology in them. In neither case are the words cited technical, as their widespread use in contemporary literature plainly shows. To the medical argument we shall return in a later chapter, as well as to other claims of individuality in Luke's style. It will be sufficient here to illustrate Luke's conformity to widespread Greek idiom by a few examples: [1]

"*biennium*" (διετία, Acts xxiv.27; xxviii.30) was known beside only in one passage, and that in the Jewish writer Philo. Now inscriptions and papyri show that it was the ordinary word for a two-year term, whether in jail or as tenant of a farm.

"accusation" (αἰτίωμα, Acts xxv.7) has been found in an illiterate papyrus of the year 95-96 A.D. about an accused donkey driver (*P Fay* 111). No other

---

[1] These examples and others will be found dealt with more fully in *The Beginnings of Christianity*, Vol. IV, or in *The Journal of Biblical Literature*, xlv, 1926, pp. 200 f.

instance was known before this discovery, and the later scribes, thinking the word rare, had in Acts changed it to a commoner word of similar spelling, αἰτίαμα

"ankles" (σφυδρά, Acts iii.7) in this spelling was equally rare, as the commoner spelling (σφυρά) in all the MSS. and correctors except the three or four oldest suggests. The original spelling was known to the Christian dictionary-writer Hesychius and now has turned up on a papyrus (*P Flor* 391) containing instructions for divination by the movements of members of the body. The use of this passage to indicate Luke's medical vocabulary is a comedy of errors.

"half dead" (ἡμιθανής, Luke x.30) in the story of the Good Samaritan is not really an unusual word, but its use in the papyri in complaints of assault and battery shows how very appropriate its expressive language is to the setting. It is scarcely a technical term of medicine! But it has been claimed as such, though, as in the preceding case, confusion with the more familiar spelling (ἡμιθνῆς) found in medical and many other writers is necessary.

"olive grove" (ἐλαιών, Acts i.12, *et al.*), as Luke seems to call the Mount of Olives, occurs in Josephus and the Greek Old Testament, but no instance in any secular Greek writers was known to lexicographers. In the papyri, however, we have abundant evidence that it was not a Jewish-Greek word. There were olive groves innumerable in Egypt, and it was used also as a proper name there, as "a vine-covered property called Olive-Grove at ———" (*P Lond* 214; *cf.* *P Fay* 118; *P Hamb* 64).

"mattress" (κλινάριον, Acts v.15) in this one of the diminutive forms occurs in no known author before Luke except Aristophanes. Professor Harnack and others have supposed it medical, though no instance of its use by doctors is forthcoming. That it belonged to everyday speech, which Aristophanes often adumbrates, was suggested by its use by Marcus Aurelius, Artemidorus and Arrian, three writers in the second

century after Christ. Now, however, a newly published papyrus (*PSI* 616) carries it back four centuries earlier to Syria and Egypt.

A single chapter of Luke's, and that, too, one of the
most secular in its style (Acts xvii), contains no less than
four words which, though not found in profane literature,
have been proved now, by their use in the papyri and inscriptions, to be good Gentile and secular words. They
are translated "rulers of the city," "turn upside down,"
"a setter forth," "bounds." [2] It is strange indeed that
none of these words has been found in any of the Greek
writers, but it must be regarded as merely a "statistical
accident." It can hardly be an accident, however, that of
the inscriptions on which occurs the first of these words,
"rulers of the city," a large majority come from Macedonia, and nearly half of these from Thessalonica, the
very country and city of which Luke employs it.

Many phrases of Luke regarded as peculiar or due to
special causes occur so regularly in the writers of his day
as to indicate rather how thorough his knowledge of Greek
idiom was. In the later chapters of Acts especially occur
many combinations of words that we can identify as sound
Greek idiom. There is, for example, his use of *litotes*. All
readers of Acts recall Paul's boast of citizenship in Tarsus
which he calls literally "a not insignificant city," but few
realize that this special combination is often used by the
Greeks in just such contexts. It was not necessary for
Luke or Paul to know Euripides' *Ion* or the (spurious)
Epistles of Hippocrates.[3] The privative compound adjective is used more often in Greek with "not" than without it,
and resembles a form of understatement affected by some

---

[2] πολιτάρχης (verses 6, 8), ἀναστατόω (6), καταγγελεύς (18), ὁροθεσία
(26). Two other words of this chapter, ὀχλοποιέω (5) and κατείδωλος
(16), still await discovery in any other ancient writing, but they
are scarcely of Luke's invention.

[3] οὐκ ἄσημος πόλις, Acts xxi. 39. Eur. *Ion* 8; Hipp. *Epp.* 1273.

English writers. So elsewhere we read, "God left himself not unattested," or "I was not disobedient." [4] Perhaps even more characteristic of contemporary Greek, both
literary and unliterary, is another *litotes* of Luke, "no
ordinary miracles," "no everyday kindness." [5] This phrase,
though it occurs nowhere again in the New Testament, is
familiar enough to readers of the papyri or of authors like
Polybius, Philo, Josephus, Diodorus Siculus and Artemidorus. It evidently came naturally to Luke. The same
may be said of his other instances of *litotes*.

In every language certain pairs of words become stereotyped. Some of them are similar in sound, like our kith
and kin, black and blue, health and wealth, name and fame.
Such a phrase is the Greek λιμοί καί λοιμοί,[6] two words
as alike in sound as "dearth" and "death," by which we
may translate them. They formed a standard combination
in the Greek from Hesiod down. Others are synonymous
pairs, like "signs and wonders," "times and seasons,"
"neither part nor lot." [7] These fixed expressions were
already as familiar to Luke as their English equivalents
have become under Biblical influence.

Again, Luke employs idiomatically certain verbs with
certain nouns as objects. His ἀναβολήν μηδεμίαν ποιησάμενος
is as regular a locution as our English "brooking no delay,"
his περιῃρεῖτο ἐλπὶς πᾶσα as our rendering of Dante,
"All hope abandon." [8] If we find in English something
familiar in such phrases as "wrapt in slumber," "deliver
the letter," "secure assistance" and "gain one's end," we
may know that they would render more distinctive idioms
in the Greek of Acts.[9]

These and many other evidences that Luke was fully at

---

[4] οὐκ ἀμάρτυρος, Acts xiv. 17; οὐκ ἀπειθής, xxvi. 19.
[5] οὐχ ὁ τυχών, Acts xix. 11; xxviii. 2.
[6] Luke xxi. 11. The parallels do not have the pair, but simply
λιμοί.   [7] Acts i. 7; viii. 21.   [8] Acts xxv. 17; xxvii. 20.
[9] Acts xx. 9; xxiii. 33; xxvi. 22; xxvii. 13.

home in the idioms of Greek are accessible to the modern connoisseur of the ancient tongue. That they are due to specific passages in Greek authors which Luke had read is very unlikely. Even his citation of the poets [10] belongs to the category of familiar quotations, not necessarily quoted first-hand. If "kicking against the goads" and "not in a corner" in the speech before Agrippa are proverbial, they too come through familiarity with educated language rather than with literature.

While we may safely deny Luke the special influence of Josephus or of medical terminology or conscious Atticism, the effect of the Greek Old Testament upon his style is unmistakable. In the birth stories it has affected both the matter and the manner, and frequently elsewhere it is quoted, echoed or imitated. It may be difficult for us to decide whether the imitation is conscious or unconscious. The Biblical flavor of Bunyan, Lincoln and other writers of Biblical English is probably unconscious. It is well to remember, however, that Luke belonged to a setting in which imitative style was not uncommon. Archaism had certainly affected Jewish literature before him; it was

[10] Acts xvii. 28. By an intelligible if not especially creditable trait of human nature, familiar quotations tend to come from near the beginning of works of literature. "We also are his offspring" would be no exception if the phrases it echoes were those which occur in line 5 of the *Phœnomena* of Aratus and in line 4 of Cleanthes' *Hymn to Zeus*. The former was familiar, two or three centuries before Luke, to the Hellenistic Jewish writer Aristobulus who quoted lines 1-9 (*apud* Eusebius *Præp. Evang.* xiii. 12, p. 666 b), and to Clement of Alexandria after him (*Strom.* v. 14, 101, quoting lines 1-6, 10-15).

According to Syriac commentators (*Horæ Semiticæ* x, 1913, pp. xii ff.), the preceding words are also a quotation. The line "For in thee we live, and move, and have our being" occurs two lines after the hexameter quoted in Titus i. 12, which Jerome assigned to Epimenides of Crete and which Diels thinks occurred precisely in the prologue of his poem. Further discussion must be left to the commentary.

already affecting Greek literature. The apocryphal books, the Wisdom of Solomon and First Maccabees, whether written originally in Hebrew or in Greek, represent an archaizing manner. Indeed, all late use of Hebrew was an artificial return to an obsolescent language comparable to the *tour de force* involved in Greek Atticism. The Greek mind was particularly sensitive to variations of style. Different dialects were artificially preserved in different classes of writing, and imitation (μίμησις) of definite authors became a rhetorical practice for young students that finished authors never outgrew. It is therefore not improbable that some of the more obvious Semitisms of the speeches in Acts are Biblical imitation. The prepositional use of parts of the body, "to the face of" (= before), "from the face of" (= away from), "on the face of" (= upon), "by the hand of," "by the mouth of" and the like, are easily adopted from any literal translation of the Bible. Similarly, in suitable passages an author readily falls into the Semitic parallelism, like "in the gall of bitterness and the bond of iniquity," "that they may turn from darkness to light and from the power of Satan unto God." [11]

Foreign words, on the other hand, Luke largely avoids, and here he coincides with the genius of the Greek language, at least with all Greek that has any literary pretensions. While English is hospitable to foreign words, and the use of foreign phrases from the French, German or Latin, like *esprit de corps, Zeitgeist,* and *deus ex machina,* is often affected and sometimes approved as a mark of culture, Greek standards strictly banned foreign and even Latin words as barbarisms. In Hellenistic and Byzantine Greek and in imperial and medieval Latin, writers who dealt with foreign history or geography were embarrassed with the difficulty and the unpleasantness of including the proper names of Semitic or Germanic or other alien civilizations

[11] Acts viii. 23; xxvi. 18.

in their own homogeneous language. This is one reason
why they use them sparingly, often so sparingly as to
obscure geographical or biographical identity.[12] The geog-
rapher Strabo explains repeatedly [13] that he omits names
of places or peoples to avoid unpleasantness of writing or
because of the ugliness and strangeness of expression, and
his successor Pomponius Mela mentions only two of the
highest mountains in Germany because the rest were "hard
to pronounce with a Roman mouth." [14] Mela also in his
preface apologizes in advance for the barbarian names he
will be forced to use, and the same is true of the prefaces
of Pliny's *Natural History,* Jerome's Latin translation of
Eusebius' Greek *Chronicle* and Appian's Greek history of
Rome. Similarly, Josephus in the first of his twenty books
of *Antiquities of the Jews* explains that the proper names
have been Hellenized for the sake of the beauty of the
writing, with a view to the pleasure of the readers.[15] Even
Latin names were turned into Greek not without apology,
criticism or ridicule.[16] The triple Roman names of persons

[12] H. Peter, *Die geschichtliche Litteratur,* 1897, Vol. II, pp.
287 f.   [13] iii. 3, 7, p. 155; xvi. 4, 18, p. 777.

[14] *De situ orbis,* iii. 3, 3.

[15] *Ant.* i. 6, 1 § 129. When his sources give lists of names, as
the officers of David in 1 Chron. xxvii, the exiles who returned
with Zerubbabel in 1 Esdras v, the Jews who put away their foreign wives in 1 Esdras ix, and the seventy elders who brought the
law to Egypt for translation into Greek in Aristeas 47-50, Josephus
omits the lists, though he regularly explains that he did not think
it necessary to enumerate the names (*Ant.* vii. 14, 8 § 369; xi. 3,
10 § 68; 5, 4 § 152; xii. 2, 7 § 57). Only the special reason of confuting those who supposed that the Jews were Egyptians and not
out of Mesopotamia induced him to transcribe from Genesis xlvi
the [five and] seventy descendants of Jacob who went down to
Egypt, though he says, "I was not inclined to set down their
names, especially because of their difficulty" (*i.e.,* of pronuncia-
tion in Greek, ii. 7, 4 § 176).

[16] Plutarch *De fortuna Rom.,* 10 (pp. 322 f.); Philostratus
Apollonius, iv. 5; Lucian *De hist. conscrib.,* 21. Dion. Hal. (*Ant.
Rom.,* ii. 50, 3) in describing the founding of religious cults in

must have seemed unnecessarily burdensome to any Greek with sense of style.[17]

It is natural, therefore, that Jerome, whose own difficulties have been mentioned, explains the fact that Luke alone of the four evangelists omits the Hebrew word *hosanna* as characteristic of one "who among all the evangelists was most learned in the Greek language," and gives as his reason that since he saw he could not transfer the exact meaning of the language he thought it better to omit than to set down that which would raise a question in the reader's mind. Beside *hosanna* the other Hebrew or Aramaic exclamations in Mark are omitted in Luke's gospel, and many of the proper names like Golgotha and Gethsemane and Bartimaeus fall away. When they are retained Luke often apologizes for them by adding "so-called," "as its name is." Probably it is literary apology quite as much as archeological explanation to his readers which leads him to speak of "a city called Bethsaida," "Capernaum, a city of Galilee," "a publican by name Levi," "Arimathea, a city of the Jews," "a man by name Joseph," " two men who were Moses and Elias," "the feast of the unleavened bread called the *pascha*," instead of the mere names found in the parallels of Mark. Even where he avoids the Semitic word by omitting it or translating it into good Greek, he uses similar qualifications, "the mountain called Oliveyard," "the place called Skull," "the gate of the temple called Beautiful," "the so-called Zealot." Perhaps the same applies to his "the day of the sabbaths," "the day of the pentecost," "the power of God called Great." Instead of repeating the names Barabbas and

early Rome lists a few deities by the names of their counterparts in Greek religion and adds "and other gods whose names it is hard to pronounce in the Greek tongue."

[17] See Norden, *Die antike Kunstprosa*, 2d ed., 1909, pp. 60 f., and Nachtrage and Index, *s.v.* "Fremdwörter," for other evidences to the same effect.

E*

Emmaus, he uses like other Greek writers a circumlocution; for the former, "he who for riot and murder was thrown into prison, whom they demanded," for the latter, "the village where they were going." Like other Greek writers, also, Luke avoids some Latin transliterations that were getting into Greek,—mostly names for money, or other governmental terms like *centurio, census,* and *quadrans.*[18] We shall find further reason elsewhere [19] for supposing that Luke was sensitive to the spelling of foreign names, using both a Greek and a barbarian (indeclinable) form for Saul, Simeon or Jerusalem. It is his unhellenized spelling of the first of these (Σαούλ rather than Σαῦλος) which leads him in the very Hellenic setting and style of the speech before Agrippa (but not in the two parallel accounts) to explain that the voice from heaven spoke to Paul "in the Hebrew language."

---

[18] Mark xv. 39; xii. 14, 42; *cf.* Matt. v. 26.   *Cf.* pp. 88 f., and *Style and Literary Method of Luke,* pp. 154 ff.

[19] See pp. 225 ff.

CHAPTER X

LITERARY TYPES

The character of a writing is partly determined by the class or *genre* to which it belongs. The writer will work quite differently if his subject is to be expressed in poetry or in prose, as an argument or a narrative, a novel, a biography, a textbook, a sermon, a letter, an apocalypse or a tragedy. And the reader of each work will form a more understanding judgment about it if he can place it in its proper literary setting and identify the literary class to which it belongs. To classify Luke's work seems, therefore, the beginning of wisdom.

All four of the gospels appear at first sight to fall under a familiar category—the biography. We call them lives of Christ like our modern "lives" and we naturally seek to understand them by the ways of modern biographies; or if we are more careful and learned, by the ancient biographical methods. We know that the βίος as a definite type of literature existed in the days of Luke and in the Hellenistic culture to which he belonged. The *Parallel Lives* by Plutarch, which were familiar to many generations of Englishmen, come from a contemporary of Luke, and classical students know of other examples in Latin as well as Greek. Tacitus' *Agricola* and Suetonius' *Lives of the Caesars* have as subjects statesmen and men of action, as do the biographies of Plutarch. But leaders of thought, philosophers and teachers also sat for portraits to the biographers. Their lives were not so full of public incident, but private anecdotes and quotations from their

sayings gave them sufficient interest.   In subject and in
form these books are therefore nearer to the gospels.   One
of the earliest and most influential was the *Recollections of
Socrates* by his pupil Xenophon (called *Memorabilia* in
Latin, ἀπομνημονεύματα in Greek).   This work consists of a series of unarranged incidents in the philosopher's life together with the teaching which they called
from his lips in the ensuing dialogue.   In the second
century of our era Arrian, the imitator of Xenophon, perpetuated in a similar composition the memory of his
famous teacher Epictetus.   The remains of this work of
pietas that have come down to us are quite without incident
or dialogue; they are the lectures, sermons, addresses, or
whatever one should call the utterances of the sage when
reported without setting.

There are other instances of purely teaching *memorabilia*
or *apophthegmata*.   Closer to the gospel in their admixture
of act and word are the so-called *Lives and Opinions of
the Eminent Philosophers* compiled by Diogenes Laertius;
but perhaps the most interesting and effective parallel to
the gospels is a work written by Philostratus in the third
century, on the Life of Apollonius of Tyana, a philosopher
and wonder-worker, contemporary with Jesus and Paul.[1]
Respecting the relation between the gospels and this work
C. W. Votaw, who has instituted a careful comparison
of "The Gospels and Contemporary Biographies,"[2] gives
the following points of likeness:

(1) The purpose in each case was a practical one,
to promote morality and religion by eulogizing and
commending the great teacher in his message and in his
example; (2) the method common to each was to recount the life in a general chronological arrangement
from humble birth to death and glorification; (3) the

[1] Both these works are now available to English readers in the
Loeb Classical Library.

[2] *American Journal of Theology*, xix, 1915, pp. 45-73, 217-249.

deeds and words were intermingled in a narrative that consisted mainly in a chain of anecdotes; (4) the story in each case was full of miracle—divine person, miraculous birth, healing miracles, supernatural knowledge and foretelling, resurrection and ascension; (5) the biography in each case was written by one who was not an immediate disciple and observer of the hero, and who wrote a generation or more after his death; (6) the information was obtained partly from oral tradition but chiefly from written memorabilia; (7) the traditional story was retold without much historical investigation or criticism, using the material at hand almost as it was; (8) the Greek style of the sources was reworked more or less, to give the writing higher quality, acceptability, and usefulness.[3]

Votaw lays stress upon the popular character of the gospels and of their classical parallels. They are not historical biographies in the sense of representing critical investigation and sifting of the facts. The writers show no disposition to relate their heroes to general history, to explain their inner development or to interpret them historically or psychologically. They are propagandists. "They eulogize and idealize their heroes, they select their best sayings and interpret them for practical use, they give the memorabilia in an atmosphere of appreciation, they commend the message to the faith and practice of all." The gospels he confesses are not the work of professional *littérateurs,* but writings "of the people, by the people, for the people."

In spite of these safeguards the comparison of the gospels with the Hellenistic biographies has been severely criticized in an interesting study of their literary classification by K. L. Schmidt.[4] For all the propagandist and popular character of the more influential ancient biograph-

[3] *Loc. cit.,* pp. 65 f.
[4] *Die Stellung der Evangelien in der allgemeinen Literaturgeschichte,* 1923.

ies, he believes they differ essentially from the gospels
in that, after all, they are literature. They represent
conscious art, intended for the literary public (though
Arrian protests that he did not intend and had not prepared for the publication of the *Discourses of Epictetus*).
For the gospels parallels must be sought in lowlier levels
of composition, and if sufficient analogous material is not
forthcoming among our remains from the same age and
civilization as the gospels, it can be readily supplied from
other writings that show the same informality and the same
origin, whether in the folk-lore or in the saint-lore of other
religions and races.

The classification of the gospels as biographies has
worked, Schmidt believes, a good deal of mischief. The
mistake was made as early as Justin Martyr, perhaps as
early as Papias. The former in any case was trying to
explain Christianity to the cultured heathen public and
therefore applied to the gospels the literary term made
familiar since Xenophon for recollections of great men
written by their disciples. He was also trying to secure
for the gospels such credence as first-hand evidence gives.
Therefore he called them memorabilia and attributed them
to the apostles or to "the apostles and those who associated with them." In the same way he parades references
to official records—the census papers of Quirinius at the
time of Jesus' birth, or the reports of Pilate dealing with
Jesus' deeds and his execution. But the gospels are not
biographies or memorabilia in the sense that Justin or
others would understand those words. An apologetic interest in their historicity has encouraged a false classification, and the effects of this error still persist. The consideration of their literary *genre*, instead of revealing their
real character, has obscured it.

The differentiating factor in the gospels that separates
them from biographies is their popular character. They
are not popular in the sense that they are written for un-

educated people by educated people, by experts for the
inexpert, by specialists catering to a general interest; but
rather in the sense that they are natural growths, self-made,
not artificial or artistic productions. Sometimes they re-
semble conscious art, as in their reliance on objective
presentation; but while such indirection of portraiture was
with the ancient Peripatetic biography a conscious device,
with the gospels it was an unconscious development. In
formal biography the individual author plays an important
rôle. He must collect and sift the materials, arrange
them in order, interpret them and present them so as to
trace the inner and outer life of the subject. He is likely
to obtrude himself on the material. In popular literature
the individual artist or writer has no importance. The
material is the spontaneous creation of a group, and the
ultimate scribe is satisfied to set down the material as it
has come to him. The art of composition is a very slight
factor compared with tradition, and in no stage in its
history has the tradition felt the strong controlling hand
of an individual artist, critic or creator. In popular literature the literary form is inherent in the material as it
has come to growth; it is not superimposed by the
composer.

All this applies to our gospels and justifies the differen-
tiation from formal literature, though the difference is
perhaps in degree rather than in kind. Schmidt admits
that the line between *Kunstliteratur* and *Kleinliteratur* is
hard to draw, and that in its earlier stages the life of
Apollonius is comparable to the gospels. With this restric-
tion much of Votaw's comparison is fully justified. All
history and biography rely ultimately on the raw material
of facts, and the proportion between tradition and composition is the varying factor. We have already seen how
tradition molded the materials of the gospels and how fully
it determined their present form. The study of the literary
classification—the models or the analogies for Luke's writ-

ing—carries us back once more to the materials themselves. It will be worth while to consider their classification again from the present standpoint, but after that there remains the question whether beside this influence of the materials a small quantum of literary and editorial art was not exercised by the final evangelist.

That Luke's gospel should not be counted a formal biography is further confirmed when one recalls that it is merely part of a longer work, and that its sequel, though full of biographical incident, is even less concerned with sketching the full career of its principal characters. The figures in Acts—Peter, Stephen, Philip and Paul—are neither taken up from their birth nor (except Stephen) followed to their death. For the readers they are "without beginning or end of days," like the transitory figure of Melchizedek. They remain more like actors in a drama than the subjects of biography; and of course historical setting, psychological development and the other traits of formal biography are lacking in Acts as they are in all the synoptic gospels. If we take Luke's work as a whole, as we should do, and not by halves, biography is not the word for it.

At this point, however, another convenient rubric suggests itself. That is history. Like biography this class of literature was known in antiquity as well as in our times. The distinction was recognized by biographers like Plutarch and Nepos,[5] but the dividing line between the two was often slight. Biographies of the leaders of the philosophic schools or of emperors (Suetonius) were published as a series, and many ancient histories dwelt on biographical details fully as much as does Luke's work. If one thinks of Hebrew history on the one hand, or Greek history on the other, one recalls the strong bias toward dealing with indi-

---

[5] Plutarch *Alexander*, 1, p. 664ᴇ, *cf. Galba*, 2, p. 1054ᴀ, Nepos *Pelopidas*, 1.

viduals. Group movements and cultural, economic and social developments are more difficult of description and more modern. As in Luke-Acts, the narratives of ancient history were often carried forward by the careers of successive individuals. The succession of statesmen in Athens, of emperors in the Roman Empire, and of patriarchs, judges, kings and prophets in Hebrew history made the most natural thread of continuous narrative. The series of Luke, John-Jesus-Peter-Paul (to omit minor characters), is it not comparable to Eli-Samuel-Saul-David or Sulla-Pompey-Caesar-Antony-Augustus? How similar contemporary Greek biography and history were in their general method of presentation may be seen by comparing Plutarch's [6] life of Coriolanus with the parallel (and source) in the history of Dionysius of Halicarnassus.

No doubt Luke's work is nearer to history than to any other familiar classification. In the Book of Acts particularly we have enough variation from concentration on persons to suggest that we are getting the history of a group—the church. Heinrici says it "is the only book in the New Testament that permits of classification in the contemporary Greek literature" and compares it for example with the later books of Cassius Dio, where Dio writes the history of his time: "Like the latter, Luke collects the facts carefully; both believe sincerely in the signs and wonders which they recount. Also Dio's method of narrating reminds of Luke's in that he tells of his experiences under Commodus in the first person." [7]

It is evident that the same objection can be made to this other formal classification as is made to biography. Luke is not the author of two books either of history or of biography, or of one book of each. If we can separate popular literature from technical history, Luke's work be-

---

[6] See below, pp. 161 ff.

[7] C. F. G. Heinrici, *Der litterarische Charakter der neutestamentlichen Schriften,* 1908, p. 91.

longs to the former, not to the latter. Schmidt himself
complains that even the latest writers, like Harnack and
Meyer, select Luke because he seems the nearest of the
evangelists to a formal *littérateur* and deal with him as
though he were an ancient historian, a successor to Polybius and a precursor of Eusebius, whereas Luke and all
the evangelists are really the transmitters of popular
tradition. Schmidt admits that Luke has more literary
aim than the others, but he is hindered by the nature of
his materials from carrying it through. "His real literary
abilities become somewhat visible in his Gospel and his
Acts of the Apostles (and there most strikingly in the
second part of his work), but viewed as a whole he is
primarily the bearer of the tradition which he passes
on."[8] His efforts at literary form only bring into sharper
outline the incurably unliterary character of his materials.

   If Luke's books do not fit the rubrics of formal history or
biography, is there any single class of folk-literature which
may be applied to them as a whole? This latter literature
has never enjoyed the clear-cut subdivision which goes with
conscious workmanship, and furthermore the materials in
Luke's writings were apparently miscellaneous from the
start. Here again we come to the standpoint of the
material and to the discovery that its units have had
separate history and hence separate form. The comparisons which we hoped to make with Luke-Acts cannot be
made with them as a whole but in parts. The analogies
are partial and sectional. The sayings of Jesus have their
parallels in the collected dicta of the Greek philosophers,
in the proverbs of the Jews and in the apothegms of the
Christian Fathers. The narratives have their parallels in
the Old Testament and in all popular history. Even the
combinations of sayings and doings, the anecdotal style,
may be illustrated as we have seen in popular Greek bio-

   [8] K. L. Schmidt, *op. cit.*, pp. 102 f., *cf.* 132 *et al.*

graphies, and of course in other literatures. There are
stories of miracles in all primitive and in most cultivated
societies. The same kinds of circumstances produce the
same phenomena, which we may call a type if we like,
provided we guard against the fallacies of assuming thereby
imitation and influence.

Luke is certainly as uninfluenced by popular types as
models to be imitated as he is by the literary canons
of Greek formal history and biography. The material itself sets the form automatically and independently. The
likenesses are worth noting none the less. Especially interesting are those analogues which come from the same age
and background as Luke. This is the interest of the life of
Apollonius of Tyana, of the rabbinic parables and of Jewish
miracle tales collected by Fiebig. The gospel controversies have their analogies with Greek dialogue, the itinerary of Acts with the travel tales of the Greeks, and the
trial of Paul and to a less degree the martyrdom of Jesus
and Stephen with the later Christian *acta* of martyrs and
their non-Christian predecessors. These, with other and
perhaps better parallels from other fields where popular
material has somehow been recorded with little literary
self-consciousness, all show how such things tend to be
told. It is necessary, however, constantly to beware of
any assumption of conscious conformity to type or even
unconscious imitation.

It might seem natural to find more inclusive names for
the types of Luke's composition in the names that his books
now bear—"gospel" and "acts." It is doubtful whether
either of them came from the original author and whether
they had already any use as designations of definite literary types. The gospel type apparently existed before
Luke in Mark. Whether that was an innovation is not
certain, but even if it were it was hardly a conscious one.
It was probably not called a "gospel" ($\epsilon\dot{v}a\gamma\gamma\dot{\epsilon}\lambda\iota\sigma\nu$) at

first; perhaps it had no distinctive name. When it was felt to be a distinctive type a new name had to be found for it. We know of no non-Christian use of the word "gospel" of a writing, though we are learning of its contemporary use in senses akin to other Christian uses. Justin Martyr seems to have thought that the name needed explanation for pagan readers. The Jewish opponents of Christianity transliterated it into Aramaic as a distinctively Christian kind of writing. As a special name it applied to the spontaneous and natural growth represented by our synoptic gospels. Once the type was established the fourth evangelist and the early uncanonical gospels conformed to it, and the apocryphal gospels imitated it, but the later literary Christian writers never resumed this form of literature.

The name "acts" (πράξεις) has a similar history, except that it was a noun more commonly or naturally applied to a writing. A few biographical works are known to have included that word in the title, but it was such a simple word that it is doubtful whether it carried any special formal connotations. It could be used of romance and mythology, as well as history, of inscriptions as well as books, and probably of magic and of other forms of non-literary composition. Its application to Luke's second volume, when the latter became detached, was entirely appropriate and was not intended as a literary classification by the originator of the name. It is if anything an effort to describe the contents rather than the form. The contents were too miscellaneous for any simple title. Possibly in this volume, too, Luke had some predecessors. In any case he had some imitators with apocryphal acts, but the name is borrowed from the canonical work rather than derived in common from any prior, well-defined type. In referring to his predecessors Luke is satisfied to call their work simply a "story" (διήγησις, Luke i.1). Probably no more technical name would be felt necessary for his own work. He calls his first volume a λόγος. One gets the impression that Greek writers of even more literary pretensions were indifferent to the use of generic names in referring to their own works or to the kindred works of their predecessors. The authors' own titles of ancient works are often lost (if they had them), but aside from naming the subject matter "concerning ——," only simple untechnical names like "compositions" or "books" predominate in cross references.

As our interest in the subject of literary form is not classification for its own sake, but for the light it throws on the origin of Luke's writings, it may be unnecessary for us to settle the controversy which such questions raise. There is a danger of "fighting about words to no profit." It is interesting to recall that the correspondence of Paul— such a spontaneous and individual product—has raised a similar dispute, whether we should think of it as formal epistles or informal letters. The dividing line which is attempted in each case is difficult to carry through. Luke's writings contain an element of both sorts. They are, at least in their original material, not literary at all. They are made of the stuff of unadorned tradition, whose art is natural and whose creation is unconscious, social rather than individual, and popular rather than literary. They retain to the end the earmarks of their origin. This we attempted to show in dealing with Luke's material.

When, however, we distinguish the procedure of the evangelist from the character of his materials, the literary element comes to light. The tradition and its popular forms he shares with the other gospels; in his literary effort he stands apart. Evidently the standards to which he aspired were more akin to formal literature than were those of the other evangelists, and yet the material in its given form was not easily transposed into formal history. However incomplete and superficial his success, he evidently tried to convert this material into literary form. He cannot be blamed for the effort as a dilettante who was incapable of success or who tried the impossible task of putting new wine in old bottles. Possibly the earlier style, evidently popular and episodic, so commended itself to him that he was loath to change it. The material at hand, both in its units and also in its general character as used by Mark, provided Luke with another standard of writing. In any case the popular form competed with the literary and Luke either could not or would not entirely abandon it. The literary element is therefore limited and is superimposed upon the non-literary form and matter. But here he differs from contemporary historians only in that the material he used was less amenable to formal use than was theirs and that he was less thoroughgoing in his editorial process.

All ancient history and biography rested in the last resort on material much like Luke's. Sometimes this material had the initial advantage of greater completeness, closer relation to the eyewitness, and more historical connection and order. In many cases the extant histories rest not directly on raw material, but on earlier histories which had accomplished for them the preliminary labor of putting the material into historical form, so that the successor had the easier task of carrying forward a process toward literary expression, or of merely combining and paraphrasing earlier rhetorical sources into a rhetorical and literary version of his own. The *littérateur* recognized the crudity (both in style and in contents) of unarranged tradition or material (ὑπομνήματα) and gladly avoided the task of forcing it into approved historical form. He preferred to let others do it, though he was glad to claim reliance on the original sources and, if it lent verisimilitude, to imitate (with apologies) or to retain their unpolished style. Yet in many formal histories and biographies the incompleteness, the dearth of historical connection and the effects of popular tradition still shine through from the untractable underlying material.

Luke's material evidently had not been artistically arranged when it came to him. No earlier evangelist had transformed the things fulfilled among the Christians into a work of literature, and Luke himself only made the change in certain quite partial ways. His final product, Luke-Acts, shows less of the composer and more of tradition than much ancient and modern literature, but the literary aspects are unmistakable and are fully in accord, as far as they go, with contemporary prose writings. The specific influences of these standards may therefore be appropriately reckoned among the formative factors of Luke's work. They will be dealt with in some subsequent chapters.

CHAPTER XI

POPULAR FORMS

In the preceding chapter a distinction has been made between the popular and the literary forms of composition, and both have been claimed as component factors in the work of Luke. The former consists of the natural forms of expression and narrative which belong to common speech and daily life; the latter applies to the formal writing of the *littérateur*, especially to the contemporary standards in Greek and Roman biography and history. The former affected Luke primarily through the material that came to him, whether oral or written; the latter enters in as part of his own editorial method. To the former, therefore, we first direct our attention.

In its origin, at least, Christian story had nothing to do with Greek literary culture. It arose from the life of Palestinian peasants and missionaries, and its language never quite lost that plebeian flavor which in the circles of culture became a ground of ridicule to its enemies and of embarrassment to its friends. In the gospels especially the strong Semitic coloring bears evidence of the near connection of the written Greek to the spoken Aramaic. The whole synoptic tradition, says Harnack,[1] is Palestinian and has had nothing to do with Gentile Christian circles except in the redaction of Luke. But the gospel story reveals its humble origin as well by the very simplicity, naïveté and artlessness of its style and matter. And herein its affinity is not merely to the writing of one land or one race, but

[1] *Luke the Physician*, p. 166.

to the whole realm of simple folk-story throughout the Hellenistic world, and to other peoples in other times in the same stage of unsophisticated primitiveness.

The popular literature of antiquity and its oral forms of expression are not so familiar to us as are the conventional forms of composition. Such material was neglected by men of culture as unworthy of the name of literature, and so was largely lost to posterity. Not enough survives to allow even a rough classification of the various conventional types, which in any case must have been more fluid than the stereotyped *genres* of belles-lettres. In recent times more attention has been given by classical scholars to the lower forms of writing. The papyri have provided examples of some kinds of vulgar composition (e.g., magic spells and exorcisms) which formerly were known only indirectly. In other cases material long available has yielded by fresh study and comparison a new insight into the popular style of narrative as it lay hiddden under the cultured redaction of the *literati* or obscured by the caricature of the satirist. All such fresh revelations concerning the lower strata of ancient writing have great significance for the New Testament, a significance, however, that is very likely to be overstated or misinterpreted. No doubt the forms of letters and diatribes have affected the manner of Paul; no doubt conventional sermon topics have affected the speeches in Acts and other hortatory passages in early Christian literature, but such influence does not preclude originality and independence of authorship.

To those who, in the novelty of enthusiasm and interest in the discoveries in these lower cultural strata, believe that all early Christian writing derives its form if not its content as well from such sources, any comparison between Luke and contemporary formal historiography will seem without value. With such a verdict the present writer cannot agree. The marks of literary affiliation in Luke are too numerous to be neglected. But at the same time it is most desirable to place beside him as well all the parallels of common speech and writing that are available. In spite of his culture even Luke's work, as Wendland declares, in many respects allies itself with the popular hero tales. If the points of comparison are less clear, that is partly due to the greater variety and scope of winged word and anonymous memoranda,[2] partly to our less perfect knowledge of the subject. The task that lies ahead is well stated by Reitzenstein:

> If it is once granted that there is no early Christian writing that had not its antecedents in the Hellenistic popular literature, it becomes obvious that theologians and philologians must labor together to distinguish the forms as sharply as possible and to determine the laws which work in each form. Only after this is done can we tell how` far the individual Christian writing is influenced by them, how far it is independent.[3]

For the present we must be satisfied with a few brief hints as to the forms of popular expression that can be compared with Luke and Acts, and with some suggestion of points of likeness between them.

Our point of departure is suggested by the pioneer work just quoted—*Wundererzählungen*—tales of wonder and miracle.[4] Throughout its history the miracle tale was connected with religion and superstition. As the readers craved the supernatural, so religion supplied the means for their satisfaction. It may be safely said that popular reli-

---

[2] ἀδέσποτα ὑπομνήματα is the expression of Plutarch *Demos.*, 5.

[3] R. Reitzenstein, *Hellenistische Wundererzählungen*, 1906, p. 99; *cf.* Norden, *Agnostos Theos*, p. 307.

[4] Besides Reitzenstein, *cf.* O. Weinreich, *Antike Heilungswunder*, 1909; P. Fiebig, *Jüdische Wundergeschichten des neutestamentlichen Zeitalters*, 1911; P. Wendland, *Die hellenistisch-römische Kultur*, 1907.

gion always preferred conviction through the miraculous to the strict requirements of truth. Even when as in the case of Lucian the wonder tale reaches the ridiculous and seems to be but caricature, the religious connection is still apparent, and the author maintains an attitude of sincere piety. But sometimes the religious element recedes into the background and the wonder tale is told purely for its own sake.

Foremost among the miracle tales are the accounts of cures. These are of course closely connected with the shrines of the gods, especially the gods of healing. On the stelae erected in gratitude to Aesculapius by cured visitors were written accounts of their cures, with full diagnosis and a description of the treatment. Some of these inscriptions are still preserved. These form at least one literary beginning of miracle tales, ἱεροὶ λόγοι. Like the testimonials of modern patent medicines such accounts were circulated widely for advertising purposes. No one can fail to recognize the analogy which the abundant cures in the gospels and in Acts afford to these tales of healing. In an age when salvation was thought of as the cure of disease, physical healing loomed large in every religion. That to a considerable extent healing was described as exorcism is due to the prevalent belief in demons as the cause of disease. While the gospels do not give any full formula of exorcism, there can be little doubt that the practice of this art affects their description of cures.

Other kinds of miracle tales in Luke and Acts find parallels in popular literature. Thus the miraculous release from prison, as of Peter in Acts xii and of Paul and Silas in Acts xvi, and the miraculous and gruesome punishment of the hero's opponents, as of Judas Iscariot in Acts i and Herod Agrippa I in Acts xii, are common conventional topics. The public competition between a true and a false prophet, like the scenes with Simon Magus in

Samaria and Bar Jesus (Elymas) in Cyprus, is also a favorite theme of Jewish and Christian literature.

Another class of popular literature, if anything so varied and unrestrained can be classified, is the travel tale (*Reisebericht*). It included journeys by land ($\pi\epsilon\rho\iota\acute{\eta}\gamma\eta\sigma\iota\varsigma$) and by sea ($\pi\epsilon\rho\acute{\iota}\pi\lambda o\upsilon\varsigma$). Some are the travel diaries of common men and soldiers, such as Lucian refers to. Some are the official records of royal admirals and the reports of deputations and expeditions. Others are the records of explorers and men of science. From the last kind, with its perennial tendency to the extraordinary and miraculous and with its wonders of nature learned by credulous investigators from superstitious natives, the transition to the purely fictitious travel tale is easy. And this in turn is parodied by Lucian in his *Icaromenippus* and his *True History,* and by others. In all these grades of literature the travel story had certain favorite themes and certain common characteristics. Everyone knows what a long series of visits to the world below followed the account told Alcinous in the Odyssey.[5] Especially common is the story of storm [6] and shipwreck on a desert island. Characteristic of their style is the brief seriatim itinerary with the names of places, companions and duration of stay such as is found in Acts.

But the most impressive characteristic of all is the frequent use of the first person. The testimony of eyewitnesses is a desideratum in all narrative, but especially in travel narrative, and nowhere is the use of the first person more abundant. It seems to have been the regular custom for the *periplus,* as the account of a coasting voyage was called, to be written in the first person—at least in its unadorned original form, although the revised works of

[5] *Cf.* C. Liedloff, *De tempestatis, necyomanteæ, inferorum descriptionibus,* 1884.

[6] *Ibid.; cf.* H. Peter, *Wahrheit und Kunst,* 1911, p. 423, and Acts xxvii.

that title are usually in the third person.[7]   The novels and
the satires of this class, however, keep the first person,
and occasionally in the revised works the original first
person shines through.   Whatever the explanation of the
"we" passages in Acts, their form is certainly nothing
extraordinary in contemporary writing.

With what other forms of popular literature should
Luke's work be compared?   In *Agnostos Theos* Norden has
suggested one line of comparison, between the speeches of
Acts and the conventional sermon of Hellenistic philosophy
and religion.   But many other types of popular literature
can be properly compared.

Especially desirable would be a fuller knowledge of the
popular religious literature of the day in its various forms.
No doubt in the conflict of religions among the lower
classes the religious tractate of all kinds flourished—
diatribe, gospel, hero-tale, sacred journey, wonder tale,
pastoral letter, prayer book, sermon, apology, and many
more.   But the greater part of this literature has perished.
Of the literature of only one Hellenistic religion have we
anything like a considerable remnant—the Jewish.   What
we have from Judaism illustrates the great variety of
literary expression which a religion could employ.   The
Septuagint in itself contains the greatest diversity, and
still other varieties, like the midrash, the homily, the allegory, the parable and the sacred epic, are known from the
remains of extra-canonical Jewish writings.   All these are
part of the inheritance of early Christian writers.

The field opened before us by but one religion seems
limitless; how much more vast it would be if we still
possessed the sacred books of Mithra, Isis, the Syrian
goddess, and the many other gods who found devotees in
the ancient world.   Sometimes we guess that certain New
Testament terms are part of the rich religious vocabulary
of the day, but how little do we really know of the literary

[7] Norden, *Agnostos Theos*, p. 323.

form and contents of that secret literature of the mysteries intended for edification, instruction, revelation and defense, in which "theological, astrological, and alchemistical and other writings mix Egyptian, Persian, Syrian, Phoenician and even Jewish teaching." [8]

> All such religious literature is in the nature of the case ephemeral and not intended for permanence; it disappears quickly, as it renews itself quickly. To judge by the glimpse we have got from the papyri we cannot make our conception of the production in this field too varied or too prolific. Only so the wealth of the literature of edification belonging to the socalled gnostics and the Christians becomes intelligible to us, a literature upon which the brightest light falls from their profane antecedents. [9]

We have repeatedly expressed the warning that such likeness in form between Luke's material and the popular parallels is not to be miscontrued. The parallels point really to no special literary grade or culture or age. They are frequent in belles-lettres as well as in folk-lore, in Jewish or Oriental tradition as well as in Greek and Roman, and indeed in quite independent bodies of literature. Neither in form nor in substance do they indicate a derivation of the Christian from the pagan material. They do not argue even a corresponding level of fancifulness, truthfulness or accuracy.

There is one part of Luke's tradition, however, which is in itself of special interest to the reader and which, if genuine, might be expected to reveal some personal, or at any rate some cultural, individuality. I mean the teaching

[8] Reitzenstein, *Die hellenistischen Mysterienreligionen,* 2d ed., 1920, p. 18.

[9] P. Wendland, *Die hellenistisch-römische Kultur,* 2d ed., 1912, p. 163. *Cf.* Deissmann, "The Letter of Zoilos," in *The Expositor,* December, 1922, and elsewhere.

of Jesus. For as nearly as we can tell Jesus was a thorough
Jew in mental background, profession and method, a successor of the prophets, a contemporary of the scribes and
a predecessor of the rabbis, and his words might be expected to reveal some of the special formal characteristics
of their provenience. The Semitic way of speech is not
like the Western. How far, then, do these characteristics
remain in the later Greek gospels?

The answer to this question is entirely reassuring. The
Semitic coloring in the sayings of Jesus is unmistakable.
Those persons who are most familiar with them may perhaps never have approached them from the viewpoint of
Formgeschichte, though rich instruction is the reward of
careful analysis. They are Oriental and Jewish through
and through. The two traits of Oriental language—figur-
ativeness and poetical form—are so abundant that prosaic
and non-figurative sayings attributed to Jesus are comparatively few. By poetic form is meant for the Jew not
so much meter or rhyme as parallelism—the poetic arrangement familiar to every reader of the lyric or gnomic literature of the Old Testament:

> Unto us a child is born,
> Unto us a son is given.

> A soft answer turneth away wrath,
> But grievous words stir up anger.

Such couplets, synonymous or antithetical, abound in
Jesus' teaching:

> He that is faithful in a very little is faithful also in much,
> And he that is unrighteous in a very little is unrighteous also in
> much.

> Give to every one that asketh thee,
> And of him that taketh away thy goods ask them not again.

The figures of speech are also equally characteristic of
both the gospels and simple Semitic style. Hyperbole we

think of as specially Oriental; paradox is perhaps found in all proverbial speech. Illustrations of the former are not far to seek in the gospels:

> Even the hairs of your head are numbered.

> Not a jot or tittle of the law shall fail.

Often hyperbole and paradox are combined by the use of two proverbial extremes—the camel and the needle's eye, the camel and the gnat, the mustard seed and the mountain, the mustard seed and the tree, bread and stones, the mote and the beam.[10] For paradox we may quote such oft-repeated proverbs as:

> Many last shall be first,
> And the first last.

> He that saveth his life shall lose it,
> And he that loseth his life shall find it.

To him that hath shall be given,
And from him that hath not shall be taken even that which he hath.

It is the figures of comparison, however, that predominate in Jesus' teaching. Metaphor, simile, parable, allegory

---

[10] The terms chosen for extremes of size are as conventional as the English "needle in the haystack." The rabbis spoke of an elephant going through the needle's eye and of recriminating critics demanding that one should remove the "mote" or the beam from between the teeth or eyes. *Cf.* G. B. King, *Harvard Theological Review,* xvii, 1924, pp. 393-404. But the most typically Jewish in idea and in subject matter is the reference to the minutest thing in the written law by the term "tittle" (κεραία), which may be assumed to be not merely the smallest letter (jot = ἰῶτα = yodh), nor even a distinguishing part of a letter, but the horns, thorns or crowns, as the rabbis called them, which were purely decorative apexes drawn above certain letters in scrolls of the sacred Torah. *Cf.* Strack-Billerbeck, *Kommentar zum N. T. aus Talmud und Midrasch,* Vol. I, 1922, pp. 248 f.

—whatever one calls them, and the lines of division between the four names just given are not readily drawn—these occur in the majority of Jesus' sayings, usually in association with the poetic manner.

> Behold I send you forth as sheep in the midst of wolves,
> Be ye therefore wise as serpents and harmless as doves.

> Where the carcase is,
> Thither will the eagles also be gathered together.

Often the parable contains two or more contrasting groups described in parallel stanzas, as the Two Builders; or two similar parables are found in pairs, as the Calculating King and the Calculating Builder, the Mustard Seed and the Leaven, the Lost Sheep and the Lost Coin. The latter groupings may of course be due to the evangelist or to preceding collectors.[11] But the parable itself is unmistakably a form earlier in its origin. It is one of the most striking results of modern study to be able to vindicate Jesus' parables, not as an individual product of his own mind, but as conforming exactly to the oral speech of his precise environment. Neither the Jewish literature that preceded, as in the Old Testament, nor that which followed much later, nor any contemporary or alien culture, offers such close literary parallels as do the sayings of the Jewish rabbis of Jesus' day, which are later recorded in the Talmud and kindred writings. There is a weird resemblance in form as one reads:

> To what is Rabbi Bun, the son of Rabbi Chiyah, like? Like a king who has hired many laborers, and there is one of these laborers who is more diligent in his work than necessary. What does the king do?

---

[11] *Cf.* p. 233, and R. Bultmann, *Die Geschichte der synoptischen Tradition,* 1921, pp. 122 f. Streeter, *The Four Gospels,* pp. 189 f., notes that such twin parables occur in all our sources.

F

He takes him and accompanies him on a walk in all directions. Towards evening the laborers come to receive their wages and he gives him pay equal to theirs. The laborers complain and say: "We have worked the whole day and this man has worked only two hours, yet he was given pay equal to ours." The king answered: "This man has done more in two hours than you have all done in the whole day." Even so Rabbi Bun did more in the Law in twenty-eight years than a distinguished scholar is able to do in a hundred years.[12]

Or illustrations in Luke may be compared with passages in the *Pirke Aboth* of the Mishna:

Luke xvii. 7-10	*Pirke Aboth* I, 3
But who is there of you, having a servant plowing or keeping sheep, that will say unto him, when he is come in from the field, Come straightway and sit down to meat; and will not rather say unto him, Make ready wherewith I may sup, and gird thyself, and serve me, till I have eaten and drunken; and afterward thou shalt eat and drink? Doth he thank the servant because he did the things that were commanded? Even so ye also, when ye shall have done all the things that are commanded you, say, We are unprofitable servants; we have done that which it was our duty to do.	Antigonus of Socho received the tradition from Simeon the Just. He used to say: "Be not like servants who minister unto (their) lord on condition of a gratuity; but be like unto servants who minister unto (their) lord without (expecting) to receive a gratuity."

[12] Jerusalem Talmud *Berachoth*, II f. 5c. *Cf. Midrash Rabbah* on Cant. ii. 6. Compare Matt. xx. 1-16. On the rabbinic parables and the gospel counterparts see the books cited by J. Klausner, *Jesus of Nazareth*, Eng. trans., 1925, p. 265 *note* 38.

Luke vi. 47-49	Pirke Aboth III, 17
Everyone that cometh unto me, and heareth my words, and doeth them, I will show you to whom he is like: he is like a man building a house, who digged and went deep, and laid a foundation upon the rock: and when a flood arose, the stream brake against that house, and could not shake it: because it had been well builded. But he that heareth, and doeth not, is like a man that built a house upon the earth without a foundation; against which the stream brake, and straightway it fell in; and the ruin of that house was great.	(Rabbi Eleazar ben Azariah) used to say: "Whosesoever wisdom is greater than his works, unto what is he like? To a tree whose branches are many, but whose roots are few; and the wind comes, and uproots it, and overturns it. And whosesoever works are more abundant than his wisdom, unto what is he like? Unto a tree whose branches are few and whose roots are many; if all the winds that are in the world come and blow upon it, they move it not from its place."

Even where the agreement in substance is not so close the likeness of method is evident. The agreements extend not only to the general form but to the formulas. The "king parables" are characteristic of the gospels as of the rabbis. The Jewish parable is introduced often by the question and answer, as in Luke's "Whereunto shall I liken the kingdom of God? It is like unto leaven"; sometimes by the double question as in the preceding verses, "Unto what is the kingdom of God like? and whereunto shall I liken it? It is like unto a grain of mustard seed." We have in the parable of the Wicked Husbandmen, as in the first Jewish instance quoted, the moral pointed by the question, "What then will the lord of the vineyard do to them?" Although the earlier question in this parable, "What shall I do?" is added to his source by the third evangelist here, and perhaps likewise in two other parables (Rich Fool, Unjust Steward), evidently neither he nor his immediate predecessors are responsible for the main features of these illustrations. It is not necessary, per-

haps not possible, to determine whether they come from
Jesus or are from the early Palestinian Christian tradition,
or in either case whether the likeness in contents shows
oral interdependence between the Jewish and the Christian
tradition.   Written relationship must probably be excluded.
The form of the Christian parable—for this is our point—
plainly represents the contemporary Jewish technique
and gives striking testimony that the Christian tradition,
running its roots back to Palestinian soil, has been molded
by that Jewish technique and has not been much revamped
by Luke or the other Greek evangelists, so as to lose its
Semitic form.

The persistence of these Jewish characteristics is the
more marked when we recall how natural it would have
been for the evangelists to eliminate them.   In the simple
popular philosophic speech of the Stoic and Cynic pamph-
let, the Hellenistic world had at hand a style of its own,
as informal as that of the Jewish scribes and as suitable
for the presentation of plain moral truths.   This type of
writing is called the "diatribe," and survives in the works
of Seneca, Epictetus, and others.   Its formulas and ways
of illustration are many of them similar to the Jewish
methods.   The short command, the rhetorical question, the
interruptive objection and other vivacious traits derived
from the dialogue constitute its formal earmarks.   Jewish
writers with Greek contacts, like Paul and Philo and
"James," easily adopted these mannerisms of the diatribe.
They are lacking, however, in the gospel sayings.   Luke
alone perhaps introduces a few: "you fool!" "you fools!"
"God forbid!" [13]   They are exceptional and the exception
again proves the rule.   Luke also perhaps tones down the
rhythmical parallelism of his material, or is less strikingly
symmetrical than Matthew, as in the story of the Two

---

[13] Luke xii. 20; xi. 40; xx. 16 ($\mu\dot{\eta}$ $\gamma\acute{\epsilon}\nu o\iota\tau o$).   The accumulation of
short precepts in Luke vi. 27 f., 35, 36-38, is, as Easton notes, "not
paralleled elsewhere in the gospels."

Builders, but how far he is from adopting the style of prose, not to say the style of Hellenistic rhetoric and philosophy, the work of Josephus reminds us.

We have already in Chapter IV contrasted with our gospels the Jewish historian's account of John's teaching. The contrast is as great in style as it is in motive and subject matter. Josephus has translated the Jewish prophetic oracle into the Greek philosophic essay. His process is even more clearly shown in earlier passages in the same work, where his actual source, the Old Testament, with all its Semitic style, is available to us for comparison. Even when he retains quite closely the content of the original, as in Nathan's parable,[14] many of the picturesque features of the original disappear, and instead of Jewish repetition we get the studied variation of phrase characteristic of the Hellenistic style. But at other times Josephus recasts the original into long, prosy moral disquisitions. So in the kindred passage, in place of Samuel's rebuke of Saul:

> Behold, to obey is better than sacrifice,
> And to hearken than the fat of rams, etc.

Josephus writes:

> The deity is not delighted with sacrifices, but with good and righteous men, who are such as follow his will and his laws, and never think that anything is well done by them, but when they do as God has commanded them: for he looks upon himself as affronted, not when anyone does not sacrifice, but when anybody appears to be disobedient to him. And from those who do not obey him, or pay him that duty which is the only true and acceptable worship, he will not kindly accept their oblations, be those they offer never so many and fat, and be the presents they make him never so ornamental,—nay though they may be made of gold and silver, he will reject them, and

[14] 2 Sam. xii. 1-4 = *Ant.* vii. 7, 3 §§ 148 f.

esteem them arguments of wickedness, and not piety.
And he is delighted with those that still bear in mind
this one thing, and this only, how to do whatever God
tells or commands them to do, and to choose rather
to die than to transgress any of those commands,
nor does he require so much as a sacrifice from them.
And when such do sacrifice, though it be but a mean
oblation, he better accepts of the honour than such
oblations as come from the richest man, etc., etc.[15]

The procedure of Luke's contemporary reminds us forcibly
of what Luke himself has refrained from doing with the
traditions of Jesus' words, and emphasizes the extent to
which the evangelist's underlying material has determined
its ultimate form.

[15] I Sam. xv. 22 = *Ant.* vi. 7, 4 §§ 147 ff.

CHAPTER XII

TREATMENT OF PREDECESSORS

The habits of literary men in the days of Luke are not difficult for us to discover. A large body of prose has come down to us from the Hellenistic age composed by Greeks and by Romans who followed the same methods. The methods of the several forms of prose composition were much alike, especially where the subject matter was a definite body of objective material like history, biography, natural history, geography, medicine or mathematics. For the technique of ancient history we have abundant materials. "These materials are not only derived from an intensive study and comparison of the writings of the historians, especially Thucydides, Diodorus Siculus, Tacitus, and Livy, but are supplemented by essays, prefaces, or long digressions discussing the general principles of historical composition. Thus Dionysius of Halicarnassus not only produced *Roman Antiquities* in twenty volumes: he also wrote several essays on literary criticism; while Polybius is constantly filling his pages with trenchant discussion of earlier and contemporary historiography. His principal complaint is against the rhetorical historians. The rhetorical studies—even those of later date, and those composed in Latin—bear testimony to the traditional problems and principles of the historians, while satire contributes its share to the illumination of the subject in the *De historiæ conscribendæ arte* of Lucian." [1] Other essays

[1] *The Beginnings of Christianity,* Vol. II, p. 8. Much of the following paragraph is also adapted from my earlier sketch where the references are given in full.

on the theory of historical composition were written, but unfortunately have not survived. However, we may confidently assume that from the surviving evidence we can recover a knowledge of the theory and practice of Luke's contemporaries.

In this study a most important question is the method of using materials. The value of history depends not only on what sources are used, but also on how they are used. In ancient times the distinction was emphasized between the materials for history and the finished product. The former were the raw stuff—the records of participants when available, official documents and personal notes, and the first-hand investigation by the historian of battlefields or his interviews with eyewitnesses; the latter was the ordered literary narrative based on the scattered evidence so laboriously collected. The difference between the two was a difference of style. The sources were crude and unpolished. From them the historian created his work of art, as the sculptor chisels the statue out of the rough stone. For history as for all kinds of scientific prose this rough raw product was supposed to exist. It was called memoranda (ὑπόμνημα, or ὑπομνήματα). This word was used of the personal observations or experience of statesmen and generals, like the familiar "commentaries" of Julius Cæsar on the wars in which he was engaged; it was used of rough notes on which geographers or scientists of other kinds based their description. In biography it was interchangeable with the word "memorabilia" (ἀπομνημονεύ-ματα),[2] such as those made by Xenophon and Arrian of

---

[2] For the confusion of the terms see the dissertation E. Köpke, *Ueber die Gattung der* ἀπομνημονεύματα *in der griechischen Litteratur,* 1863, p. 2. Both words imply the primitive character of the writing but I suppose rather differently. In ὑπομνήματα the rough style and fragmentary scope of the materials are emphasized, in ἀπομνημονεύματα the personal recollection of the eyewitness, *e.g.,* Xenophon. Justin Martyr (*cf.* p. 130) calls the gospels ἀπομνηονεύματα of the apostles, etc., rather than of Jesus. It was perhaps because

their teachers in philosophy. The life of Apollonius to
which we have already referred is claimed by its author
Philostratus to be based on the memoranda of the hero's
pupil and companion, Damis. In such cases the eyewitness naturally speaks in the first person, as does the
author of Acts occasionally, but even Cæsar's memoranda
use the third person.

The most important distinction between the source and
the derivative is the distinction of style. The memoranda
are bald, unadorned prose. They are therefore unfit for
publication until they have been worked over into rhetorical style. The contrast in style is constantly mentioned
and the rhetorical principles which history must follow
are set forth in full. Plutarch describes the commentaries of Aratus as "written carelessly and by the way as
fast as he could and in such words as first came to his
mind." The same lack of rhetorical adornment was felt
by Cicero in the case both of his own sketch of his con-
sulate and of the commentaries of Cæsar. Lucian criti-
cizes one who published, "putting together naked memoranda of what had taken place, quite trivial and mean in
style, such as some soldier might compile who jotted down
each day's events, or some artisan or sutler who followed
the army about." For the real historian such material is
the *corpus vile*, "memoranda, one might say" or "a body
still without beauty and unrevised," to which he must
bring the adornment of style and diction, figures of speech
and prose rhythm. When such material gets into circulation, the author apologizes for it as unfinished and un-
prepared for publication. Sometimes authors have left us
works only partly revised. Thus it is believed that certain
books of Thucydides which quote original records verbatim
have come from him without final editorial revision, while

of the autoptic implication of the "we" passages that Clement of
Alexandria says of Acts that Luke ἀπομνημονεύει and Tertullian
calls the book *commentarius Lucæ*.

F*

his last book is notably lacking in speeches.   In the last
eight books of Strabo the excerpts from his sources are
given in their original form, but not elsewhere.   In such
cases one can see clearly the editorial method.   It is more
conspicuous when original and revision are both extant.

It must not be supposed that revised works rest always
directly on first-hand material.   More often, at least in the
works that have survived, the authors are dependent on
earlier literary writers.   To follow others is much easier
than to get material for oneself.   Their methods, however,
are quite the same.   The predecessor's language is not
retained but is paraphrased, being thus transformed into
the vocabulary and mannerisms of the author who uses
him.   The contents of the material is identical, and often
the agreement between two writers in arrangement or in
occasional unusual word conclusively proves the literary
relationship which the similarity of substance suggests.
The exact relationship is, as in the case of our gospels, not
always easy to guess.   Besides the direct dependence of
one writer on the other the probability often exists that
they both copy a common source or that the later derives
from the earlier through some intermediate writer.

Finished publications of this sort not only avoided
quoting the wording of their source; they even avoided
mentioning the secondary source by name.   It was usual
to refer to many predecessors, as Luke does, in the preface, but their names, especially the name of the particular
author who is being paraphrased, are not given, though
sometimes when alternative views are offered they are referred to by the general expression, "several have said"
or "as some write."   Even verbatim quotations from the
poets are often anonymously introduced, and Luke conforms to this custom when in the speech at Athens, instead
of mentioning Epimenides, Aratus or Cleanthes by name,
he represents Paul as saying what we should perhaps
print thus:

. . . that they should seek God, if haply they might feel after him and find him, "though he is not far from" each one of us;

"For in [him] we live, and move, and have our being";

as certain even of your own poets have said,

"For we also are his offspring."[3]

"One may consider it a fixed rule of ancient writers," says Gutschmid, "not to name expressly their main sources." There are exceptions of course, as when the author of Second Maccabees, who belongs to a literary level much like Luke's, explains that he is epitomizing a five-volume work of Jason of Cyrene into one volume. Also when an author disagrees with his main source he sometimes names it. It is usually only when conflicting and variant versions of the same event are compared that authors' names are given.

Such comparison and contrast of several authorities are by no means the prevailing habits of composition. It requires more trouble and interferes with smooth style. It is easier to follow a single writer consecutively and, if it becomes necessary to abandon him, to follow another writer in the same way. "One source at a time" is a principle that classical students have come to count the

[3] The "some" (ἔνιοι) of the historians often means "the source I am following" (for examples see below, pp. 162 and 170 *note* 2); or perhaps more often, as in the agreements of Tacitus and Plutarch (see E. G. Hardy, *Studies in Roman History*, 1906, p. 316), "the authority referred to either by name or anonymously in my source." But in Acts "some of your own [poets]" may be a real plural, and the indefinite pronoun (τινες) may be a different formality like the literary formulæ, "someone somewhere" (που, πού τις), affected by Philo, the author of Hebrews, and Clement of Rome, not to mention pagan writers. For the poetical quotations see p. 122, *note*. On the citing of sources see the chapter in E. Stemplinger, *Das Plagiat in der griechischen Literatur*, 1912, pp. 177 ff.

usual course of procedure. That this was the method of Luke seems to be suggested by the evidence in his use of Mark. Instead of interweaving his sources as Matthew did, and as even the more mechanical editors of the Pentateuch appear to have done sometimes, Luke takes over the main sections of Mark in unbroken blocks. It is possible that the alternating blocks are derived similarly from a continuous writing.

These general observations on the habits of ancient writers will be confirmed by any serious student of Hellenistic literature and can be illustrated profusely. Enough has already been said to show that the habits then were different from the professed methods of our own time. The ancients may often have expressed ideas which are more in accord with modern standards than was their own practice; but in the weight they laid upon form they show a relative indifference to fact, and in their reliance upon second-hand sources a lack of diligence in seeking and testing older material. To be sure, they praise truth as their goal, they make great claims of diligent research, they emphasize the value of the evidence of eyewitnesses or of well-informed sponsors for their story and they condemn plagiarism. Sometimes their words are justified by their practice, but at least in the unacknowledged use of written material they had no inkling of our modern demand for quotation both verbatim and acknowledged. Unacknowledged paraphrase and the free plundering of the work of predecessors were entirely ethical by their standards, condemned by neither law, taste nor etiquette. Copyright, quotation marks and footnotes did not belong to that age. Verbatim quotation was usually avoided, but for literary rather than moral reasons. Macrobius apologizes for it: "Let no one blame me if I narrate the things that I borrow from diverse reading in the same words in which they are told by the authors, since the present work promises not a display of eloquence but a collection of facts worth knowing." That is, as Ulpian says, "verbatim copying is inartistic." Strabo conversely says that his repetition of subject matter must not be blamed if he is not found guilty of saying everything in just the same way.

Plutarch's *Life of Coriolanus* is a good illustration of the method of paraphrase. Except for a few characteristic digressions by Plutarch it contains no historical information that could not be derived from the corresponding sections in the *Roman Antiquities* of Dionysius of Halicarnassus. But the biography greatly reduces the diffuse narrative and omits certain data of the annalistic historian, as the annual election and names of the consuls, though in one instance it notes that "for the consuls was still left of their rule a little time," following Dionysius, "the time of rule remaining to the consuls was brief." [4] The very long speeches in Dionysius are omitted or condensed to a few lines, though occasionally an earlier illustration is retained, like the famous fable of Menenius Agrippa concerning the body and its members,[5] or the comparison to the embassy of the Sabine women made in the appeal of the Roman matrons to the mother of Coriolanus.[6] There is some freedom in the arrangement of matter, some syncopation

[4] Plutarch *Marcius* 28 = Dion. Hal. *Ant. Rom.*, viii. 15, 3.

[5] Plut. 6 = Dion. Hal. vi. 86. Dionysius of course derived the fable in turn from his source. For once he does not invent the ideas put into the mouth of his speaker, and he signalizes this exceptional course by the following apology: "He (*i.e.*, Menenius Agrippa) not only in other respects seemed to use as far as he could words that were convincing and suited to the desire of his hearers (these Dionysius supplies in his usual diffuse manner, chapters 83-85), but also at the close of his address he is said to have told a certain fable, fashioning it after the manner of Æsop with great resemblance to the situation, and to have won them over especially with this; for which cause his speech deserves to be remembered and is reported in all the ancient histories" (vi. 83).

[6] Plut. 33 = Dion. Hal. viii. 40, 4.

of similar episodes, and of course difference in editorial
comment. In the most similar passages there appears a
studied variation of wording. The description of the
divine portents if compared makes an illuminating and
typical illustration.[7] A briefer example is the description
of the personnel of the second delegation to Marcius
(Coriolanus). The later writer has substituted the past
tense "voted" for the historical present "vote," as Luke
often does with Mark's historical presents. The passages
are as follows:

Dionysius viii. 38, 1	Plutarch 32
They vote that both the hierophants and the diviners and all the others who had any sacred honor or service which they had received in connection with the state religion . . . having with them the emblems of the gods who are served and worshipped, and clothed in the sacred garments, should go in a body to the camp of the enemy, carrying the same message as the former (messengers)	For as many as were priests or celebrants or keepers of the mysteries or who had the art of divination from birds which from of old was ancestral, all these they voted should proceed to Marcius, adorned as was the rule for each one during the ceremonies and should say the same things

In such cases there is often no significant agreement
of wording, so independent is the later writer's composition and so complete the paraphrase. At other times
there is the telltale identity of phrase. It has been often
noted that in the biography Plutarch does not once mention Dionysius by name, but in the comparison of Alcibiades
and Coriolanus he speaks of Dionysius as holding a view
which Plutarch introduces in chapter 26 of the biography
with the words, "But some say." Throughout that section
the wording of Dionysius repeatedly appears if a verbal
comparison is made:

[7] Plut. 24 = Dion. Hal. vii. 68-69, and Plut. 37 = Dion. Hal.
viii. 55-56.

Dion. Hal. viii. 2, 2

The Romans and the Voluscians happened then to have cessation of war and armistice and two years' truce made a little while before

Plut. 26

Two years' truce and armistice had been made by them

Dion. Hal. viii. 11, 1

They choose (as) generals plenipotentiary for the war both Tullus and Marcius

Plut. 27

[Marcius] is appointed with Tullus general plenipotentiary for the war

An identical and uncommon word (δυσανασχετέω) appears in this parallel:

Dion. Hal. vii. 35, 2

The plebeians being disgruntled at the revilings called him bitter and harsh and more hateful than all enemies

Plut. 18

The plebs was enraged and was clearly disgruntled and embittered by what he said

Even when the words are slightly changed or differently applied their occurrence in parallel passages shows the influence of the earlier writer on the later one. Thus Plutarch uses the compound verb for the simple one (a substitution often introduced by Luke into Mark) in the following passage:

Dion. Hal. vii. 37, 1

to postpone to as remote a time as possible until the anger of the multitude should wither

Plut. 19

in order to have length and time in which the plebs would become of a better mood, their anger withering away

A thorough examination of the two narratives in the Greek texts shows how simply the material of one writer is transferred to another without any acknowledgment and with almost complete change of diction.[8]

[8] This comparison is recommended by Fr. Leo, *Die griechisch-römische Biographie*, 1901, p. 172, as extraordinarily instructive for one's understanding of the whole later prose literature.

A similar parallel, though often a closer one, is found in the works of Josephus, who in his *Antiquities* covers much of the same ground as he had included in his earlier work on the *Jewish War*. Laqueur has recently published an interesting study of Book XIV of the former, showing how the author has changed his political motives and attitudes from those revealed in corresponding sections of the *Jewish War*.[9] But the comparison is equally useful for our inquiry into the current method of reproducing earlier material.

In this case the later version is the more diffuse and adds besides new editorial comments such new information as a long list of documents and the dates of events. As Luke iii.1-2 adds to Mark a careful dating of John the Baptist's ministry, so Josephus adds such phrases as the following:

> *Antiquities* xiv. 4, 3 §66. For when the city [Jerusalem] was captured in the third month on the day of the Fast in the 179th Olympiad, in the consulship of Caius Antonius and Marcus Tullius Cicero, etc.
>
> 14, 5 §389. He [Herod] thus receives his kingdom, obtaining it in the 184th Olympiad in the consulship of Cnaeus Domitius Calvinus (second consulship) and Caius Asinius Pollio. (*cf.* 16, 4 §487.)

But the rest of the book is almost entirely a paraphrase of the previous work.[10] In the earlier chapters the paraphrase is free, but with the characteristic slackening of care found in such editorial revision the later chapters retain sentence after sentence almost intact. Two passages, the first mention of Herod the Great and the account of his

[9] R. Laqueur, *Der jüdische Historiker Flavius Josephus*, 1920, Chapter V.

[10] This view of the relation between these parallel versions in Josephus is the simplest and most probable. It is assumed in the following discussion which aims merely to illustrate Josephus' literary method. An alternative view is suggested at the end of the chapter.

capture of Jerusalem with the help of Roman troops, may
be given in somewhat literal translation as illustration:

B. J. i. 10, 4 f. §§ 203-205	*Ant.* xiv. 9, 1 f. §§ 157-160

But saying this at the same time also he [Antipater] restored the country through his own efforts perceiving that Hyrcanus was unenergetic and too sluggish for the kingship. Accordingly he constitutes Phasael the eldest of his sons general of Jerusalem and the environs while the next one, Herod, he sent on the like terms to Galilee, quite young. But he being vigorous by nature straightway finds material for his disposition. So having learned that Hezekiah the chief-bandit was raiding the adjacent parts of Syria with a very large band, he catches and kills both him and many of the bandits. This he considered especially gratifying to the Syrians. At least Herod's praises were sung at every village and in the cities as having restored to them peace and their property. As a result of this he becomes known also to Sextus Cæsar who was a kinsman of the great Cæsar and ruler of Syria.

Saying this, he [Antipater] restores the conditions in the country. But perceiving that Hyrcanus was slow and unenergetic he appoints Phasael the eldest of his sons general of Jerusalem and the environs while to the next one, Herod, he entrusted Galilee, being extremely young, for he was only fifteen years old. But his youth did him no harm; on the contrary, being noble of disposition the boy finds immediately an opportunity to demonstrate his prowess. For having learned that Hezekiah the chief-bandit was raiding the adjacent parts of Syria together with a very large band, he catches and kills him and many of the bandits that were with him. But the Syrians were exceedingly pleased with this act of his. For he had cleared their country of banditry for them when they longed to be rid of it. At least they sang his praises for this at every village and city as having secured peace for them and the safe enjoyment of their possessions. On account of this he became known also to Sextus Cæsar who was a kinsman of the great Cæsar and administrator of Syria.

B. J. i. 18, 3 §§ 354-356.

Herod took care that in subduing then the enemy he should subdue also his Gentile allies. For the foreign force was eager to view the temple and the holy things in the shrine, but the king encouraging some and threatening others actually sent some also with weapons, counting victory more intolerable than defeat if any of the secret objects should be seen by them. He had prevented already also pillaging about the city, vigorously protesting to Sossius if after emptying the city of both goods and men the Romans would leave him king of desolation, and (saying) that he judged even the rulership of the world a slight exchange if at the cost of so extensive slaughter of fellow countrymen. But when he (Sossius) declared that he was justified in permitting his soldiers to pillage in return for the siege he (Herod) said he would distribute gratuities to each out of his own funds. And having thus bought up the rest of his native place he fulfilled his promises. For he remunerated each soldier handsomely, and in proportion the officers, and most royally Sossius himself, so that none departed lacking money.

The passage in *Antiquities* xiv.16, 3 §§482-486 parallel to the above omits "then" and "already," and (if the readings of MSS. chosen by Niese in his text may be trusted) changes the tense or mood of the verbs "sent," "hindered," "judged." It substitutes for "counting" the synonymous "supposing," for "native place" "city," and for the final clause, "none departed lacking money," "all departed well provided with money." Otherwise both the wording and the word order of the two passages are identical.

The changes in such short sections cannot be classified, and many of them are significant neither as matters of thought nor as matters of language. They are probably made often quite unconsciously. Some of them are exactly identical with changes in Luke. The addition of Herod's age is like Luke iii. 23. The addition of the participle "being" to the adjective is like the same changes in Luke.[11] As Josephus changes "straightway" to "immediately," Luke does the same with Mark.[12] When such

[11] Luke vi. 3; xxiii. 50 and other cases where a participle is added to Mark. See Cadbury, *Style and Literary Method of Luke*, p. 149.

[12] παραχρῆμα in Luke viii. 44, 55; xviii. 43; xxii. 60 for εὐθύς in Mark's parallels.

changes recur repeatedly, as does the omission of "native place" [13] or the addition of the name of God,[14] they may reflect the difference of viewpoint which the new circumstances of writing (new purpose or new audience) imply. But while Josephus' references to God imply a more Jewish spirit in his later writing, Luke's additions suggest

[13] πατρίς. Beside the above passage compare:

B. J.	i. §201	the wall of his native place torn down by Pompey	*Ant.* xiv. §156	the wall destroyed by Pompey
Mark	vi. 1	he came to his native place	Luke	iv. 16	he came to Nazareth where he was brought up (but "native place" in iv. 23 and 24)

[14] Examples from this section are:

B. J.	i. §287	it happened to rain	*Ant.* xiv. §391	God having rained . . .
			§391	as though from God's providence
	§304	in a very severe snowstorm	§414	God sending snow
	§331	then also a kind of supernatural (δαιμόνιόν τι) portent befell him	§455	then one could see good will for the king from God
	§341	he was satisfied to have suffered nothing	§463	by God's providence he escaped

A. Schlatter, *Wie sprach Josephus von Gott?* 1910, does not note this tendency in *Ant.*, though he comments (p. 38) on δαιμόνιος as a favorite adjective in *B.J.*, which occurs only once in *Ant.* (xiii. § 314, where it is taken over from *B. J.*, i. § 82). It is quite vague and so more appropriate for Gentile readers as above § 331.

rather that he is interpreting the cryptic Jewish phrases of Mark for Gentile readers:

Mark	iv. 14	the word	Luke	viii. 11	the word of God
	viii. 29	the Anointed		ix. 20	the anointed of God
	xiv. 62	at the right side of Power		xxii. 69	at the right side of the power of God
	xiv. 61	the son of the Blessed		xxii. 70	the son of God
	xv. 32	the Anointed		xxiii. 35	the anointed of God

The parallels within Josephus show the same characteristics as the parallels between two different writers that stand in the same relation of source and copyist. It is possible that in the sections compared Josephus is not really copying his own work, but using twice over the same source. If so, the *Antiquities* is not derived from the *War* as Luke is derived from Mark, but both works of Josephus paraphrase and transmit a common source as Luke and Matthew appear to have done with Q. In that case the close agreements that appear from time to time are even more striking as showing that, though the underlying source was used not once but twice, it was copied with so little verbal change.

CHAPTER XIII

TREATMENT OF PREDECESSORS:
A PARALLEL FROM JOSEPHUS

Perhaps still better than the examples given above for illustrating Luke's method and the methods of his age is Josephus' treatment of 1 Maccabees, in the section of his *Antiquities* preceding the one which we have just been considering. Here again we have a Hellenistic revision of a Semitic narrative, though Luke makes far less pretension to the literary style than does Josephus, while Luke's sources were perhaps none of them quite so unhellenic as 1 Maccabees. For some eighty pages Josephus is simply transferring nearly the whole of 1 Maccabees, from the first act of Mattathias down to the burial of Jonathan, including even the final statement that the sepulchral monuments built by Simon "are preserved to this day." [1]

---

[1] 1 Macc. i. 1-xiii. 30 = *Ant.* xii. 5, 1 § 240-xiii. 6, 6 § 211. (References in the latter passage will be given hereafter simply by the number of the book and the use of the section numbers in Niese's edition.)

For the sake of simplicity I shall speak throughout this chapter as though Josephus used 1 Maccabees directly. This may well be the case, but the reader should be warned that many scholars following Destinon suppose that there was a less immediate filiation, and that Josephus owes his knowledge of 1 Maccabees to an unnamed writer who had already combined it with other materials dealing with Seleucid history. The question is too complex for discussion here, or perhaps for decision, and in any case does not affect the value of the parallels as illustrating the ancient manner of using sources. See H. St. J. Thackeray in Hastings, *Dictionary of the Bible*, V, 465; and G. Hölscher in Pauly-Wis-

Yet Josephus never mentions this his main source. He once cites by name Polybius, only to reject the explanation of Antiochus Epiphanes' death, which he says Polybius gave.[2] His digressions from the account of 1 Maccabees usually conclude with a cross reference to other passages in his own works,[3] and after digressing he always returns to his main source just where he has left it. He possibly mentions his own earlier and independent summary narrative of the period, but he makes no use of it or apparently of any other continuous source. Thus he observes the usual custom of naming sources without using them and using sources without naming them.[4]

His expansions are such as would come from his own knowledge of Judaism or of the geography of Palestine or of the Old Testament. He draws military manoeuvers out of a single reference,[5] inserts the distance between opposing armies and supplies the motives of actors. Otherwise scarcely a single detail of this whole section requires any explanation other than the free borrowing and interpreting and revising of the Greek text of 1 Maccabees. Except for two passages containing digressions of 1 Maccabees which Josephus evidently aims to arrange in chronological order, the sequence of events and even of sentences is identical. That Josephus is not independently translating the Semitic original of our Greek 1 Maccabees is repeatedly proved by unexpected agreements in the Greek

---

sowa-Kroll, *Real-Encyclopädie der classischen Altertumswissenschaft*, Vol. IX, coll. 1963-9 (bibliography up to the year 1916, *ibid.*, 1999 f.).

[2] xii. 358 f. In reality the explanation is not Polybius' own, but that of his source, to which Polybius refers by the typical "as some say" (xxxi. 11).

[3] xii. 388; xiii. 36, 61, 108, 112, 119, 173, 186. According to the view suggested in *note* 1 above, even these cross references were taken over from the source.

[4] See above, pp. 158 f.

[5] *E.g.*, xiii. 5, 3 §§ 138 f.

wording. His process, however, is usually to substitute for each word a synonym, as though his main object was to avoid using the words of his source. As in the gospels, the unusual place names diverge in spelling in the parallel passages. This is due to the uncertainty of scribal transmission, but the later writer in each case often proves superior to the best MSS. as textual evidence for the earlier writing.[6]

Josephus' paraphrase varies in its closeness to the original. The dialogue parts and the exhortations of generals are most freely recast. Like Luke he often turns direct discourse into indirect. In general the narrative follows the original, sentence by sentence, but the structure of the sentence is changed. Parentheses are altered so as to be embodied in the main sentence; rapid change of subject is avoided. The so-called paratactic construction of the Semitic style in which verb follows verb with "and" is reduced by the use of subordinate clauses and genitives absolute, or by substituting for the first of two verbs a participle. "But" and other conjunctions take the place of "and." All this is likewise the method of Luke's treatment of Mark.

Semitic proper names are Hellenized in spelling or omitted by Josephus. Like Luke, Josephus adds to the name of a city an explanatory phrase, "this was a city." For Modein, when first mentioned, is substituted "Modais, a village of Judaea," just as in Luke's narrative we have at its first occurrence the full phrase "Capernaum, a city of Galilee," "Arimathea, a city of the Jews."[7] Semitic idioms are omitted or translated. Sometimes, however, even Josephus seems to misunderstand the Semitic idioms

---

[6] H. St. J. Thackeray has found that it is possible to determine which of the two extant old uncial MSS. of 1 Maccabees represents more nearly the text behind Josephus.

[7] *Ant.* xii. 341 = 1 Macc. v. 37; 265 = 1 Macc. ii. 1; Luke iv. 31, *cf.* Mark i. 21; Luke xxiii. 51 = Mark xv. 43. See also p. 125.

which are literally reproduced in the Greek of 1 Macca-
bees, such as "Galilee of the Gentiles," "the land of the
Philistines," "daughters" of a city, in the sense of suburbs.
See the following parallels:

1 Macc. v. 8 he took Jazer and its daughters and returned to Judæa	*Ant.* xii. 329 he captures the city of the Jazorites and taking as captives their women and children and burning the city he returned to Judæa
v. 15 there were gathered against them people from Ptolemais and Tyre and Sidon and all "Galilee of the Gentiles" (ἀλλοφύλων)	331 there were gathered together men from Ptolemais and Tyre and Sidon and the other nations of Galilee
v. 65 Hebron and her daughters	353 the city Hebron
v. 66 the land of the Philistines (γῆν ἀλλοφύλων)	353 the alien territory (τὴν ἀλλόφυλον χώραν)
v. 68 to Azotus the land of the Philistines	353 to Azotus

Besides Hebraisms, vulgarisms in 1 Maccabees disappear under Josephus' revising hand. In the verbatim
copying of the phrase, "they put loaves upon the table," [8]
he substitutes the correct form (ἐπέθεσαν) for the incor-
rect (ἐπέθηκαν). For the simple δείλης, "evening," he substitutes δείλης ὀψίας, "late evening," according to the principle expressed by Moeris: "evening (δείλης) by itself the
Attic writers do not say, but evening alone by itself is
used by the later Greeks." [9] He substitutes for common
words like "see" and "know," more varied and specialized
meanings such as "perceive," "discover," "learn," "ascertain," and supplies an object when one is missing. He

---

[8] *I.e.* Of shewbread, 1 Macc. iv. 51 = *Ant.* xii. 319.

[9] 1 Macc. x. 80 = *Ant.* xiii, 97. J. Pierson, *Moeridis Atticistæ
lexicon Atticum*, 1759, p. 132. The use of ὀψία by itself was
likewise condemned by the Atticists and is avoided by Luke,
though not by Mark and Matthew in the parallel passages (*Style
and Literary Method of Luke,* p. 187).

varies the monotonous "went" into "departed," "set forth," "withdrew," "arrived," etc.[10]

In such a process of paraphrase certain common words of the source almost regularly disappear and favorite expressions of the editor come into prominence. Lists of both kinds for Josephus and 1 Maccabees could be prepared, as has been done for Mark and Luke.

In some cases the aversions or preferences of the two later editors agree. Thus a certain Greek word for "tribulation" ($\theta\lambda\iota\beta\omega$, $\theta\lambda\iota\psi\iota s$), occurring nine times in 1 Maccabees and four times in Mark, is never retained by either copyist,[11] for example:

Mark iv. 17 tribulation or persecution arising	Luke viii. 13 in time of trial
Mark xiii. 19 tribulation	Luke xxi. 23 distress
1 Macc. ix. 27 and there was great tribulation in Israel which had not been since the day when no prophet appeared to them	*Ant.* xiii. 5 but this disaster to the Jews having been such as they had not experienced after the return from Babylon, etc.

On the other hand, both copyists gladly substitute for a simple verb the choice "perceive" ($\kappa\alpha\tau\alpha\nu o\acute{\epsilon}\omega$), and both have the same liking for one of the Greek synonyms for "return" ($\dot{\upsilon}\pi o\sigma\tau\rho\acute{\epsilon}\phi\omega$). Almost regularly Josephus avoids certain favorite words of 1 Maccabees for "army" ($\delta\acute{\upsilon}\nu\alpha\mu\iota s$, Josephus $\sigma\tau\rho\alpha\tau\iota\acute{\alpha}$, etc.),[12] "camp" ($\pi\alpha\rho\epsilon\mu\beta o\lambda\acute{\eta}$),[13] "encamp" ($\pi\alpha\rho\epsilon\mu\beta\acute{\alpha}\lambda\lambda\omega$), "send" ($\dot{\alpha}\pi o\sigma\tau\acute{\epsilon}\lambda\lambda\omega$, Josephus usually $\pi\acute{\epsilon}\mu\pi\omega$), "fort" ($\dot{o}\chi\acute{\upsilon}\rho\omega\mu\alpha$, Josephus usually $\phi\rho o\acute{\upsilon}\rho\iota o\nu$),

[10] For similar changes in Mark made by Luke see *Style and Literary Method of Luke*, pp. 175 ff.

[11] The same substitute for it is used in the following:

Mark iii. 9 $\delta\iota\grave{\alpha}$ $\tau\grave{o}\nu$ $\check{o}\chi\lambda o\nu$ $\check{\iota}\nu\alpha$ $\mu\grave{\eta}$ $\theta\lambda\acute{\iota}\beta\omega\sigma\iota\nu$ $\alpha\dot{\upsilon}\tau\grave{o}\nu$	Luke v. 1 $\dot{\epsilon}\nu$ $\tau\hat{\omega}$ $\check{o}\chi\lambda o\nu$ $\dot{\epsilon}\pi\iota\kappa\epsilon\hat{\iota}\sigma\theta\alpha\iota$ $\alpha\dot{\upsilon}\tau\hat{\omega}$
1 Macc. ix. 7 $\dot{o}$ $\pi\acute{o}\lambda\epsilon\mu os$ $\check{\epsilon}\theta\lambda\iota\beta\epsilon\nu$ $\alpha\dot{\upsilon}\tau\grave{o}\nu$	*Ant.* xii. 423 $\tau\hat{\omega}\nu$ $\pi o\lambda\epsilon\mu\acute{\iota}\omega\nu$ $\dot{\epsilon}\pi\iota\kappa\epsilon\iota\mu\acute{\epsilon}\nu\omega\nu$.

[12] Except *Ant.* xii. 272; xiii. 38.

[13] Once in Josephus, *Ant.* xiii. 175.

"hostages" (ὅμηρα, Josephus always masculine ὅμηροι), "border" (ὅριον, Josephus regularly ὅρος). Similarly, Luke usually avoids the favorite verbs of Mark for "seize" (κρα- τέω), "lead" (φέρω), "depart" (ὑπάγω), and his adverbs "often" (πολλά) and "again" (πάλιν).[14]

In other cases the habits of the two revisers are oppo- site, or at least different. While Luke frequently sub- stitutes for the simple verb of Mark a compound of the same stem, Josephus unless he changes the verb alto- gether usually reduces the compound verbs by omitting a prepositional prefix, especially when there are two of them. Luke substitutes the past tense for Mark's his- torical present. Josephus frequently does just the reverse. The approximate number of occurrences of this present in the parallels is:[15]

Mark	151	Luke	4
1 Macc.	2	*Ant.* (dependent sections)	131

A more complete contrast of editorial habit could scarcely be imagined. Mark's periphrastic "began to" is often re- moved by Luke. Twice at least Josephus seems to intro- duce it:

1 Macc. iv. 39 they wailed with great wailing	*Ant.* xii. 317 he began to lament with his associates
1 Macc. xiii. 2 he collected the people and exhorted them and said	*Ant.* xiii. 197 having called to- gether the citizenry into the temple then he began to exhort them

Like Luke, Josephus often supplies the subject of a singular verb, so that we are reminded that the actor of the scene is Judas, Nicanor, Jonathan or the like. Simi- larly, when Mark or 1 Maccabees uses the plural verb, their editors by referring the action to a single subject like

[14] See Hawkins, *Horæ Synopticæ,* pp. 12 f., 24; and Cadbury, *Style, etc.,* pp. 172-4, 199 f.

[15] The first three numbers are taken from Hawkins, *Horæ Synopticæ,* 2d ed., pp. 143 ff., 213.

Jesus or Judas give the scene more definiteness.[16]   As Josephus repeatedly infers chronological sequence by substituting for the simple "and" of 1 Maccabees more definite expressions of time,[17] so the initial "and" of Mark is represented in Luke by "after this," "on one of those days" (and more often in Matthew by "in that time (hour)," "then," etc.).   Sometimes each writer deliberately changes his sources, as when Josephus says Nicanor fell last rather than first, or Luke puts the cure of the blind beggar on entering rather than on leaving Jericho.[18]   Both editors supply details which make the scene more intelligible or striking or which are obvious inferences, and both avoid difficult passages or interpret them with doubtful success. As Josephus twice omits the Asideans, Luke twice omits the equally obscure group called Herodians.[19]

Especially in the matter of Semitism the two editors make an interesting contrast.   Sometimes the very idioms which Josephus eliminates from his sources the evangelist Luke retains or even adds.

1 Maccabees	Josephus, *Antiquities*
iv. 24 returning, they sang praises and gave blessing to Heaven (Luke xv. 7, 18, 21) because (he is) good (;) for ever (is) his mercy. *Cf.* ix. 46. 1 Macc. never uses "God" or "the Lord."	xii. 312 he returned rejoicing and sang God's praises on account of the successes accomplished. *Cf.* xiii. 13
ix. 55 was struck	*Cf.* xii. 413 a stroke from God (see p. 167 *note* 14)

[16] Cadbury, *op. cit.,* pp. 150 f., 165 f.; *cf. e.g.,* 1 Macc. iv. 36-61 = *Ant.* xii. 316-326.   Scribes of Mark and of 1 Maccabees were subject to the same two tendencies.   See the textual apparatus of 1 Maccabees in Charles, *Apocrypha and Pseudepigrapha of the Old Testament,* or in Fritzsche, *Libri apocryphi Veteris Testamenti Græce.*

[17] xii. 354, 362, 389; xiii. 4, 103, 180.

[18] *Ant.* xii. 409 = 1 Macc. vii. 43; Luke xviii. 35 = Mark x. 46.

[19] 1 Macc. ii. 42; vii. 13; Mark iii. 6; xii. 13.

ii. 27 let him come after me (Luke ix. 23 = follow after, Matt. x. 38 [Mark viii. 34])

xii. 271 let him follow me

vi. 60 and the word was pleasing before (Acts vi. 5 verbatim the same) the king and rulers

xii. 381 Lysias having said this, both the army was pleased and the generals at the advice

x. 60 he found favor before them, xi. 24 he found favor before him (Luke i. 30; Acts vii. 46)

xiii. 83 he enjoyed brilliant honor from both, 124 having been honored by him

ix. 1 he added . . . to send (Luke xx. 11, 12 = Mark xii. 4 again he sent, 5 another he sent) *Cf.* ix. 72; x. 88

xii. 420 again . . . he sent *Cf.* xiii. 33, 102

ix. 10   μὴ γένοιτο   (Luke xx. 16 added to Mark xii. 9) that I should do this, should flee from them

xii. 424 may the sun never see this happen, that I should show my back to the enemy

ix. 23 and it came to pass (Luke viii. 40 added to Mark v. 21, Luke ix. 28 added to Mark ix. 2, and elsewhere) after the death of Judas. *Cf.* v. 1; vi. 8; vii. 2; x. 88

xiii. 2   after the death of Judas

x. 7 in the ears of (Acts xi. 22)

xiii. 39   while they heard

v. 28, 51 by the mouth of the sword (Luke xxi. 24)

xii. 336, 347 omits

v. 45 from little unto great (Acts viii. 10)

xii. 345 omits

The famous phrase of Daniel, "abomination of desolation" (βδέλυγμα ἐρημώσεως), is understood by Josephus as "the desolation of the shrine"; by Luke as the "desolation of Jerusalem."   Compare:

1 Macc. i. 54 They built the abomination of desolation on the altar of burnt offering	*Ant.* xii. 253 having built on the altar of burnt offering an altar ($\beta\omega\mu\delta s$), the king slaughtered swine upon it.
Mark xiii. 14 but when ye see the abomination of desolation standing where he ought not, let him that readeth understand, etc.[19a]	Luke xxi. 20 but when ye see Jerusalem compassed with armies, then know that her desolation is nigh.

Josephus twice omits references to the cessation of prophecy. In the second case, when it is used for an era, he substitutes the return from Babylon.[20] Luke sometimes avoids the suggestion that John is Elijah, though he predicts that he comes in the spirit and power of Elijah.[21] And twice when it is suggested that Jesus is one of the prophets Luke makes plain that this involves the resurrection of one of the old time prophets:

Mark vi. 15 others said that he is a prophet like one of the prophets	Luke ix. 8 (it was said by) others that some prophet of the ancient ($\dot{\alpha}\rho\chi\alpha\iota\omega\nu$) ones has arisen
Mark viii. 28 but others (said) that (he is) one of the prophets	Luke ix. 19 but others (said) that some prophet of the ancient ($\dot{\alpha}\rho\chi\alpha\iota\omega\nu$) ones has arisen

Precisely the same addition is made by Josephus in the following passage:

1 Macc. ix. 54 Alcimus gave orders to tear down the wall of the inner court of the sanctuary and he tore down the works of the prophets.	*Ant.* xii. 413 Now when the high priest Alcimus wished to tear down the wall of the sanctuary which was old and built by the ancient ($\dot{\alpha}\rho\chi\alpha\iota\omega\nu$) prophets, etc.

[19a] An explicit reference to Daniel (*e.g.* ix. 27; xi. 31; xii. 11) is not given in 1 Macc. or Mark but is added by Josephus *Ant.* xii. 322 and in Matt. xxiv. 15.

[20] 1 Macc. iv. 46 = *Ant.* xii. 318; 1 Macc. ix. 27 = *Ant.* xiii. 5.

[21] Luke i. 17; but Luke has no parallel to Mark ix. 11-13, or to Matt. xi. 14.

Attention has often been called to the addition by Luke of the word "right" to the hand that was withered and the ear that was struck off. It has been thought to indicate that the third evangelist was a doctor. It is rather due to the free interpretation to which editors are accustomed. So Josephus substitutes for "hand" "right (hand)" in the account of the escape of Bacchides.[22]

These extended illustrations of the contemporary methods of using sources are not intended to suggest that there was a recognized technique in such matters or that likeness in detailed changes means dependence upon explicit standards of paraphrase. The methods of several authors differ, and even one author, as Josephus shows us, handles some parts of his material much more freely than other parts. Sometimes a sentence or section of the source was read and recast; sometimes (and this on the whole is the method of Luke) the sentence structure and even most of the wording were retained. In the former case exchange of synonyms is less striking than in the latter, but in neither case must the change be considered to have been always deliberate, or the substitution always significant. Even changes which look like conscious improvement in style or diction are not like the proof-reader's blue pencilings, but come naturally in the process of paraphrase. The fact that the rule-books actually prescribe such changes as editors make does not mean that the editors have read the rules and are definitely applying them. They are merely following their own taste, which in such cases agrees with the better usage which the rule-books record.

With this caution we may conclude by giving some illustrations of Luke's own paraphrase of Mark. I begin with

---

[22] Mark iii. 1 = Luke vi. 6; Mark xiv. 47 = Luke xxii. 50; 1 Macc. ix. 47 = *Ant.* xiii. 14. In *Ant.* viii. 408, occurs the same change with reference to the hand that Jeroboam stretched out to seize the man of God and that was withered. *Cf.* 1 Kings xiii. 4 and *Ant.* viii. 233.

the subject just mentioned—the rule-books of the Atticists. These glossaries by Moeris, Phrynichus and others were intended to instruct students on the correct usage (ancient or cultured) over against the uncultivated popular language, just as modern English handbooks are written to warn against the most frequent misspellings, mispronunciations and misuses of words. Several of Mark's words avoided by Luke are thus condemned. For example, Luke substitutes for needle ($ραφίς$) the synonymous $βελόνη$, for which we may quote Phrynichus: "$βελόνη$ and $βελόνη$-seller are old established words, but one would not know what $ραφίς$ is." [23] Moeris, another purist, explains that the word $ἀπάτη$ means "deceit for the Attic writers, but for the later Greeks pleasure." Luke possibly thought that Mark was using it in the popular sense when he spoke of the "cares of this age and the $ἀπάτη$ of riches and cravings with regard to other things." In any case he omits it by rendering simply "cares and wealth and pleasures of life." [24] Five lines later the same Moeris says, "$ἄρτι$ the Attic writers [use] of 'a little while ago,' but the later Greeks say it also of 'now.'" Matthew (like John, Paul and other New Testament writers) uses the word freely, but Luke in passages parallel to Matthew's "from $ἄρτι$," or "until $ἄρτι$," [25] always expresses the thought differently.

The later editors do not avoid all the words condemned by the purists. There is much in Luke as in Josephus still characteristic of the Hellenistic or popular Greek.[26]

[23] Mark x. 25 = Luke xviii. 25. C. A. Lobeck, *Phrynichi eclogæ nominum et verborum Atticorum,* 1820, p. 90.

[24] J. Pierson, *Moeridis Atticistæ lexicon Atticum,* p. 65.   Mark iv. 19 = Luke viii. 14.

[25] Matt. xxiii. 39; xxvi. 29, 64; xi. 12.

[26] Lagrange, *Évangile selon S. Luc,* pp. cxxiv f., lists nearly thirty words in the gospel alone which Luke employs contrary to the preferences of Phrynichus. Even the Atticists did not agree and anti-Atticists took delight in unearthing instances of the

But their changes in diction never appear to be in the direction of less elegant Greek. Even if Luke once uses the diminutive word for "ear" (ὠτίον) that Phrynichus condemns, it is to his credit that he had used the preferred word (οὖς) in the preceding verse, where the other evangelists use only ὠτίον (Matt., John), or still worse ὠτάριον (Mark, John). There are other cases where Luke, perhaps for the sake of variety, perhaps from indifference, lapses into the colloquial diminutive after using the more correct forms.[27]

Luke's improvement in expression and sentence structure may be represented even in English by a continuous literal translation of parallels with Mark. It should be recalled that Greek required that every sentence should be connected by a conjunction and that it eschewed foreign words and disliked repetition. The following quotation shows how Luke removes Mark's asyndeton by adding "for" (Mark, verse 36) or "therefore" (37), drops the Latin "quadrans" (42) and the use of brass [28] for money (41) and the Aramaic "amen" (43), avoids the repetition of "David himself," "treasury," "poor," "cast" (not to mention "and"), and improves the loose structure of sentences by inserting "loving" (38) and "who" (40), and by rearranging the final apposition (44).

Mark xii. 35-44	Luke xx. 41-xxi. 4
35 And Jesus answering said, teaching in the temple, "How say the scribes that Christ is son of David? 36 David him-	41 But he said to them [i.e., the scribes], "How do they say that Christ is David's son? 42 For David himself

condemned words in the older classics. Thus in the case of the two words for "needle" mentioned above, Helladius turned the tables when he said "ῥαφίς is more archaic than βελόνη" (Photius *Bibliotheca, cod.* 279, ed. Bekker, 1824, p. 533b, 6 f.).

[27] Luke v. 17 ff. κλίνη. . . κλινίδιον; xviii. 15 ff. βρέφη . . . παιδία.

[28] χαλκόν of money in general (*cf.* Latin *aes*) was according to Pollux ii. 92 a popular Greek expression: ἡ τῶν πολλῶν καὶ ἰδιωτῶν χρῆσις τὸν χαλκὸν ἀργύριον λέγει.

self said in the holy Spirit, 'The Lord said to my lord, Sit on my right until I make thy enemies the footstool of thy feet.' 37 David himself speaks of him as lord, and whence is he his son?"

And the large multitude heard him gladly, 38 and in his teaching he said; "Look out for the scribes wishing to walk in robes and greetings in the market places 39 and front seats in the synagogues and the places of honor at banquets, 40 they devouring the houses of the widows and for excuse praying at length. These will get more abundant judgment."

41 And having seated himself opposite the treasury he watched how the multitude cast brass into the treasury, and many rich cast many (coins), 42 and one poor widow coming cast two mites which is a quadrans, 43 and calling his disciples he said to them, "Amen I tell you that this poor widow has cast more than all who cast into the treasury. 44 For all from their surplus cast, but she from her lacking cast everything which she had, her whole wealth."

says in the book of psalms, 'The Lord said to my lord, Sit on my right 43 until I make thy enemies the footstool of thy feet.' 44 David therefore calls him lord, and how is he his son?"

45 But while the whole people were hearing, he said to his disciples, "46 Beware of the scribes wishing to walk in robes and loving greetings in the market places and front seats in the synagogues and the places of honor at banquets, 47 who devour the houses of the widows and for excuse pray at length. These will get more abundant judgment."

1 But looking up he saw the rich casting into the treasury their gifts

2 but he saw a certain indigent widow casting there two mites

3 and he said, "Truly I tell you that this poor widow has cast more than all.
4 For all these from their surplus cast into the gifts but she from her lack cast all the wealth that she had."

Besides the literary improvements mentioned, this passage will yield others by a careful examination of the Greek texts.[29] It also illustrates a few special habits of speech

---

[29] *Cf.* on the last paragraph Streeter, *The Four Gospels,* p. 172: "In four verses we find no less than four examples of the most

G

on the part of Luke and a substitution of "in the book of psalms" for "in the holy Spirit." [30]

When, as often happens, Luke's paraphrase is more free the changes are more striking. The following kindred passages are in many respects typical:

Mark	Luke
xi. 18 the chief priests and the scribes . . . sought how to destroy him, for they feared him,	xix. 47, 48 the chief priests and the scribes sought to destroy him, and the leaders of the people, and they did not find
for all the multitude were astonished at his teaching	the way how to do so, for the whole people hung upon his words listening
xiv. 1, 2, 10, 11 and the chief priests and the scribes sought how arresting him by craft to kill him, for they said, "Not at the feast lest there be a tumult of the people."	xxii. 2-6 and the chief priests and the scribes sought the way how to destroy him, for they feared the people. But Satan entered into Judas called Is-
And Judas Iscariot, who was one of the twelve, departed to the chief priests in order to deliver him to them, but they when they heard rejoiced and promised to give him money and he sought how he could opportunely deliver him	cariotes, being of the number of the twelve, and he departing discussed with the chief priests and police the way how he might deliver him to them, and they rejoiced and made a compact to give him money and he agreed and sought opportunity for delivering him to them without a crowd

Of Luke's more significant changes of Mark we shall have occasion to speak later from time to time. The following passages will illustrate the additions (marked with square brackets) which may be accounted for as due to

characteristic features of Mark's style—a 'context supplement,' a 'duplicate expression,' the idiom ὅ ἐστι, and the Latinism κοδράντης —all of which we may note Luke is careful to revise away."

[30] The last change certainly makes it clearer to a Gentile reader that a citation of Scripture is meant, but it is noteworthy in view of Luke's usual interest in the holy Spirit (see Chapter XVIII).

his natural elaboration of his source in paraphrase, like the conjectural and visualizing additions in Josephus:

iv.35   the demon came out from him [having done him no harm]

vi.1   his disciples plucked the heads of grain [and ate them rubbing them with the hands] (Matt. xii.1 similarly adds "were hungry" and "ate")

viii.5   and as he sowed some fell on the path [and was trodden upon] and the birds of the heaven ate it up

xxii.45   coming to the disciples he found them asleep [from sorrow]

To the same purely literary process may be due, for example, Luke's references to perplexity or expectancy (ἀπορέω, προσδοκάω). Additions to Mark are again indicated by square brackets:

iii.15   [But while the people were in expectancy and all men were debating in their hearts about John, whether perhaps he was the Christ, John answered saying to all,] "I baptize you with water," etc.

viii.40   the multitude welcomed him [for they were all expecting him]

ix.43   [while all wondered at all that he did] he said to his disciples, etc.

xxi.25   there shall be signs in sun and moon and stars; [and upon the earth distress of nations in perplexity at the sound of the sea and surge, men growing cold from fear and expectancy of the things that are to come upon the world], for the powers of the heaven shall be shaken; and then, etc.

xxiv.3   but entering in they found not the body of the Lord Jesus; and it came to pass [while they were perplexed about this], behold two men, etc.

CHAPTER XIV

SPEECHES, LETTERS AND CANTICLES

A prevailing convention among ancient historians was the custom of inserting speeches of the leading characters into the narrative. This convention was quite in accord with the current demands of style, as the speeches offered the writer an opportunity for variety and for the display of his rhetorical powers. Like the chorus in a Greek play they served to review the situation for the reader, and they brought out the inner thoughts and feelings of important persons. They often occupied large sections of the historical work, approximately one-third of Dionysius of Halicarnassus and one-fifth of Thucydides. They were the objects of special care and pride on the part of historians interested in style, and were the parts of history most appreciated by literary connoisseurs. The speeches of Thucydides were said to have been studied by Demosthenes. Later critics accounted them the supreme achievement of that historian.[1] They are still the most renowned part of his work. Livy's speeches numbering, it is supposed, originally over two thousand (some four hundred of them are still extant!) were highly praised by Quintilian.[2] It is noteworthy that the only parts of Sallust's *Histories* which have survived consist of speeches and letters. On the other hand, unfinished works or parts of works are lacking in speeches,[3] and historians like Polybius who deprecate the rhetorical tendency in history avoid

---

[1] Dion. Hal. *De Thucyd.* 34.   [2] x. 1, 101.
[3] Dion Hal. *De Thucyd.* 16.   See above pp. 157 f.

the excessive use of speeches themselves and criticize it in others.[4]

Aside from rhetorical style, the chief requisite of these speeches was appropriateness to the speaker and the occasion. They must be "in character." Lucian in warning against excess of rhetoric adds: "If ever it is necessary to introduce anyone who will deliver an address, see to it that his words are especially appropriate to the character of the speaker and relevant to the situation; further, that they are as clear as possible. But at such a time you are permitted to play the orator and to exhibit your rhetorical skill." [5] In almost identical words Dionysius praises Thucydides' speeches as "suited to the persons and relevant to the situations." [6] Indeed, Thucydides himself had long before explained the custom in a classic passage:

> As to the speeches that were made by different men, either when they were about to begin the war or when they were already engaged therein, it has been difficult to recall with strict accuracy the words actually spoken, both for me as regards that which I myself heard, and for those who from various other sources have brought me reports. Therefore the speeches are given in the language in which, as it seemed to me, the several speakers would express, on the subjects under consideration, the sentiments most befitting the occasion, though at the same time I have adhered as closely as possible to the general sense of what was actually said (i. 22).

It is evident that the ancient writers and their readers considered the speeches more as editorial and dramatic comment than as historical tradition. Neither the form

---

[4] See *Beginnings of Christianity*, Vol. II, p. 14, *note 6*.

[5] *De hist. conscrib.* 58.

[6] *De Thucyd.* 36. The classic English discussion of the speeches of Thucydides is by R. C. Jebb in the collection of essays edited by E. Abbott in 1880 entitled *Hellenica.*

of direct quotation nor the appropriateness of the words
to the speaker and his occasion proves that the writer
had any actual knowledge of what was said, or indeed
that a speech was delivered at all.   The practical difficulty
of knowing what was said was greater for many historians than for Thucydides, who wrote contemporary
history.   Those who dealt with the remoter past and those
who chiefly relied on earlier histories either invented their
speeches wholesale or rewrote the fictitious speeches of their
predecessors.   Even contemporary historians probably relied more on their dramatic imagination and sense of fitness than on knowledge, oral memory or written record.
It might seem that the published speeches of Caesar,
Cicero and others would be used by later histories.   On
the contrary, they were regularly omitted, either because
they were accessible to the reader,[7] or because uniformity
of style was demanded and the historian preferred inventing speeches with a free hand to revising actual documents.
To include verbatim original speeches would have introduced an alien and unhomogeneous style.   Contrary as it
seems to our modern standards, it may be confidently affirmed that many an ancient writer paraphrases without
acknowledgment the narrative of his source, but when he
professes to report the speech of a general or statesman
he deliberately rejects the same source's earlier version,
whether authentic or unauthentic.

Some actual illustrations from writers of about Luke's
time have been given elsewhere.   "When Livy follows
Polybius for the facts of his narrative he almost regularly
makes a change in the occasion and form of his speeches.
So Plutarch and Tacitus agree very closely in their account
of Otho but give entirely different reports of his last address. . . . The speech of Caesar to his soldiers in Dio
Cassius is very different from the brief address reported
by Caesar himself on the same occasion.   When the actual

[7] See *Beginnings of Christianity*, Vol. II, p. 14, *note 5.*

speech had been published the historian usually mentions the fact as a reason for omitting any speech of his own." [8] He does not include the published speech. As further illustration we may note how Livy repeatedly merely refers to extant speeches.[9] The speech of Claudius as given in Tacitus [10] differs widely from the words preserved on an original brass tablet found at Lyons which records the speech.

It would be erroneous to suppose that no actual tradition was ever represented in the speeches. Probably there were variations from the general custom as we have described it. Josephus, for example, often retains in his longer speeches any nucleus in his source that seems to him appropriate. Illustrations from the Old Testament have been given above.[11] His introduction of new speeches sometimes seems to us rather infelicitous, as in the incident of Potiphar's wife,[12] or when he represents himself as standing outside the walls of Jerusalem within earshot though out of the range of weapons, and appealing to its people to surrender by delivering to them a long review of history.[13] Plutarch, who reduces rather than expands speeches, retains, as we have seen, the famous parable of Menenius Agrippa and other significant illustrations from the speeches of his predecessor Dionysius.[14] The famous *"Væ victis!"* of the Gauls under Brennus at Rome he preserves in essence though in different Greek wording, probably from the same source,[15] at the same time tacitly ac-

[8] *Ibid.,* Vol. II, pp. 13 f.

[9] 38, 54, 11; 39, 42, 6; 45, 25, 3; 49 fragm.

[10] *Ann.* xi. 24. *Corpus inscr. Latin.* XIII, 1668.

[11] Pp. 153 f. An illustration of his treatment of a speech from 1 Maccabees is given in *Beginnings of Christianity,* Vol. II, p. 27.

[12] *Ant.* ii. 4, 3-5.   [13] *B. J.* v. 9, 3 f.   [14] See pp. 161 f.

[15] Dion. Hal. xiii. 9 (13); Plutarch *Camillus* 28. Probably the proverbial reply of Camillus on the same occasion (now dated 387 B.C.): "The Romans' tradition is to ransom their country with steel, not gold," was also from the source. Plutarch elaborates neither of these into speeches.

knowledging his procedure by saying that it had become
proverbial. It is likely that other writers whose sources
we cannot now control sometimes employed in their speeches
phrases which had at least earlier if not primitive authenti-
cation.

The author of Luke-Acts apparently conforms to the
customs of his age. In the sayings of Jesus, it is true, his
procedure is different. There he deals with discourse material which was valued for its own sake rather than as
adornment for narrative. It was largely poetic or figura-
tive in form and ethical in subject matter, and was regarded as authoritative for Christian conduct. This material he takes over from earlier sources and presents to
his readers with only slight change of wording. In so doing Luke like the other evangelists (except John) is following the Semitic rather than the Greek method of handling materials. For the Semitic mind did not distinguish
the substance from the form of what was said. It would
not undertake to hand down sayings of a prophet or rabbi,
a Jesus or a Mahomet, with the same freedom that it would
transmit a narrative. Their words were retained as an
essential vehicle of their thought. A Semite scarcely has
any word for "think" except "speak." He could not conceive of thought without words any more readily than he
could conceive of soul without body. Even Luke falls in
line with this general habit in his treatment of the older
records of Jesus' teaching.

In contrast with this incidental teaching or table talk
or talk by the way, the author of the Third Gospel offers
only one speech in which Jesus is represented as addressing a regularly constituted assembly. This is the speech at
Nazareth,[16] and like the corresponding addresses of self-
defense in Acts and in other writers it may be more largely
attributed to the editor than to his sources. A similar story
was indeed to be found in Mark's account of Jesus' rejec-

[16] Luke iv. 16-27; *cf.* Mark vi. 1-6.

tion in his home town, but in Luke it is placed as a program at the outset of Jesus' ministry. In modern terms it is a "keynote speech." It is a sermon regularly delivered as part of the synagogue service, drawn from a public "lesson" read from the Scriptures, illustrated with historical or haggadic examples. The anachronism produced by moving to the beginning of his ministry the reference to earlier works in Capernaum shows that Luke is not working up the whole speech without use of existent matter. The proverb that a prophet is without honor in his own country lay before him in Mark's account, but there is much about the thought of the speech as well as the style that points to the author's free composition.

The same impression is made by many of the numerous speeches in Acts, though one cannot speak more positively than in terms of impression, or more inclusively than so as to leave the possibility that some of the speeches are closely dependent on written sources or oral information. Many of the addresses are, like that at Nazareth, sermons or defenses on the basis of Scripture texts or of history. Many are before constituted authorities and on prearranged occasions. Even the more casual addresses are far removed in form and subject matter from the sayings of Jesus. Unlike their silent master in the gospels, the followers of Jesus in Acts are represented as making defenses before governors and kings, the Jewish Sanhedrin or a Gentile judgment seat.

That the style of all these addresses is that of the evangelist no one can deny. How much if any of their contents has an earlier tradition, oral or written, Greek or Aramaic, is a question often debated, and in the absence of external evidence not settled with finality in the case of a single one of them. The supposition of some authentic written or oral information is most attractive in the case of Stephen's speech and of the speeches of Paul at Athens and Miletus. It must suffice to leave the matter here with

G* `

a reminder that the editor's influence is probably to be estimated as more rather than less extensive than has often been our custom. The arguments by which the speeches in Acts are made to yield evidence of earlier origin, whether from the speakers themselves or from prior documents, can usually be met by equally plausible considerations of a negative kind. In any case, more probable than the hypothesis of much direct recollection of words actually spoken is the surmise that the author has like other historians more or less successfully composed speeches suited to the speakers and occasions out of his own imagination.[17]

The letters, decrees and other documents in ancient history had frequently an origin similar to that of the speeches. Dionysius, for example, treats the letter of Nicias as though it were one of the speeches, and the creation of Thucydides himself. Fronto agrees with this judgment and similarly assigns to Sallust himself the letters appearing in his works.[18] Secondary writers like Josephus, besides inventing letters, sometimes transfer the letters in their sources bodily, whether the latter be genuine or not. It is often difficult to determine which is the case. The transfer is rarely accomplished without revision of diction, so that both earlier letters and fictitious compositions bear the earmarks of the redactor's style. Assertion of official origin is no guarantee. Josephus takes over references to archives or public tablets from his sources,[19] while his statement about the letter of Areus king of Sparta that "the letters were square and the seal an eagle attacking a dragon," and even the conventional sentence in the same

[17] An excellent essay on the speeches of Paul in Acts by P. Gardner is included in the volume, *Cambridge Biblical Essays*, 1909.

[18] Dion. Hal. *De Thucyd.* 42; Fronto *Epp.* ii. 1 (p. 126, ed. Naber).

[19] *Ant.* xii. 10, 6 § 416 = 1 Macc. viii. 22.

correspondence, "if you are well and things public **and** private are going on to your liking it would be as we desire, and we also are well," [20] are scarcely more authentic than the parallels in 1 Maccabees to which they are added.[21]

The two letters in Acts addressed respectively:

> The apostles and the elders, brethren, unto the brethren who are of the Gentiles in Antioch and Syria and Cilicia, greeting:
> Claudius Lysias unto the most excellent governor Felix, greeting:

are so characteristic of the author's style as to support the presumption that he is responsible for them. Their variation of expression or content [22] from the parallel narrative is quite compatible with identity of authorship. The absence in Luke of the familiar parade of proofs from the official archives is brought home to us by the contrast of Justin Martyr, who refers [23] to the census records of Quirinius and the *acta* of Pilate as mentioning respectively the birth and the death of Jesus.

For the songs or canticles in the first two chapters of Luke, Jewish writings provide better parallels than do Greek. Such lyric insertions occur in the Old Testament narratives, in some instances being older than the prose context, in some cases later, and in some being the work of the prose author himself. Later Jewish literature shows the tendency to add or include lyric passages in the narrative.

---

[20] See J. Armitage Robinson, *St. Paul's Epistle to the Ephesians,* 1903, p. 279; F. Ziemann, *De epistularum Græcarum formulis sollemnibus quæstiones selectæ,* 1910, pp. 302 ff.

[21] *Ant.* xii. 4, 10 § 227 = 1 Macc. xii. 20-23; *Ant.* xiii. 5, 8 § 166 = 1 Macc. xii. 6 ff. Josephus adds also in both places the name of the envoy, Demoteles.

[22] Especially xxiii, 27 and 30.

[23] *Apol.* 34, 2; 35, 9; (48, 3 *v.l.*). Tertullian also cites both.

Two curiously located additions are the prayer of Jonah
"out of the fish's belly," and the Song of the Three Children
"in the burning fiery furnace" (Daniel iii in the Greek).
The First Book of Maccabees has several lyric passages, and
so do the apocryphal books of Baruch and Tobit and some of
the apocalyptic literature.   In most of these cases there is
obvious imitation of earlier Hebrew poetical material and
adoption of earlier phrases.   Even in the canonical psalter
and in the Psalms of Solomon, not to mention the prayer
and (Hebrew) hymn in Ecclesiasticus li, many parts are
like centos dependent on the older liturgy.

The songs or prayers of Luke's nativity stories belong
to the same category.   Not only does their setting have Old
Testament precedents (notably in the Song of Hannah),
but also their style and thought is redolent of the older
hymnology.   They are a striking and beautiful feature of
Luke's overture.   They are quite in his own vocabulary,
though only occasionally later does he return to the poetic
and Biblical lyric style.[24]   It is, of course, not impossible
that the *Benedictus,* the *Magnificat,* the *Gloria in Excelsis*
and the *Nunc Dimittis* come from a Greek source like the
sayings of Jesus, from a Semitic source as is the case apparently with the lyrics of 1 Maccabees, or from oral tradition.   The relative merits of such alternative explanations
can be settled, if at all, only by detailed study of the text.
If they are older than Luke they are nevertheless illustra-
tive of the literary craftsmanship of later Judaism and early
Christianity.   If, as seems to me at present more likely,

---

[24] *E.g.,* in the praise of Luke vii. 16, the warnings peculiar to
Luke in xix. 42-44; xxiii. 28-31, and in parts of Luke xxi, the
prayer of Acts iv, the rebuke of Acts viii. 20-23, the farewell of
Acts xx, the commission of Acts xxvi. 16-18, and to a less extent
elsewhere in the speeches of Acts.   When Luke expands or combines Old Testament quotations he naturally uses Biblical style
in the patching, so that, to use his own phrase, "the patch from
the new will agree with the old."   See, for example, Luke iv. 18;
Acts ii. 19; viii. 21-23; xv. 18, as well as the Canticles *passim.*

they are mainly the evangelist's own composition, they illustrate, as do the speeches and letters, how the author conforms to the customs of his literary inheritance—customs often quite different from our own.

CHAPTER XV

LITERARY FORMALIA

The influence of literary conventions is often more obvious in the formalia of a writing than in its main contents. The letters of Paul, for example, and other New Testament epistles reveal the epistolary customs of their time principally in the greetings at the close and in the somewhat stereotyped address at the beginning with the thanksgiving that often follows it. The numerous contemporary letters now available in the papyri show at once how conventional and how limited are the formalia of these New Testament writings. In like manner Luke has adopted a few quite obvious and superficial literary conventions without carrying through his work the standards of composition which these affiliations might seem to imply.

His preface is one of the most evident marks of the litterateur. Neither the ancient Greek writers nor the Semitic authors used prefaces. They came into vogue in the Hellenistic age and were used by all kinds of formal prose writers, whether Greek or Roman. It is noteworthy that in the Greek Bible the only other prefaces are by the grandson of Jesus ben Sira, who translated his work into Greek (Ecclesiasticus), and by the good Greek stylist who wrote the Second Book of Maccabees. But for the Greek and Latin historians, geographers, scientists, doctors and other prose writers of the time the preface was a usual thing and even poets provided their works with prefaces (sometimes in prose).

The contents of the preface were prescribed by rhetorical

194

rule-books, largely on the basis of the technique of the orator's exordium. Both kinds of beginnings have the same name (προοίμιον). For historical prefaces one or two sets of instructions have come down to us, including that in Lucian's essay on *How History Ought to be Written*.[1] But it would seem that the circumstances of the case determined quite naturally what a preface should include and that the rules were more useful in preventing the bad taste of rhetors than in correcting the natural expression of a sensible writer. Certain subjects were often mentioned in prefaces, and probably for the same reason, viz., their naturalness to the occasion. As in Luke's preface, we often get references to preceding writers on the same theme (sometimes with such odious comparisons as will commend the later author), to the author's knowledge of the subject, to his decision to write and to his purpose in writing. In the preface is mentioned the official addressee of a work, to whom it is dedicated and whose association with the subject matter is sometimes given as explaining why he is addressed. The author's name is often included in the preface, usually at the end of it (Dionysius of Halicarnassus, Appian). Earlier writers of history began with their names (Thucydides, Hecataeus). But where the title and author of a work were named on a separate tag, as was probably the case with the *Antiquities* of Josephus, with the *Library* of Diodorus Siculus and with Luke-Acts, neither of these appeared on the inner text of the roll.

Modern scholars have classified the items in prefaces and have suggested that the recurrence of the same topics in so many authors was due to a certain convention in preface writing. Other critics both ancient and modern have explained the likeness as due to imitation, influence or plagiarism. Neither explanation is necessary, though in the case of some writers it may be correct. The likeness of circumstances often led different writers to deal with

---

[1] *De hist. conscrib.* 52-55.

much the same subjects and in much the same way. Parallels between the first sentence of Luke, for example, and certain medical prefaces or the *prooemia* of Josephus's *Jewish War* or *Antiquities* are not close enough to suggest literary dependence. It is possible to illustrate from a great variety of prefaces a number of the expressions in Luke. It is in the bare fact of his using a preface rather than in its details that Luke's relation to literature is apparent. "In fact the preface of Luke is the one place of the New Testament whereof one may say that in it the world shines through most plainly." [2]

The literary quality of prefaces manifested itself in certain incongruous and excessive uses on the part of would-be authors. Intended as they were to provide a semblance of literature to quite prosy compositions, the prefaces were often in marked contrast with the style of the technical books to which they were attached. Even the most incapable writers made an effort at style for this frontispiece, so that a well-known student of ancient literary prose describes it as self-explanatory, according to a consistent rule of antiquity, that a *prooemium* should be in a different style from the treatise itself, especially a technical treatise. [3] It is natural that the demands of rhetoric should be most carefully observed in the preface of any formal work. The writer must be sure here at the start to make a favorable impression. The words must be choice and elegant, the sentences well balanced, and the whole preface whether long or short rounded off with a good *clausula*. Men like Cicero, who were everywhere careful of their style, no doubt took particular pains with their prefaces, but also poorer stylists here at least exerted themselves. Even purely scientific works had artistic prefaces.

[2] Franz Overbeck, *Christentum und Kultur*, 1919, p. 79.
[3] E. Norden, *Die antike Kunstprosa*, 1898, p. 432. For the bearing of this rule upon the transition at Luke 1. 5, see *post*, p. 223.

It has been pointed out [4] that Polybius himself, who was no rhetor but a writer notoriously indifferent to matters of style, felt bound out of respect for the taste of his contemporaries to employ in his preface some rhetorical methods. A careful review of the prefaces of Byzantine historians shows that even in the times of greatest literary decadence scarcely a single preface is to be found that would have to be described as barbarously unpolished.[5]

This interest in the style of prefaces led to the custom of writing prefaces for practice, to the habit among some writers of treating in prefaces subjects quite alien to the contents of the main work, to the writing of prefaces as separate units, and apparently to the fault of prolonging them out of proportion to the body of the work. Desire for originality or for variety in an author's numerous writings was often responsible for the more far-fetched prefaces. Cicero in one of his letters throws an interesting light on his own practice. He had composed for himself a supply of *prooemia* from which he selected one for use as needed. So it came about that by a slip of the memory he used exactly the same preface for two different works.[6]

Luke's preface is not to be accused of all these faults, as our taste would now call them. His preface is not too long, like those which Lucian satirized as "the head of a colossus of Rhodes on the body of a dwarf," "for," as the author of 2 Maccabees observes, "it is foolish to expand what precedes the narrative and to cut short the narrative." [7] It is remarkably brief, a single sentence, pregnant with

[4] H. Lieberich, *Studien zu den Proömien in der griechischen und byzantinischen Geschichtsschreibung*, 1. Teil, 1898, p. 20.

[5] *Ibid.*, 2. Teil, 1900, p. 60.

[6] Cicero *Ad Att.* xvi. 6, 4, referring to the prefaces of his *De gloria* and *Academicus*, Book III.

[7] Lucian *De hist. conscrib.* 23; 2 Macc. ii. 32; *cf.* Aristeas *Epist. ad Philocratem* 8: "But that we may not be guilty of garrulity by being too lengthy in prolegomena we shall revert to continuous narration."

ideas, even though it is obscure and less explicit than many
a modern reader would desire. It is germane to the subject matter in spite of the fact that it stands off sharply
from the initial scene instead of giving what Lucian called
"an easy and unforced transition to the narrative." [8] Possibly it was written after the whole work was finished, as
is often the case with modern prefaces and apparently with
ancient prefaces also. It does, however, show an unmistakable effort at stylistic excellence, in marked contrast
with the very simple and Semitic idiom of the following
narrative, and in this respect aligns itself with the process
of superficial acceptance of literary conventions which so
many other prefaces reveal. The rhetorical balance of the
sentence, its closing rhythm, its choice diction, are all matters of linguistic technique familiar to the New Testament
grammarian. That in some of his longer words the writer
has overshot the mark and sacrificed clearness to sonorous
style is a suspicion that may be honestly voiced, even if it
cannot be proved. There is without it sufficient evidence in
the preface of literary conformity.

When an ancient work required more than one volume,
what may be called a secondary preface often occurs.
Each of the later books began with summaries of the preceding book and of the book just begun. Sometimes the
latter summary occurs instead at the close of the preceding
volume, or even in both places. In Acts it is omitted altogether and the review of the preceding book—"I wrote the
first book, Theophilus, about all that Jesus began to do and
to teach until the day when," etc.—leads over into a repetition of the closing scene of the gospel, so that no summary
of the following book is given. This sentence lacks the
systematic arrangement which we often find in contemporary transitions of the sort, and there is some difference
in the manuscripts as to the wording of its latter half. For

[8] *De hist. conscrib.* 55.

these reasons some scholars have supposed that it originally
concluded in the conventional way and has been tampered
with. As it stands, however, it is not unparalleled in
Luke's writings. It exhibits a brevity of summary not
unlike the preface of the gospel and does provide what
Lucian would call "an easy transition to the narrative."
Possibly the author himself is responsible for the anacolu-
thon. Something of the same kind is found elsewhere, e.g.,
Josephus *Antiquities* xiii.1:

> How the nation of the Jews recovered their freedom
> when they had been brought into slavery by the Mace-
> donians, and how many and great struggles their gen-
> eral, Judas, went through, till he was slain fighting
> for them, we have shown in the preceding book. But
> after the death of Judas all the wicked, and those that
> transgressed the laws of their forefathers, prevailed
> against the Jews, etc.

The use of these secondary prefaces was not universal.
Many historical works pass from book to book as though
no break occurred. In many cases the division into books
and even such *argumenta* as now occur in the texts were
not the work of the original writer. On the other hand,
rhetorical writers elaborated the several volumes as separate units and provided each with an artistic preface,
lengthy and quite alien to the subject matter. Among historians the use of book prefaces was not universal. We are
told that "Ephorus wrote thirty books, prefixing a preface
to each." [9] Diodorus Siculus followed the same custom out
of self-defense, wishing, he said, "to prevent those who are
in the habit of revising the books from injuring other people's compositions." [10] Jerome says, "To avoid the con-
fusing of the number of books and the spoiling of the order
of the different volumes over long spaces of time I have
prefixed to the several books little prefaces (*praefatiuncu-*

Diod. Sic. xvi. 76, 5.   [10] Diod. Sic. i. 5, 2.

lae)." [11]   There is reason to believe that books without prefaces, since they were circulated on separate rolls, often became mixed in order.   The simple linking preface may be illustrated as follows:

> In the preceding book after pointing out the causes of the second war between Rome and Carthage, I described the invasion of Italy by Hannibal, and the engagements which took place between the belligerents up to the battle on the river Aufidus at the town of Cannae.   I shall now give an account of the contemporary events in Greece from the 140th Olympiad onwards.   (Polybius iv. 1, 1.)

> The book before this, being the sixteenth of the whole work, began with the reign of Philip son of Amyntas.   In it were included all the acts of Philip until his death and those of the other kings and peoples and cities so far as they occurred during the period of that reign, which was twenty-four years. But in this book we shall record the events that followed beginning with the reign of Alexander. While including the things done by that king until his death we shall record along with them contemporary happenings in the known parts of the world. (Diodorus Siculus xvii. 1, 1 f.)

> The facts regarding Alexandra the queen and her death having been clearly presented by us in the book before this, we shall now tell the things subsequent to and related to those facts, making nothing else our aim except that we should not, either from ignorance or from weariness of memory, omit any of the events. (Josephus *Antiquities* xiv. 1, 1.)

> In the first book, Cassius Maximus, I gave an account (ἐποιησάμην τὸν λόγον as in Acts i. 1) of the

[11] Cited from G. Engel, *De antiquorum epicorum, didacticorum, historicorum prooemiis*, Marburg, 1910, p. 75, *note* 1.

materials of the art and of the teaching as to how dreams ought to be interpreted, etc. . . . But in this book I shall make the differentiations that are necessary. (Artemidorus *Oneirocritica* ii. 1.)

In connection with the prefaces to Luke's works should be mentioned the address to Theophilus which occurs in both of them. This custom of dedicating books to individuals is more or less familiar today, but in antiquity it first prevailed in the Hellenistic age and followed its own conventions. Sometimes a letter was used, prefixed to the book or sent separately. In that case the regular forms of a letter were employed, though if the body of the work followed immediately it was natural to omit the closing "farewell." At its briefest the letter was reduced to its lowest terms: "Hyginus to M. Fabius cordial greeting," or "Lucian to Cronius greeting." More commonly the name of the addressee was inserted in the vocative in the text of the preface, and if a preface was lacking, even in the body of the work. This was done near the beginning— almost never as the first word, because initial vocatives were eschewed in Greek and Latin—and also often at the end. When the work was in more than one volume it was customary to mention the addressee at the beginning of each volume, as is done in Acts. The vocative address often occurs not only at the beginning of each volume, but also the end of the last, as in Plutarch's *Quaestiones Conviviales* (nine volumes addressed to Sossius Senecio), Dioscorides' *Materia Medica* (five volumes addressed to "dearest Areus"), Josephus's *Contra Apionem* (two volumes addressed to "Epaphroditus most excellent of men," "Epaphroditus most precious to me" or simply "Epaphroditus"). It is evident from contemporary examples that the addition of "most excellent" in Luke i. 3 and its omission in Acts i. 1 is a variation entirely consonant with the habits of the time. If Theophilus had been mentioned also at the end of

Acts, we should have been spared any doubt we may now feel as to whether the author really intended to close his work with its present ending or expected to continue in a third volume.

The formal effect of this custom was to give the treatise a personal appearance. Thus books are often mistaken for letters or called letters when, as sometimes happens, the original title is lost. This is illustrated by the "letter" of Aristeas to Philocrates and the so-called Epistle to Diognetus, to mention only two writings associated with the study of the Bible. Neither of these treatises was really a letter at all. The latter also illustrates a curious result (already mentioned in Chapter I) of the habit of including in the text the name of the addressee but not the author's name or title of the work. When the latter have been forgotten, scholars must designate the work by the name of the person addressed, no matter how little that tells us about the work. Beside the anonymous early Christian tract or apology, *Ad Diognetum,* just mentioned, there is a famous rhetorical work, often attributed to Cornificius, which is known from its addressee as the *Ad Herennium.* By the same nomenclature the third and fifth books in our New Testament would together become simply the *Ad Theophilum.*

The relation of the addressee to the work and to its author varied. He was often a personal friend or fellow author. Sometimes he had inspired the work or asked to have it written. Sometimes he was the author's *patronus* and repaid the honor by underwriting the cost of publication. Sometimes he was chosen to lend prestige to the book, as nowadays by a different custom in British books the patron actually writes the foreword. Sometimes he was simply a person appropriate to the book's contents. In the preface to his essay on *The General,* dedicated to the general Veranius, the tactician Onasander writes (about 58 A. D.):

It is fitting, I believe, to dedicate monographs on horsemanship, or hunting, or fishing, or farming, to men who are devoted to such pursuits; but a treatise on military science, Quintus Veranius, should be dedicated to Romans, and especially to those of the Romans who have attained senatorial dignity, and who through the wisdom of Augustus Cæsar have been raised to the power of consul or general, both by reason of their military training (in which they have had no brief experience) and because of the distinction of their ancestors.

Other considerations, however, determined the person to be addressed. Textbooks were dedicated to the author's son, as typical of those whom he would instruct. Kings, emperors or others in authority were addressed, sometimes perhaps in the hope of securing favor for the author or his cause. Josephus says explicitly that the Epaphroditus to whom his works were dedicated had provided him the incentive, but modern scholars have thought he was chosen, some because of his influence at court, others (e.g., Laqueur) as the literary patron and ultimate owner of publication rights. Theodor Birt, an authority on ancient book-lore, has repeatedly argued that in many cases the person addressed was given or was sold these rights by the author.

With so many alternatives to choose from, the dedication of Luke-Acts to Theophilus does not prove much about Theophilus. In any case the relation of author to addressee was usually formal and it rarely affected the contents of the work. The imagined addressee is dropped from view as the writer proceeds, and the consciousness of personal relation is not maintained as it would be in a long but really personal letter. We cannot be sure that Theophilus would be more interested in "all that Jesus began both to do and to teach" than the second-century emperors were in the works dedicated to them on Greek word accent (twenty volumes by Herodian), on military strategy (by Aelian and Polyaenus), on the sayings of kings and generals (by Plutarch), on geography (e.g., Arrian's Periplus of the Euxine Sea), not to mention dictionaries (e.g., Pollux) and many defenses of Christianity by the apologists (Quadratus, Aristides, Justin, Melito, Apollinarius, Miltiades, Athenagoras and probably others).

Theophilus may or may not have been typical of the reading public for whom the work was intended. For, strange as it may seem to us, what the address to an individual really shows is that the work was intended not for an individual, but for a public—that is, it was published as a finished product and in accordance with the literary conventions. The real readers may be different. Plutarch, in the work already named, seems to reveal the fiction for a moment when, in his preface to the second volume of his work addressed to Senecio, he writes: "The readers must not be surprised if after dedicating the work to thee, we include some of the discussions in which thou hast had thyself a part." [12] That the dedication as well as the prefaces and arrangement into books were part of the formalia of belles-lettres was recognized by Photius when he says of Olympiodorus that, though "he professes to have provided only the material for a book or the material of history, so lacking in form and shape did the character of the language seem even to himself, nevertheless he both divides the history into books and tries to adorn it with prefaces and dedicates it to Theodosius the emperor." [13] As was to be expected, no other books of the Bible contain such a phenomenon as Luke's formal address to "the most excellent Theophilus."

Among the formalia of Luke's writings should be reckoned perhaps the elaborate dating of the ministry of John the Baptist:

[12] *Quæst. Conviv.* ii. *præf.* (p. 629E).   [13] Photius *Bibl., cod.* 80.

> In the fifteenth year of the government of Tiberius
> Caesar, when Pontius Pilate was governor of Judaea,
> and the tetrarch of Galilee was Herod, and Philip his
> brother was tetrarch of the country of Iturea and
> Trachonitis, and Lysanias was tetrarch of Abilene, in
> the highpriesthood of Annas and Caiaphas, the word
> of God came upon John the son of Zechariah in the
> wilderness. (Luke iii. 1.)

Occasional references to contemporary or local rulers are
perhaps natural in any writing, and Luke's mention elsewhere of Herod the Great, of Augustus and Quirinius, and,
of Claudius indicates only the contact with Gentile history
which his story illustrates throughout. In other cases
officials and the numbers of years or months are mentioned by Luke because they actually are part of the story,
but in this case the naming of the exact imperial year
and the inclusion of four local rulers and of the religious
leaders suggests that a more formal dating was intended.

The papyri show us that in Egypt official documents and
letters were regularly dated by using the year of the
Ptolemy or of the emperor and the month and day of the
local calendar. But not infrequently in more formal documents the names of some further incumbents in office were
named, perhaps as eponymous officials, without indication
of the year of their term. In Egypt these additional officials were often priests and when too numerous to name
were omitted, as the following examples show:

> Thirty-fifth year, month Pharmouthi. In the reigns
> of Ptolemy Euergetes, son of Ptolemy and Cleopatra,
> gods Epiphanes, and of queen Cleopatra his sister and
> of queen Cleopatra his wife, goddess Euergetes, and
> the rest of the associated datings. (*P. Giss.* 36, 7 ff.,
> April or May, 135 B. C.)
> In the reign of Ptolemy, who is also surnamed
> Alexander, god Philometor, year 14, in the priesthood
> of the priests, priestess, and basket-bearers, whatso-

ever their respective names, on the second of Choiak.
(*B.G.U.* 998.   17 Dec., 101 B. C.)

Such legal dating was no doubt used in other countries,
as the inscriptions indeed sufficiently testify, and one is led
to wonder whether Paul's letters once carried such dates.
It is not here, however, that we should seek the direct
models of Luke, but rather among the historians, who in
spite of notorious lack of interest in precise chronology
occasionally give similar details.   Annals, for example,
which were narratives arranged year by year, often distinguished each year by more than one reckoning.   The
Acta Pilati (A) in adjusting the year mentioned by Luke to
the form of official *acta* supplies for it the Roman consuls
and the Olympiad reckoning and adds the day and month
by the Roman calendar.   Dionysius of Halicarnassus tells
for each year of his *Roman Antiquities* the names of the
Roman consuls, and every fourth year the number of the
Olympiad and other information, in this manner:

> In the seventy-ninth Olympiad, of which Xenophon
> of Corinth was victor, the archon at Athens being
> Archedemides, Titus Quintius Capitolinus and Quintus
> Fabius Vibulanus receive the consulship (ix. 61).

The completest parallels to Luke occur, however, in
special passages in other historians where they are mark-
ing like the evangelist the real starting-point of their narrative.   Josephus in his account of the Jewish war says,
"it began in the twelfth year of the government of Nero,
in the seventeenth of the reign of Agrippa, in the month
Artemisium," and in a cross reference to that work at the
close of the *Antiquities* he gives the same era as "the second
year of the procuratorship of Florus and the twelfth of the
rule of Nero." [14]   But the most remarkable parallel is the

---

[14] *B. J.* ii. 14, 4 § 284; *Ant.* xx. 11 § 257.   A different though elaborate and interesting chronological effort is found in Josephus'

famous synchronism by which Thucydides dates the beginning of the Peloponnesian War with the attack on Plataea:

> In the fifteenth year [of the armistice concluded
> after the conquest of Euboea] in the priesthood at
> Argos of Chrysis then in her forty-eighth year of
> service, in the ephorship of Ainesias at Sparta, in the
> archonship among the Athenians of Pythodorus with
> two months still to serve, in the sixth month after the
> battle at Potidaea, at the beginning of spring, came
> men from Thebes, etc. (ii. 2, 1)

This full synchronism, including the chronological data
of three prominent states, is as unique in Thucydides as the
parallel is in the writings of Luke. Evidently both felt
the value of one full dating at the starting-point. It is
noteworthy that even Eusebius of Caesarea, though he had
written a chronographical outline of history and retained
an interest in the reckoning of time, nevertheless gives in
his *Church History* an elaborate dating only for Jesus'
birth [15]—his real beginning. Professor Schwartz is justified when he says of Luke: "The evangelist is employing
here a form which he has taken over from an alien
sphere . . . it is derived from secular historiography
which has the habit of making prominent important events,
especially those with which the principal narrative begins,
by means of circumstantial datings and synchronisms." [16]
It must not be forgotten, however, that he has combined
it with the Old Testament formula, "the word of the Lord

dating of the beginning of Solomon's temple in *Ant.* viii. 3, 1
§§ 61 f., based on the nucleus in 1 Kings vi. 1. He adds the Jewish
and Macedonian names of the second month, the number of years
since Abraham, since the Flood and since the Creation, the year
of Hiram's reign, and the number of years since the founding of
Tyre.

[15] *H.E.* i. 5, 2.
[16] E. Schwartz, *Zeitschrift für die neutestamentliche Wissenschaft*, xi, 1910, p. 102, referring to Luke iii. 1 f.

came to —— son of ——," which occurs at the beginning
of so many prophetic oracles with a date, and which has
been used perhaps by later editors in a somewhat different
introduction to the several books, summarizing the duration
of the prophet's work, e.g.:

> The word of God which came upon Jeremiah son
> of Hilkiah, one of the priests, who was living in
> Anathoth in the land of Benjamin, the message of
> God that came to him in the days of Josiah son of
> Amos, king of Judah, in the thirteenth year in his
> reign; and it came in the days of Joachim son of
> Josiah, king of Judah, until the eleventh year of
> Zedekiah son of Josiah, king of Judah, until the
> captivity of Jerusalem in the fifth month (Jer. i. 1-3
> LXX).

Evidently Luke is closer to the "profane" form, but
whether, as Schwartz further claims, it was more than he
could handle is a question that depends on our judgment
about the accuracy of his combination.[17]   That writer does
well to emphasize the difficulty in antiquity of such synchronisms, a difficulty which the student of antiquity knows
only too well, but which is hardly dreamed of by a reader
in our own day who takes historical dates for granted.[18]

---

[17] It is suspicious that he has two Jewish high priests, that the
tetrarchs become literally "rulers out of four," and that a Lysanias of Abilene belongs in history two generations earlier.   The
dates have been recently defended by E. Meyer, *Ursprung und
Anfänge des Christentums*, Vol. I, pp. 46-51, and by C. Cichorius,
"Chronologisches zum Leben Jesu," in *Zeitschrift für die neutestamentliche Wissenschaft*, xxii, 1923, pp. 16-20.   See M. Goguel,
Jésus de Nazareth: mythe ou histoire? 1925, p. 236 (Eng. Trans.,
1926, p. 240): "The value of the data which he gives is a question
of small importance.   The interesting thing is that he had considered it necessary to give them."

[18] We are rudely reminded of our own uncertainty in this regard
when Assyriologists in the light of recent discoveries quietly move
backward six years (from 607-6 to 612 B.C.) a date so important
and so comparatively modern as the fall of Nineveh.

In any case the passage in Luke is an unusual effort. But of this as of the other formalia it may be said that they are so slight in extent and so alien to much of the surrounding matter that they emphasize the difference rather than the likeness of the Christian evangelists when put in comparison with the Hellenistic authors.

PART III

THE PERSONALITY OF THE AUTHOR

CHAPTER XVI

LANGUAGE AND STYLE

The third factor to be considered in the work of Luke is the author's individuality. His sources represent the deeds and records of predecessors. His general language, method and viewpoint he shares with others of his group. There remains, however, something distinctive in his writing, as there is something distinctive in everyone's writing —his own personality. To distinguish this and to isolate it for study is never easy even for contemporaries, and it is especially difficult for us to do so for the evangelist because of our remoteness in time, thought and knowledge. Often a writer himself is as unaware of his own special characteristics as he is of the conventions of his group. He has of course some conscious viewpoints and some definite aims. These we shall postpone for later examination. At this stage we wish rather to consider, so far as it can be detected, the author's own personality as one of the determining factors in the making of Luke-Acts. But our only clue to this influence is the resultant character of the work itself and the author's unconscious self-revelation there.

Even a man's language is individual. His printed diction is nearly as distinctive as his voice or as his handwriting. With some men the favorite or peculiar idioms are more numerous and striking than with others, but nearly every writer has something of his own. If these idiosyncrasies are too prominent and peculiar, we call them mannerisms. Under less odious titles phenomena of the same kind can be recognized in everyone. As far as we can tell, Luke's style is particularly individual. Though he often agrees with the current ways of speech he nevertheless has certain distinctive habits of his own.

It is usual to compare him with other New Testament writers or merely with the other evangelists, and to call characteristic of Luke or "peculiar" to him the words and expressions confined to his writings or occurring most frequently in them. In view, however, of the limited extent of the gospels, of the New Testament or even of the whole Greek Bible, and in view of the fact that the selection of these special canonical groups of Greek writings is from the linguistic viewpoint unrepresentative and arbitrary, the occurrence of certain words or ways of speech exclusively or principally in Luke and Acts is often merely an accident. Examples which are selected in this way as "peculiar to Luke" are often neither characteristic of him nor unusual in contemporary Greek, and the stress which is frequently laid upon them is quite unscientific. Of over seven hundred words used in Luke and Acts but not found elsewhere in the New Testament many are certainly words that Luke's contemporaries, even the other evangelists, might have used if they had been dealing with the identical subjects. Nearly all of them are words found outside of the New Testament, usually in several writers in different places and times and with various grades of culture. It would be absurd to suppose that because the Greek nouns innkeeper, eyewitness, kinswoman, mist, tanner, fathom, orator and others occur not once in the whole Greek Bible outside of Luke and Acts, any more significance thereby attaches to them than to their English equivalents.

It must be recalled that with our limited knowledge of the ancient language even words found only once in all the range of known Greek—the so-called *hapax legomena*— are curiosities to us rather than personal idiosyncrasies of the writers. They indicate limitation in our knowledge rather than in their own currency. A new discovery might at any time remove such a word from the category, as the papyri have done with several New Testament *hapax legomena*, e.g., the word for "accusations" in Acts xxv. 7, which, instead of being unique, is now found in an illiterate complaint about two dead pigs over-driven by a donkey driver, written at the end of Domitian's reign and first published in 1900. This and other examples we have already cited in an earlier chapter. Under such circumstances any effort made in our modern ignorance to select the really characteristic locutions of our author can be no more than tentative. A few illustrations only will be attempted, chosen as far as possible for their intelligibility to English readers; and probably none of them is unique.

Among the initial phrases that occur most often in his writings is the Semitic idiom "it came to pass," followed by more than one construction, as a comparison between Luke and Acts shows us. Another phrase and a more unusual one is "on one of those days" and the like. Luke also says "he spoke a parable" rather than "spoke in a parable" or "in parables." He differs from the other evangelists even in the way he expresses "he spake unto." [1] Almost limited to him in the New Testament is the simple dative "by name," though it occurs in papyri. Other differences from Matthew and Mark appear in comparing parallel passages. Interesting though not unique is his use of the article before questions, so that literally he says, for example, "And they began to inquire with each other the who then might be of them he that was to do this. And there arose also rivalry among them, the who of them seemed to be greatest." His words for "immediately" and for "master" (in address of disciples to Jesus) are not those which the other evangelists use.

[1] εἶπεν δὲ πρός

Like many other writers he combines pairs of words. Some of these pairs are fixed idioms of the language, like the examples we have given in Chapter IX; others are spontaneous and temporary combinations. Only one occurs frequently enough in Luke and infrequently enough elsewhere to deserve mention here—the association of "authority and power." [2] It is barely possible that an observant contemporary would have detected something resembling mannerism in his use of certain participles as nouns—translatable in English as "the happening," "the sayings"—and in his frequent use of the word "sufficient" in a weakened sense, as our "considerable." The last, however, occurs only less frequently in other writers like Paul and in papyri. The adjective "safe" used with the article in the sense "the facts" does not occur often, I think, in other writers, as it does in Acts. Even the noun "safety" is used in the same way in Luke's preface. [3] Yet the former of these I have found at least three times in the papyri (twice in the same writer, again perhaps a personal idiom) and once in Lucian. [4]

The forms of emphasis in Luke are among the characteristics of his style. A favorite though scarcely unusual method is his insertion of "all" or "every." It occurs in such literary passages as the speech at Athens: "in all things . . . all things . . . he giveth to all men life and breath and all things . . . every nation . . . on all the face of the earth . . . he is not far from each one of us . . . he commandeth men that they should all everywhere repent . . . he hath given assurance unto all men"; or in the exordium of the rhetor Tertullus: "we accept it

---

[2] But see Rev. xvii. 13; *Test. XII. Patr.* Reuben 5 v. *l.;* Herodian v. 1, 1.

[3] τὸ ἀσφαλές Acts xxi. 34; xxii. 30; xxv. 26; ἀσφάλεια Luke i. 4. The adverb is perhaps more common in this sense, as in Acts ii. 36.

[4] *Vera historia* i. 26. For instances in the papyri see *Beginnings of Christianity,* Vol. II, p. 509.

in all ways and in all places, most excellent Felix, with all thankfulness," and also in phrases like, "O full of all guile and all villany, thou son of the devil, thou enemy of all righteousness"; "All his adversaries were put to shame: and all the multitude rejoiced for all the glorious things that were done by him"; "Give to everyone that asketh thee"; "We ourselves also forgive everyone that is indebted to us." [5]

This last passage suggests another form of emphasis in Luke, the use of the pronoun αὐτός translated "they themselves," "he himself," "on that day," "this night," "in that very hour (time or house)" and the adverbial "together" (ἐπὶ τὸ αὐτό). So the contemptuous "this," used of Jesus so often in Luke's account of the passion, adds to the pathos of the scene.[6] Like the author of Deuteronomy, Luke used the emphatic "today." "Today is this scripture fulfilled in your ears," "Today is salvation come to this house," "Today shalt thou be with me in paradise," "Wherefore I testify to you today," etc. The beatitudes and woes in Luke are marked by "now," and in Acts we have in the speeches a different "now therefore," "for the present," as well as the emphatic "today." His insertion of "each day" in the Lord's Prayer and in the saying about taking up the cross, and his advice about forgiving the brother who sins and repents seven times "per day" are notable because of their absence from the parallels.

From the tradition of Jesus' words came the *"amen* I say unto you." Luke often replaces the Aramaic adverb with "truly" or "really" or "yes," but the emphatic "I

[5] There is no "everyone" in Matthew's parallels to the last two sentences.

[6] Compare its emphatic, triumphant or contemptuous use in Luke xix. 14; xx. 14; xxi. 4; xxii. 56, 59; and often in Acts, *e.g.*, "this Jesus," "this Moses," "this babbler," "this Paul," vi. 14; vii. 40; xvii. 18; xix. 26.

say unto you" he likes to use not only before an important saying as in his sources, but at the close of a parable or argument or upon reiterating a solemn pronouncement.[7] There is also the negative "no, I tell you." He adds many other like words: "I will show you," "know this," "make up your mind," "put these words in your ears," "let this be known to you and give your ears to my words," "hear these words," "listen!"[8] The Semitic "and behold" is one of his favorite expressions; he alone emphasizes numbers by "behold."[9]

Luke is the evangelist who, like the "Elohist" in the Old Testament, doubles the vocatives: "master, master"; "Martha, Martha"; "Simon, Simon"; "Saul, Saul." Similarly, he doubles the cry, "Crucify, crucify him."

In classical Greek the word order was so flexible that emphasis could be effectively expressed by the position of words, but the later vernacular language lost much of this fine capacity for indicating shades of tone and meaning. In the New Testament the author of the Epistle to the Hebrews is perhaps a partial exception. He was sensitive to both the rhythm and the emphasis that can be obtained by arrangement of words. One of his habits, the conclusion of a clause by the name Jesus, finds some parallels in the speeches in Acts.[10]

Possibly Luke's style is not altogether constant. Like the rest of us, he has the habit of soon repeating a word when he has once used it. Hence certain words and expressions occur in one part of his writings and others in

---

[7] Luke xi. 51; xii. 5; xiii. 27; xiv. 24; xv. 7, 10; xviii. 8, 14; xix. 26.

[8] Luke vi. 47; xii. 5. Luke x. 11; *cf.* Acts ii. 36. Luke xxi. 14; ix. 44. Acts ii. 14, 22; vii. 2; xv. 13. In these too he resembles the "diatribe," *cf.* p. 152.

[9] Luke xiii. 7, 16; xv. 29; xix. 8; *cf.* Acts ii. 7.

[10] Heb. ii. 9; iii. 1; iv. 14; vi. 20; vii. 22; xii. 2, 24; xiii. 20; Acts ii. 36; iii. 20; iv. 27; x. 37; xiii. 23, 33. *Cf.* v. 42; xvii. 3.

another part. It is unwise to attribute these phenomena to his sources, for his Greek sources at least are largely recast in his copying of them. The accumulation of idioms that seem Semitic may be due to translation of a Semitic source, but they may be due also to the mood or style in which certain parts of his story were written. It is not impossible that in addition to the quotations which are from the Greek Old Testament other passages in this work are influenced by its vocabulary or style.

There are other influences to which traits of his style have been variously attributed, though with less probability. The fact that he shares with Paul alone of New Testament writers quite a number of words and expressions has been thought by some to prove or confirm his personal acquaintance with the apostle to the Gentiles. But the inference would be justified only if the examples of verbal agreement cited were really unusual words. The same fallacy regularly inheres in the argument from vocabulary, whether employed by Krenkel to show Luke's knowledge of Josephus, or by Hobart and others to prove that the evangelist was a physician.[11] While he undoubtedly has much in common with the diction of the Septuagint, Paul, Josephus and the medical writers and with many other bodies of Greek writing taken one at a time, these facts give little clue to his individuality of speech. Of the first named alone can we feel sure that he had actual knowledge, since he regularly quotes the Greek Bible. In this he resembles all the early Christian writings known to us except Matthew and Revelation, which seem to have had in addition other channels of contact with the Hebrew Scriptures.

---

[11] M. Krenkel, *Josephus und Lucas*, 1894; W. K. Hobart, *The Medical Language of St. Luke*, 1882. I have dealt with the medical language of Luke at length in my *Style and Literary Method of Luke*, pp. 39-72 and in *The Journal of Biblical Literature*, xlv, 1926, pp. 190-209.

Such individuality as this or any other writer betrays must be found in the combination of elements, in the actual scope and limitation of his diction, rather than in statistical comparison with any arbitrary or accidental collection of writings. Who of us has not in our speech much in common with the English Bible, with medical writers, with Phillips Brooks or Macaulay or whatever English writer you will? We recognize the fallacy when as an argument for Baconian authorship Shakespeare's plays are made to yield many words of legal meaning found also in Francis Bacon the lawyer. By the same token our evangelist could be made a lawyer as well as a doctor on the basis of many legal terms which he uses, especially in the closing chapters of Acts,[12] while in the story of the shipwreck, if we are to believe Wellhausen,[13] the doctor and lawyer are metamorphosed into an expert mariner.

If the style is the man, then the man with whom we have to do is for his time and station a gentleman of ability and breadth of interest, whatever his past reading and training may have been. His vocabulary no purist could wholly commend, but no ignorant man could entirely equal it, though he could always understand it. It had the

---

[12] The early fragment, known as the Canon of Muratori, refers to Luke as *studiosus iuris,* which no doubt means in Latin a full-fledged lawyer, but if it translates a Greek original like Acts xxi. 20, it means zealous for the Jewish law. Apropos of a suggestion that Paul obtained from this companion not only medical but legal professional advice, Hilgenfeld many years ago made merry over Luke's degrees: "Luke, who is introduced to us by the New Testament not merely as a D.D. but as an M.D. (Col. iv. 14), has now further conferred upon him by Aberle an LL.D., so that the Faculty of Law shall have claim to his insignia. That Luke must have been not only an attorney, but also a very good one, he says may be concluded from his writings. All that Luke now lacks is the Ph.D. hood, which, forsooth, he can probably get without much trouble." (*Zeitschrift für wissenschaftliche Theologie,* vii, 1864, p. 442.)

[13] *Noten zur Apostelgeschichte,* pp. 18, 21.

qualification which is the chief requisite of any vocabulary —it could express what its owner wished to express with ease and accuracy.

It is in this connection that we would describe more fully what has been already mentioned—the variation of style in Luke's writings. The literary men of antiquity understood the imitation of classical models of style. They required that speeches invented for the actors of history should (at least in contents) be varied and appropriate to the several speakers and occasions. They taught that different types of writing—argument, description, etc.— had each its appropriate style, and even that in descriptions the style should be varied in accordance with the things described.[14] They were able to write whole essays in an archaic Attic style and even in the other extinct dialects of their famous models. The historians like Dionysius of Halicarnassus, Josephus, and Dio Cassius imitated not merely the vocabulary but whole scenes of Thucydides. Arrian and Josephus imitated titles of works and number of volumes from their predecessors.

Luke's sensitiveness to style seems much less artificial and really more far-reaching. It may therefore be accounted a personal characteristic rather than something he shared with contemporary technique. J. H. Moulton writes:

It would be hard to find ancient parallels for the variation of style he shows as his story changes its scene. A modern novelist will see to it that his country yokel and his professor do not talk the same dialect; and he will often try to make a Lancashire weaver or a Cornish miner approximate to the speech actually current in those areas. Similarly, Aristophanes makes a Megarian, a Bœotian, a Spartan

[14] P. Scheller, *De hellenistica historiæ conscribendæ arte*, 1911, p. 56.

H*

woman speak their own dialect fairly correctly. But this is only partial illustration: it suits Luke's accurate reproduction of the reported dialogues that came to him in rough translations like that we postulate for Q. But it is not going as far as Luke when he steeps his style in Biblical phraseology, drawn from the Greek Old Testament, so long as his narrative moves in Palestinian circles, where the speakers use Greek that obviously represents a foreign idiom—like Shakespeare's Fluellen with his Welsh English. That Luke should do this fits in well with his presumed history. A proselyte who made his first acquaintance with the Old Testament in its Greek version was likely to feel for that version as no Hebrew could feel, accustomed to keep all his reverence for the original. His imitation of the translation-Greek of his model —e.g., in the construction καὶ ἐγένετο καὶ with a finite verb, which yields to the *acc. et infin.* in Acts—reminds us of the Biblical style of John Bunyan, and other English writers whose education it was to be *homo unius libri.* That Luke instinctively departs from that style when his subject takes him away from the Biblical land and people, is equally natural. It is mostly in these parts of his work that he makes what concessions he does make to the book style.[15]

This explanation of the variation in Luke's style is shared by Harnack and many other scholars. From modern literature perhaps a partial parallel may be found in *The Cotter's Saturday Night.* There literary English and broad Scotch are interchanged as the theme changes, the former appropriately used in the stanza of dedication, in those on the family Bible reading and in the patriotic conclusion, the latter in the intimate picture of "the lowly train in life's sequestered scene." For the description of domestic piety and religious devotion in Scotland, Robert Burns found the literary style of an imposed civilization

[15] *A Grammar of New Testament Greek,* Vol. II, pp. 7 f.

more natural than his native patois, while the cosmopolitan author of the "Gospel of the Infancy" adopts for his Palestinian idyll the provincial idiom of the Septuagint. Each prefers to follow his Bible, alien though its style is to him, rather than to translate religion into his own natural ways of speech.

The fact of variation in Luke-Acts is unmistakable to every careful reader of the Greek text, and some of it may be observed even in English. The main data seem to be as follows:

The most Biblical style appears in his first two chapters in the birth stories beginning, "There was in the days of· Herod, king of Judaea, a certain priest named Zacharias, of the course of Abijah: and he had a wife of the daughters of Aaron, and her name was Elisabeth." The style and even the subject matter are evidently affected by the Old Testament in the narrative, while the Canticles are reminiscent in grammar and in poetic structure, as well as in phraseology, of the older psalmody.

The contrast of the preface which immediately precedes brings this Semitic quality into strong relief, for the preface is a single long sentence, well balanced, periodic, with some choice Greek words and inflections, while what follows is a string of coördinate clauses with many unidiomatic phrases. Here at least the contrast may be due to the literary exertion of the author in conforming in his preface to the conventions of artificial style. The rhetoricians recognized the necessity of different styles. Aristides says in his *Ars rhetorica,* "While the flowing and loose structure is appropriate for narrative and emotional passages, the periodic structure is appropriate for declamations and *prooemia* and arguments." [16] The *prooemia* of which he speaks are doubtless the exordia of orations rather than the prefaces of histories, but the rule for both was the

---

[16] i. 13, 4 (Spengel, *Rhetores Græci,* Vol. II, p. 508).

same, for, as Cicero expressed it, "I do not find that history ever has been provided separately with rhetoricians' rules." [17]

When we pass on from the birth stories into the body of the gospel, there is no such notable change of style, but a fairly uniform narrative without such extensive Old Testament echoes, yet with no great literary pretensions. We can see by Mark how Luke improves the Greek of his source while he nevertheless quite obviously introduces some very plain Semitisms.[18]

The Book of Acts begins in much the same style, though there are slight signs of improvement from the point of view of purity of Greek, like the cessation of "and it came to pass and" mentioned by Moulton, the decrease of the Semitic construction ἐν τῷ with the infinitive so frequent in the gospel,[19] and the greatly increased use (not always correct use, however) of the good Greek particles μέν and τε and of the genitive absolute.

As Acts progresses the style becomes prevailingly more secular and perhaps reaches its climax in the speech of Paul before Agrippa, where in grammar alone Professor Blass noted half a dozen quite classical idioms unusual in the New Testament. The most casual reading will show how the Old Testament quotations become infrequent in the later chapters of Acts. This of course is due principally to the absence of such arguments from prophecy as occupy the speeches addressed to the Jews in the earlier part of the book. On the other hand, a number of the most choice and idiomatic phrases of secular Greek appear in the closing

---

[17] *De oratore* ii. 15, 62.

[18] These editorial Semiticisms are particularly evident at junctures of sources or where Luke is freely reworking the transitions from scene to scene. Some examples are among those listed on p. 176. The Semitic element is well illustrated in such passages as Luke ix. 44-45, 51-53.

[19] This occurs about thirty times in Luke, in Acts ii. 1; viii. 6; ix. 3; xi. 15, and not at all thereafter.

chapters, as we noted in Chapter IX.[20] No exact line of
transition can be drawn, no gauge of relative purity is
available. The contrast or gradual change could not be
shown by statistics. The Greek reader relies on general
impression, and the English reader can do no more than
accept the verdict.

Perhaps a more tangible evidence of Luke's sensitiveness
to style appears in some variation in his proper names.
The most famous is his change at Acts xiii.9 by the use
of the simple ancient formula for *alias*: "Saul who is also
Paul." Before that verse he speaks of Saul, after it of
Paul. The transition from the Hebrew to the Roman name
is scarcely to be attributed merely to the mention in this
context of the proconsul Sergius Paulus. Still less is it
likely that Paul, a Roman citizen by birth, first acquired
the Latin *cognomen* on this occasion. It is rather due to
the author's feeling for the nomenclature appropriate to
the setting. Therefore when Paul's career is fairly started
among the Gentiles, the author shifts to the Roman name.
It is at about the same stage in the story that the author
drops as his designation for Gentile adherents to Judaism
the name "God-fearers" and substitutes the less Semitic
"God-worshipers." A change of a different kind occurs a
little later, though not quite so decisively and permanently,
from "Barnabas and Saul (Paul)" to the order "Paul and
Barnabas."

There is similar evidence in this author's use of indeclinable forms of Semitic names. Something has been said
above of the aversion felt by Greek writers to the use of
barbarous proper names and of Luke's share in this aversion. If they are common nouns he translates them, if
proper names he often omits or apologizes for them. One
of the difficulties these words presented beside that of sound
was inflection. They did not always lend themselves to
the regular ways of Greek declension, and the Greek trans-

[20] Some of these are cited on pp. 120 f.

lators of the Old Testament and their successors often in despair left them as indeclinable. Josephus with his higher literary ambition usually contorted them into some Greek declension, generally by adding simply -os, as had been done, for example, with the name which when used of the patriarch was spelled "Jacob," of contemporaries "Jacobos." Now in several names Luke varies his usage, and the occurrence of the less regular Greek form is significant. For example, Saul, "Saulos," besides his Roman name Paulus is sometimes addressed as "Saoul." This spelling is limited, however, to passages where he is directly addressed in the Semitic language, viz., by Ananias of Damascus and in the three accounts of the voice at his conversion.[21] The last of these passages shows in two ways Luke's sensitiveness to style. For the voice of Jesus only the vernacular "Saoul" seems possible, but since the vision is being told to Agrippa and a Gentile court the author feels constrained to explain and apologize, as it were, for the barbarism, and therefore adds here, as he does not in the two parallel passages, that the voice spoke "in the Hebrew (Aramaic) language." We have evidence elsewhere in Acts that the author was sensitive to matters of language—of Lycaonians, Egyptians, Jerusalemites and Maltese, not to mention Parthians and Elamites and all the polyglot company at Pentecost.

Peter like Paul has more than one name. The commonest is the Greek nickname "Peter," whose Aramaic equivalent "Cephas" is entirely absent from these writings. Before that name is given Luke uses only [22] the name "Simon," which is at once a good Greek proper name and

---

[21] Παῦλε is used by Agrippa (xxvi. 24) and by God in his vision to Paul during the storm *as reported by Paul to his Gentile fellow sailors* (xxvii. 24).

[22] An exception is "Simon Peter" read by many MSS. at Luke v. 8, but I think it may be a scribal change made under the influence of the usage in John, especially of John xxi.

a fairly close equivalent of Simeon. "Simon" is used also once or twice at the close of the gospel, not in narrative, but in words of Jesus or his disciples. Cornelius and his Roman officers regularly refer to him as "Simon surnamed Peter," apparently treating the names as a Latin *nomen* and *cognomen*. The literal Semitic form of Simon Peter's name, "Simeon," occurs only once, and that in the speech of James at the council of Jerusalem. "John surnamed Mark" or "John" becomes the straight Roman "Marcus" (Mark) only as he starts out with Barnabas for service outside of Palestine.[23]

Possibly place names vary for similar reasons. There are two forms of the name Jerusalem used interchangeably with no obvious uniform rule for their variation, yet it has been often noted that the indeclinable form "Yerousalem," which most nearly transliterates the Hebrew, decreases in Acts as the story moves out of its Palestinian setting, while the declinable "Hierosolyma," used in Gentile writers and associated by popular etymology with the Greek word *hiero-* and the name Solymi, increases. For Judaea the indeclinable "Juda" occurs only in the birth stories. The word Israel (Israelites, children of Israel) occurs on the lips of various speakers and in the narrative parts of the birth stories. Elsewhere the equivalent is used, the Jews.[24]

Similar, too, is the way in which in his speeches Luke puts in the mouth of certain speakers religious terms which he entirely or almost entirely avoids in the speeches of other characters and in his own narrative. Here are a few examples:

[23] Compare A. Deissmann, *Bible Studies*, 1901, p. 317, *note*.

[24] The substitution is most evident at Luke xxiii. 35-37 = Mark xv. 29-32. The apparent exception at Acts v. 21 is a full phrase borrowed from the Greek Old Testament. In the latter part of Acts non-Jews are spoken of by the usual term Ἕλληνες, but in the earlier Palestinian sections only the expressive and unique Ἑλληνισταί occurs (vi. 1; ix. 29; xi. 20 *v. l.*), I suspect in much the same sense.

"Son of man" (of Jesus) only on Jesus' lips.   This is
true of the other gospels and of all early Christian literature except a few passages where there is plain reference
to Daniel's description of the Son of man at the right hand
of God. Stephen's dying words in Acts are one of these.

"Father" (of God) only on Jesus' lips and once when
Peter is echoing a saying of Jesus (Acts ii. 33; cf. Luke
xxiv. 49 and Acts i. 4).

"Master" (ἐπιστάτης, of Jesus) in address to Jesus
and only by his disciples, a usage peculiar to Luke among
the evangelists.   Compare

"Teacher" (διδάσκαλος of Jesus) in address to Jesus
only by others than his disciples. (Luke xxi. 7 is, with
Luke's indefinite subject, no exception.)

"Gospel" (the noun) only twice, once each in the mouth
of Peter and of Paul (Acts xv. 7 and xx. 24), before Christian gatherings.

"Church" first in Acts v. 11.

For Paul's supposed profanation of the temple the Jews
use κοινόω when addressing fellow Jews (xxi. 28) and
βεβηλόω when addressing the Gentile court of Felix
(xxiv. 6).

"Foreigner" (instead of Gentiles) only in words spoken
in the presence of the foreigner (Luke xvii. 18 ἀλλογενής;
Acts x. 28 ἀλλόφυλος).

"Nation" (ἔθνος, of the Jews) six times, but only in
"reports of discourses, in which the *official* terminology,
such as was customary before a Gentile tribunal, would
naturally be used.   These passages only show how carefully St. Luke handled matters of style." [25]

This variation of language may not always have been
conscious. To a writer of native imagination and dramatic
instinct it could come quite naturally.   In the cases mentioned it is too obvious to be accidental and too irregular
to be entirely mechanical.   In some respects it coincides

[25] Harnack, *Acts of the Apostles*, p. 50. Conversely Acts never
uses ἔθνη in addresses by or to foreigners. Contrast especially x. 2
(λαός) with 22, and xxiv. 5 (οἰκουμένη) with xxi. 21, and xxviii. 17
with 19.

with the practice of the other evangelists.[26] It may explain some other characteristics of Luke. The sense for appropriate distribution of religious terminology in the words of the several speakers may account in the case of Peter's addresses for their so-called primitive Christology, such as the absence of emphasis on Jesus' death for sin, the stress on his resurrection and even the use of the term "servant ($\pi\alpha\hat{\imath}s$) of the Lord" in a quite limited section of Acts.[27]

[26] The other synoptic evangelists, however, have habits which Luke does not share, such as their well-known avoidance of "the Lord" for Jesus in narrative, which F. C. Burkitt calls "a singular indication of historical feeling on the part of our evangelists" in the matter of nomenclature, and their avoidance (except in connection with Jesus' appointment of missionaries) of "the apostles" for the twelve disciples. In address to Jesus, Mark uses "Rabbi," which Luke avoids, I think not because it was pedantic (Burkitt), but because it was not Greek, while Luke uses freely in address, besides "teacher" and "master" (see above), the vocative "Lord," which Mark limits to the address of the Syro-Phœnician woman. (Compare Streeter, *The Four Gospels*, pp. 212 ff.) Yet Luke never represents his followers as referring to Jesus as "the Lord," or "the Lord Jesus (Christ)," except after the resurrection and when speaking to other Christians. The Western Text neglects this nicety, as for example, at Acts xiii. 33; xiv. 10; xvi. 4; xviii. 8.

The name "Christian" is another illustration. It is put by Luke into the mouth of Agrippa in deriding Paul. If as First Peter and other early Christian use (and non-use) of the name suggest it was applied at first always by non-believers to believers (as a nickname?), Luke's limitation to this passage is most appropriate and his restraint from using it even in narrative is noteworthy, since evidently in his day it was not uncommon. Otherwise he would hardly have called attention to the circumstances when the believers were "for the first time" ($\pi\rho\acute{\omega}\tau\omega s$) called Christians (Acts xi. 26). At xxiv. 5 they are first called Nazarenes (by a Jew).

[27] W. Bousset, *Kyrios Christos*, 2d ed., 1921, p. 56, points out that this unusual title, found twice in the prayer of Acts iv as "thy holy servant," occurs elsewhere throughout early Christian literature mainly in liturgical passages, and that "Acts uses the title 'Son of God' only once, and that in a place where the preaching of Paul is characterized concisely, ix. 20." It is char-

Luke may be doing here some successful archaizing. In the case of Paul's addresses it might explain whatever Pauline theology or phraseology can be detected in them.

The transitions noted in the style and even in the spelling of the names also suggest further curious literary habits. I cannot escape the feeling that, whatever the real origin of the "we" in Acts, its sudden and regular appearance in every instance when Paul's party is about to take ship is somehow connected with similar mental habits of the editor. It seems to me less likely that the author had regularly joined Paul at the moment of embarking or, if he was embodying a written diary, that this became so regularly available at just that juncture in the narrative, than that for some unknown reason the point of embarkation had the effect of making him shift his narrative suddenly to the first person, only to relapse obscurely and without cause into the third person sometime later when the party of travelers was on shore.[28]

Style is deeper than mere diction, and when one turns acteristic of Luke's sense of style, that in other combinations beside "holy servant" his speeches affect the adjective, as "holy covenant" (Luke i. 72), "holy prophets" (Luke i. 70; Acts iii. 21), "this holy place" (Acts vi. 13; xxi. 28), "holy angel" (Acts x. 22, contrast x. 3; xi. 13). Only "holy Spirit" comes frequently in narrative as well as discourse.

[28] The Books of Maccabees offer some interesting though perhaps accidental analogies to some of these features of Luke-Acts: (1) As in Acts, the lyric passages of 1 Maccabees and consequently its Old Testament echoes occur almost entirely in the first chapters. (2) "While the author, where he speaks in his own person, names his people *promiscue* τὸν 'Ισραήλ and 'Ιουδαίους, he uses the latter name regularly in international transactions and official documents." (Grimm on 1 Macc. viii. 23; on xii. 6 he makes a similar observation on the use of δῆμος.) (3) The author of 4 Maccabees, though he can Hellenize names as well as any one, perpetrating even the adjectives 'Ισακεῖος and 'Αβραμιαῖος consistently uses 'Ελεάζαρος in the narrative, indeclinable 'Ελεαζάρ in discourse.

to analyze Luke's work in a broader view the criteria of individuality are even less definite. In addition the more general traits of his work, whether they seem distinctive, commonplace or contradictory, whether artistic or not, were doubtless due to his sources in very large measure. For good or for ill he had to depend on earlier material, and his own taste and skill could not always stamp themselves upon it. It must always be a matter of uncertainty how much of the undoubted charm of the Lucan parables is due to the evangelist, how much to the author of a written source, how much to tradition, how much to Jesus. We may place more confidently to Luke's praise or blame the various features of the speeches in Acts. In the narratives we shall be again quite doubtful. At most we can record phenomena, whatever their source, and express esthetic judgments no matter how tentative.

An interesting feature of Luke's narrative is the wider parallelism between the careers of his heroes, especially Jesus, Peter and Paul. Not only are certain words and ideas put in the mouth of more than one of them, as when Paul assures his shipmates in the words of Jesus that not a hair of their head should perish, or when Stephen forgives his executioners and commends his "spirit" at death; but incidents in their lives become parallel and are even interchanged. The threat to destroy the temple is omitted by Luke from the charge against Jesus only to reappear in the charge against Stephen. The same transfer occurs to the false witnesses, the charge of blasphemy and other details of Mark's passion narrative. By adding Jesus' appearance before Herod as well as before Pilate, Luke represents the Master himself as tried "before both governors and kings" like Paul before another Herod and other procurators, as was predicted by Jesus for his followers, and for the Messiah by the "first" psalm, which mentions both "kings of the earth" and "rulers." It may be conjectured that the arrangement in Luke's gospel of

Jesus' prolonged progression to Jerusalem and death has been affected by the geographical character of Paul's career, particularly by the latter's ominous approach to Jerusalem and his often anticipated arrival at Rome. The scheme of the former, "throughout all Judaea beginning from Galilee even unto this place" (Jerusalem), "through all Judaea (and) beginning from Galilee," reverses the plan for his followers: "beginning from Jerusalem"; "in Jerusalem and in all Judaea and Samaria and to the end of the earth." [29]   While the gospel has a single goal, Jerusalem, repeatedly mentioned, the later career of Paul contains both this one and another.   The evangelist's small but characteristic word "must" ($\delta\epsilon\hat{\iota}$) makes these two *foci* plain: "After I have been there [Jerusalem], I must also see Rome"; "As thou hast testified concerning me at Jerusalem, so must thou bear witness also at Rome." Acts repeatedly predicts the fate of Paul as do the synoptic gospels the fate of Jesus.

Notice has often been taken of the balancing of the careers of Peter and Paul, in such experiences as curing one lame from birth, raising the dead, working miracles wholesale by the slightest contact, escaping from prison and confuting sorcerers.[30]   That the writer introduced this parallelism in order to give the apostles equal ranking seems quite unlikely, although such an apologetic motive in a kind of Petrine-Pauline controversy has been sometimes attributed to him.   But he may have been affected by a tendency to assimilation or to the stereotyping of incidents of which he himself was quite unconscious.   It was scarcely intentional repetition when he put similar words, proof-texts and arguments into the mouth of both Peter and Paul.[31]   It should be observed in the parables

[29] Luke xxiii. 5; Acts x. 37; Luke xxiv. 47; Acts i. 8.

[30] Acts iii. 2 = xiv. 8; ix. 36 ff. = xx. 7 ff.; v. 16 = xix. 12; xii. 6 ff. = xvi. 25 ff.; viii. 18 ff. = xiii. 6 ff.

[31] Acts ii. 24 ff. = xiii. 35 ff., etc.

of the Wise and Foolish Builders and of the Servants with
Money to Invest that Luke does not carry symmetry into
the wording of parallel stanzas nearly so far as Matthew
does in his version of these passages. Here it looks as
though he aimed at variation of phrase, as is quite evidently
the case in his account of the deaths of Ananias and of
Sapphira. That he knew well the Biblical idiom of parallel
clauses is shown not only by his quotations from the Old
Testament, but by his canticles and even by such poetic
snatches as occur later in his work.

It has been truly observed that Luke seems to be fond of
parallel pairs. The birth stories of John and Jesus illustrate this symmetry, each with its conditions of antecedent
improbability and its sign of assurance, each with its
annunciation to a parent, and each with a parent's song of
thanksgiving. Jesus' parables are in pairs. Just as in
Matthew we have the like parables of the Wheat and Tares
and the Drag Net, of the Hid Treasure and the Precious Pearl, so in Luke we have the similar pairs of the
Mustard Seed and the Leaven, of the Lost Sheep and the
Lost Coin, of the Importunate Neighbor and the Importunate Widow. Possibly this pairing is older than Luke,
who derives the first three from Q and who seems to have
separated the last pair in spite of obvious resemblance
between them, a resemblance extending down to his own
wording. In adding the short parable of New Wine after
Old and the long parable of the Prodigal Son, Luke seems
to have really spoiled the symmetry of pairs of parables
by an extraneous third. Two historical examples are
used to illustrate a point, either the unpreparedness in
the days of Noah and of Lot (only the former in Matthew),
or the attention paid to Jonah's preaching and Solomon's
wisdom (both in Matthew), or the honoring of foreigners
by the prophets Elijah and Elisha, or the two recent disasters in Jerusalem, or the two ineffective insurrections of

Theudas and Judas.[32]   As double illustrations of identical thought we may quote the prudent builder and the
prudent warrior, the two sleepers and the two grinders.[33]
   It is interesting that in many instances the pairs involve
in the first case men, in the second women.   Thus in the
last pair the grinders were women, and so were the owner
of the lost coin, the importunate widow, and the user of
leaven.   It is the mother of Jesus who corresponds to
the father of John, receiving the promise of the child and
(if the *Magnificat* belongs to Mary) offering a song of
praise.   Further, we have men and women parallel in the
two acknowledgments of the infant Jesus, by Simeon and
by Anna, in the two sabbath cures peculiar to Luke, and in
Peter's two patients in Sharon, Aeneas and Dorcas.   According to Luke, Jesus raised from the dead a widow's
son as well as Jairus' daughter.   We may compare Paul's
two converts named at Athens, Dionysius and Damaris,
his two hosts named in Macedonia, Lydia and Jason, and
of course the famous couple Aquila and Priscilla, as well
as the infamous Ananias and Sapphira.
   Luke's parables suggest as characteristic of the author
contrast as well as parallelism.   Thus two figures stand
opposed to each other—the rich man who fares sumptuously
against Lazarus full of sores, the older son who breaks no
commandment against his dissolute and spendthrift brother,
the self-righteous Pharisee against the repentant publican.
With these last two contrasts should be compared the parable of the Two Debtors and the figures of Simon the
Pharisee and the sinner woman in the associated incident.
The same kind of contrast occurs in Luke's parables of
Dissimilar Guests [34] and in the superiority twice revealed
by Samaritans over Jews.   Luke brings together the
incidents of the friendly exorcist (in Mark) and the un-

---

[32] Luke xvii. 26-30; xi. 31-32; iv. 25-27; xiii. 1-5; Acts v. 36-37.
[33] Luke xiv. 28-32; xvii. 34-35 (verse 36 is not genuine here).
[34] Luke xiv. 7-11, 12-14, 15-24.

friendly Samaritans, and Jesus' rebuke of his disciples' attitude in each case. The generosity of Joseph Barnabas immediately precedes as a foil the "peculation" of Ananias and Sapphira. A beautiful pair of vignettes is contained in the incident contrasting the way of Martha and the way of Mary. The Beatitudes become in Luke four blessings and four matching woes. The use of opposites in parables is found in Matthew and apparently often among the rabbis; the contrasts of the judgment day are naturally quite common everywhere, but some of these and other comparisons may owe at least part of their sharpness of coloring to Luke.

Many narratives in Luke and Acts possess undoubted dramatic quality. It is not necessary for the reader to confuse the sentiments of piety and reverent imagination with pure artistic sense in order for him to appreciate the vividness and simplicity of the parables peculiar to Luke. Certain scenes in the story are marked by a like effective use of a few details. The account of the shipwreck is a notable instance of description. For sheer wealth of nautical details it is without a rival in ancient literature. There is a vividness and rapidity running nearly all through the work. Doubtless the tradition already provided much of this element. Perhaps Luke himself is not responsible for it. Indeed, we can see from comparing Mark that he has often merely retained or even reduced the vigor, the naïve detail, the natural art of his sources. Luke's art is doubtless natural also rather than conscious, and modern writers are wont to lay more artistic purpose to his credit than the unadorned simplicity of his style warrants. Their attribution of conscious taste or skill is often as ill-founded as the medieval tradition which reported that Luke had been a painter. But even avoiding excess we may acknowledge much artistic quality in parts of his writings.

There are two traits of Luke's style that may be mentioned by way of illustration—the sense of suspense and the quality of pathos.   In both of these Mark's gospel was also notable, and Luke has doubtless merely preserved a primitive aspect of the tradition.   The sense of mystery about Jesus in Mark has been mentioned in an earlier chapter.   Luke has similar notes of his own in his gospel. Jesus creates wonder, perplexity and expectancy.   The frequent referencs both in Luke and in Acts to the feelings of the multitudes "remind one in a remote way of the function of the chorus in Greek tragedy." [35]   Luke tells us that Herod not only was perplexed about Jesus, but had desired to see Jesus for a long time and hoped to see a miracle performed by him.   As the long journey to Jerusalem draws to a close, suspense grows great.   "He was nigh to Jerusalem and they supposed that the kingdom of God was immediately to appear."   At Jericho a blind man with the sensitiveness to new sounds characteristic of his kind, "hearing a multitude going by, inquired what this meant," while Zacchaeus "sought to see Jesus who he was, and could not for the crowd, because he was little of stature, and he ran on before and climbed up into a sycamore tree to see him."   At Jerusalem his disciples were irrepressible and "the people all hung upon him, listening."   Though Luke earlier often omits the insistence of the crowds about Jesus he once makes the remarkable statement that "many ten thousands of the multitude were gathered together, insomuch that they trod one upon another."   Luke mentions the perplexity at the tomb and implies a similar perplexity at the ascension.   "Perplexity" and "expectation" are two notes of his apocalyptic viewpoint, and this must be considered later.

There are many illustrations of the effective use of suspense in Acts, such as the two occasions when the author

[35] J. de Zwaan, *Harvard Theological Review,* xvii. 1924, p. 102; see his list of (b) instances.

discloses the Christians praying for escape from what he euphemistically calls "all the expectation of the Jews," or the storm at sea with its two full weeks of "waiting" and an anxious night of "wishing for the day." From the multitudes "waiting for Zacharias" in the temple in the first chapter all the way to the Maltese barbarians "waiting a long time" to see Paul swell or fall down dead from snake bite in the last chapter, the reader of this vivid narrative is repeatedly brought into moods of sympathetic expectancy, hope, fear, surprise and suspense. He shares the impatience of Peter knocking at the door of Mary the mother of Mark in Jerusalem, or of Paul restrained from venturing into the theater at Ephesus, the surprising *dénouement* of the return of the prodigal son or of the haling of Paul before Gallio. There is no slowness of movement, no lack of tension, no flagging of interest. One wonders what happened to the men who vowed they would neither eat nor drink till they had killed Paul. But our suspense is for Paul rather than for them as he rides by night under escort to Antipatris, and the author liberally supplies us with tension (not to say "thrills") by his recurrent "plots of the Jews" and by his premonitions of Paul's impending fate.

Of the quality of pathos Luke has no monopoly among the evangelists. Mark's passion narrative, anticipated as it is by hints of conflict and danger, is a moving story. Luke could scarcely improve on it, though Jesus' tears over Jerusalem, his words to the women on the *via dolorosa* and to the "penitent thief" on the cross, and (if they are genuine) the bloody sweat in the garden and the forgiving of his executioners—these and other details peculiar to Luke all suit admirably the emotional and dramatic requirements of the occasion. The story of Emmaus is one particularly full of pathetic disappointment. "We hoped that it was he who should redeem Israel." The readers, who by a kind of dramatic irony have not "their eyes holden that they should not recognize" the third wayfarer until the breaking of bread, share nevertheless the sad face, the burning heart, the amazing report from the tomb and the glad assurance that "the Lord is risen indeed."

The scenes of bereavement at Nain and Joppa are briefly but effectively told. As on two occasions Luke adds to Mark that the child was an only child, so at Nain we have an only son and a widowed mother and the very moment of burial. How vivid and natural and effective is the picture by that other bier when "all the widows stood by Peter weeping, and showing the coats and garments which Dorcas made, while she was with them"! Peter need be no connoisseur of needlework to be deeply affected by the human demonstration.

There are many farewell scenes and farewell words in literature, many even in Jewish and Christian literature, but none, not even the famous chapters in John's gospel, is more touching than the speech of Paul at Miletus to the Ephesians, and the prayers, tears and kisses there and at subsequent stages of his fateful journey. Even Paul's own anxious words when in writing to the Christians at Rome he asks them to pray for his success and safety in his ministration to the saints in Judaea, though dictated by him right out of the identical situation, scarcely make the intense strain more vivid and foreboding. That, so far as modern readers are concerned, the author of Acts and indeed all history has left us still in suspense is doubtless not due to his intention. If not through a third volume, at least through other sources, the first readers would know just how "acceptable to the saints in Jerusalem" Paul's collection proved and certainly whether after the two years in his own lodging at Rome he was at last "delivered from the disobedient Jews." Even we, as the work now ends, are left with the reiterated anticipation that his missionary churches among which he "went about preaching the kingdom . . . should behold his face no more."

CHAPTER XVII

SOME SECULAR INTERESTS

It is evident from what has been already said that Luke was a man of some contacts with culture. Jerome found proof of this in his omission of the Semitic word "hosanna" and called him *inter omnes evangelistas Graeci sermonis eruditissimus* and attributed it to his profession as a doctor. J. H. Moulton found proof of it in his use of the potential optative and wrote, "We are left then with Luke as the only littérateur among the authors of New Testament books." Others have found the same distinction in the formality of his preface; still others in his references to contemporary history. The Book of Acts seemed even more secular both in subject matter and in style. In the fifth century it needed defense as having religious value. To many of Chrysostom's contemporaries it was either unknown or so clear and straightforward as to make a poor basis for the theological treatment then prevailing in homiletic gymnastics. Jerome admits that the Acts of the Apostles seems to sound like bare history (*nudam sonare videntur historiam*), but claims that, since its writer is Luke "whose praise is in the Gospel," all his words alike are medicine for the sick soul. The language of both volumes is, Jerome admits, "more elegant and smacks of secular eloquence, and employs Greek quotations rather than Hebrew." His quotations of the poets, as we have said, perhaps do not go beyond the category of familiar quotations, nor do his proverbs, "Physician heal thyself" and "It is hard for thee to kick against the goad," but like his idiomatic use of turns of phrase they show that he is somewhat at home in the Greek *milieu*. The comment in Acts xxviii. 2, "the barbarians showed us no common kindness," if the contrast between "us" and "the barbarians" could be pressed, would prove the author to be a Greek at least in this wider sense of one born to the language.

Luke seems to have a cosmopolitan outlook. He understands the political background of the Mediterranean cities, he mentions emperors by name, and municipal and provincial authorities not only by name, but also—which is even more difficult—by the correct terms for their office. He ridicules the frequent Hellenistic royal title "Benefactor" (Εὐεργέτης). He seems to know something of Roman law with its regulations for local jurisdiction and for the protection of Roman citizens. He is aware of the friction between Jews and Romans and of the difficult and delicate middle position of the Herods. He notes the hostility between Herod Antipas and Pontius Pilate [1] and the courtesy of a visit of welcome paid by another Herod (Agrippa II) to an incoming procurator, Porcius Festus. He describes the political and economic relations of a third Herod (Agrippa I) with his Phoenician neighbors. On one occasion Luke undertakes to enumerate the contemporary rulers of four tetrarchies which at one time or another belonged to the Herodian domain. He calls the praetorium at Caesarea the praetorium of Herod.

There are other allusions to the Herodian *ménage* of a quite casual nature,—to a business manager of Herod named Chuzas, one of "The Prince's Playmates" of Herod named Manaen, a chamberlain of Herod named Blastus. Women of the family are mentioned—Herodias, Drusilla and Bernice. They were all infamous in their marital relations, but Luke does not dwell on the scandals (he omits the story of the royal danseuse at Herod's birthday

---

[1] Perhaps he mentions in "the Galileans whose blood Pilate had mingled with their sacrifices" the cause of the hostility.

dinner and her gruesome prize), though he hints that they and their paramours were "reproved" "with words of truth and temperance" dealing with "justice and self-control and judgment to come." It is Luke alone who mentions that Herod Antipas both threatened Jesus and desired to see him and took a part in his trial. It is quite casually that he mentions the presence first of this prince and then of another Herod in Jerusalem at "the days of unleavened bread." Luke's story of a certain man of noble family who went to get a kingdom and to return, only to be followed by an embassy of his own citizens trying to prevent his coronation, sounds like a chapter out of Herodian history.[2]

The Herods represented the more secular side of Palestinian life. They were philhellenes. A Greek evangelist might know them better than he knew their subjects. It is often supposed that Luke or his readers were less familiar with Palestine than with the other parts of the Mediterranean world. It has been even thought possible to place Theophilus in Italy, since when Luke's story carries him that far west he gives up such explanations as "a city of Galilee named Nazareth," "Capernaum a city of Galilee," "the country of the Gerasenes, which is over against Galilee," "a village named Emmaus, which was threescore furlongs from Jerusalem," "Perga of Pamphylia," "Antioch of Pisidia," "the cities of Lycaonia, Lystra and Derbe," "Philippi, which is the first city of the division of Macedonia, a colony," "Tarsus of Cilicia," "Myra of Lycia," "a certain place called Fair Havens, to which the city Lasea was near," "Phoenix, a harbor of Crete facing north-east and south-east," and the like, but names without locating them—Syracuse, Rhegium, Puteoli and even such little places (without apology for the Latin) as

---

[2] Luke like Matthew omits Mark's obscure terms "Herodians" and "leaven of Herod." It is not certain what he means by calling Antipas "that fox."

Appii Forum and Tres Tabernae. But the explanations
of names are not really distributed along geographical
lines and may be due to the influence of sources or to other
causes. It is not easy to tell whether the author, when he
speaks in this manner, does so from familiarity with a
place or from unfamiliarity. What may seem to be an
explanation due to ignorance may be really local color due
to knowledge.

There are reasons for believing that Luke tried to make
himself at home in all parts of his narrative, even in Palestine where his style has a more Semitic flavoring.[3] If that
is so his own acquaintance with a place is not readily distinguished from his historical imagination. Had he seen the
hill on which Nazareth was built, or looked across to Jerusalem from the descent of the Mount of Olives? Did he
really understand better than Mark, for example, the relation of the latter to Bethany, Bethphage and Jerusalem?
How shall we explain the fact that he uses a "sabbath day's
journey" to measure the distance between them, and even
dates the closing of navigation in the Mediterranean by the
Jewish Day of Atonement, calling it simply "the Fast"?
In Luke alone we have references to contemporary events
in Jerusalem like Pilate's massacre of Galileans and the
accident at the tower of Siloam. Did he know the temple,
with its courts, gates and porticoes, as well as Straight
Street, Damascus, "the objects of devotion" at Athens, and
the theater at Ephesus? Was he equally familiar with the
service of Levitical courses at the incense altar in Jerusalem and the worship of Zeus-before-the-City at Lystra,
"the Great Power" at Samaria, and the meteorite of Artemis at Ephesus? Did he know the synagogues equally
well—the one at Capernaum "built" by the Roman cen-

---

[3] Harnack believes the author of Acts knew Palestine at first
hand. His discussion in *The Acts of the Apostles*, pp. 71-87, is
of interest, as indeed is the whole of Chapter II on the geographical references in Acts.

turion, that at Jerusalem named "Synagogue of the Freed-
men," and the one at Corinth next door to Titius Justus?
It would be interesting if he did, for modern archeology
has unearthed among the few remains of first-century synagogues precisely the following: the foundation of a contemporary synagogue at Capernaum, the lintel of one at
Corinth with the later inscription SYNAGOGUE OF THE
HEBREWS, and at Jerusalem an inscription to a benefactor,
Theodotus son of Vettenus, who, himself apparently a
freedman, had "built" a synagogue for the use of persons
from abroad.

It is hard for us to say where Luke's local color is most
abundant and most accurate. We can say that everywhere
he has an eye for the interesting detail, though he does not
always indulge it. It was easy for him to add in Palestine
the note that on the sabbath the women rested according
to the commandment, or at Athens to echo in his phraseology the famous charge against Socrates just four hundred
and fifty years before of introducing "strange gods," but
did he appreciate as some suppose that in Macedonia women
had more share in public life, or that, as most recent discoveries suggest to us, in the hellenization of the native
Lycaonian religion Zeus and Hermes were particularly connected, or that just near Lystra was the scene of the
story of these same two "gods coming down in the likeness
of men" to Baucis and Philemon? Ramsay treats the journeys of Paul in Acts and the letters to the Asian cities
in Revelation as though they were as full of allusion and
local color as the Odes of Pindar, while according to Nestle
and Rendel Harris we are to believe that Luke's language
is as reminiscent of the Greek poets as Tennyson or Swin-
burne. This is going too far. On the other hand, it is
scarcely fair to accuse Luke or Paul of indifference to the
beauties of Athens. Even if its idolatry stirred their
spirits and seemed to them "superstitious," the objection
was its inappropriateness, since "deity" even as a Gentile

concept (τὸ θεῖον) is too great for material worship, for
its "manufactured temples," and for its "gold, silver and
marble carved by human craft and skill." The writer
does not exclude sightseeing at Athens, while at Jerusalem
he calls attention in quite the idiomatic phrase of the secular guide book or travelogue to the temple's "decoration
with beautiful marbles and dedicatory monuments." [4]
Apart from possible personal knowledge, such references
imply a catholicity of interest consistent with what we
may gather otherwise of Luke's viewpoint.

It has been sometimes thought that Luke betrayed his
ignorance of Palestine and his own foreign provenience
through slight changes in the gospel records. Attention is
called to the story of the paralytic in which, instead of a
roof presumably of thatch which could be "dug open," as
Mark described, Luke represents the house as having a
roof of "tiles." The mud-built huts of Palestine are perhaps reflected also in two sayings of Q which refer to
thieves as "digging through." In one of these also Luke
avoids the word, though not in the other. Again in the
story of the Two Builders, while Matthew has rivers run
against the houses like a swollen Judaean wady, Luke's
description sounds more like a flood upon the plain. Both
the tile roof and the inundation of the Orontes suit, we
are told, Antioch, the traditional home of Luke, better
than Palestine. Be that as it may, we hardly have enough
evidence here to be decisive.

For Luke's local connections various other bits of internal evidence have been cited. We have already mentioned the argument which suggests that either he or Theophilus is most at home in Italy. The intermittent "we"
passages, if the pronoun is regarded as strictly limited to
the movements of the author of the whole work, suggest one
who belonged at Philippi when not traveling with Paul.

---

[4] Luke xxi. 5 λίθοις καλοῖς καὶ ἀναθήμασιν κεκόσμηται, contrast
Mark xiii. 1.

Ramsay has conjectured that the man of Macedonia who appeared at Troas to Paul in a vision of the night was none other than the evangelist himself, who proudly refers to his native place as "the first city of the district of Macedonia and a Roman colony." It is at Philippi that the "we" ends and at Philippi that it later begins again on Paul's final journey from Greece to Jerusalem.

For Antioch of Syria, where tradition places Luke's birth, the internal evidence is even more striking. Large sections of the book represent Antioch as the center of the story, the starting-point for a Gentile Christianity and for the name Christian, and the "home base" of Paul's work for foreign missions. A proselyte of Antioch is mentioned by name among the Seven at Jerusalem, and later five teachers resident at Antioch are listed. One of these, Lucius of Cyrene, was apparently at an early time identified with the author Lucas. There is now some evidence that the names are really equivalents. Further, in a very early form of the text (commonly called "Western"), the first appearance of the pronoun "we" is at Antioch.[5] These combinations, however, are more interesting than convincing. It is unnecessary and unlikely that in such a work the author should thus betray his own home associations.

Perhaps we are on safer ground when we suggest that Luke writes from the urban standpoint. Now the contrast between city and country is familiar to readers of the Bible, not always to the advantage of the city, as the stories of Enoch built by Cain, of Babel, and of Sodom and Gomorrah testify. There was much in the nomadic tradition of the Hebrews agreeing with the modern sentiment, "God made the country but man made the town." But the city came to its own in Jerusalem, real and ideal, so that the tree of life, which in Genesis is found in a garden, in Revelation grows on the city streets. The coun-

[5] Acts xi. 28.

I

try background characterizes the gospels, but Paul's figures come from the experience of the city (or more probably one should say not from experience at all, but from
the largely urban commonplaces of moral instruction).
Luke even more clearly than Paul has the metropolitan
viewpoint.   While Paul's letters show that for his missionary work he treats the Roman provinces as units
(Galatia, Asia, Macedonia, Achaia, and even Illyricum and
Spain "according to the measure of the rule which God
assigned"), we can best understand his biographer as one
who thought in terms of cities, or of city states, or of city
stations on itineraries.   The Book of Acts deals almost
entirely with cities; the missionary work is nearly limited
to them.   Harnack in his careful study of geographical
terms in Acts notes how rarely there is reference to the
country in the rural sense of the word and makes some
interesting remarks about the use of the word "city":

> The mission was for the most part carried on in
> cities, as also the Jews of the Diaspora were chiefly
> settled in the cities.   Hence we read in viii. 40 of
> Philip: "he preached the gospel to all the cities" (*scil.*
> of Philistia); again James says (xv. 21) that Moses
> has "in every city in the synagogues them that preach
> him"; and Paul admits (xxvi. 11) that he persecuted
> the Christians not only in Jerusalem, but also fol-
> lowed them up "even unto the cities outside"; Paul
> and Silas pass through (xvi. 4) "the cities" and revisit
> (xv. 36) city by city the communities that were founded
> on the first journey; Paul declares that the Spirit
> "city by city" prophesied sufferings that were about
> to come upon him (xx. 23) and "the multitude of the
> cities round about Jerusalem" crowded into the city
> to be healed by the apostles (v. 16).   It is character-
> istic of the exactness of the author [or shall we say
> his urban viewpoint?] that he often marks the fact
> that something took place outside the city.   Stephen
> was stoned "outside the city" (vii. 58); the temple of

Zeus in Lystra was situated "before the city" (xiv. 13); Paul was dragged "outside the city" (xiv. 19); the place of prayer in Philippi lies "outside the gate" (xvi. 13); and the disciples in Tyre accompany Paul "even to outside the city" (xxi. 5).[6]

Harnack also comments on the precision with which the municipal officials are mentioned.

The same phenomena meet us in the Gospel of Luke. There as in Acts "city" is often added to the proper name, Capernaum, Nain, Bethsaida, Arimathea. Jesus' parents travel to the "city of David" and return to "Nazareth, their own city." The census of Quirinius was taken by cities. Jesus' teaching was by cities or by cities and villages, as was that of his disciples. He also was taken "outside the city" to be hurled to his death, and it is on his approach to Nain or Jericho that his works of mercy are wrought. It is noteworthy that so much of Luke's gospel seems, like the Book of Acts, to be a procession toward a city as its goal. The multitude who came together to hear Jesus' parables resorted to him "out of every city." Even the most rural scenes in Luke do not leave the city very far in the background. According to his gospel, Jesus' withdrawal apart to the desert place where the Five Thousand were fed was really "to a city called Bethsaida." The demoniac who met him across the sea of Galilee came "out of the city" and returning reported his cure not throughout Decapolis as in Mark, but "in the whole city." Luke alone puts the healing of the leper "in one of the cities."

Luke seems to think it worth while to note the city as the scene or scope of what he has to tell, even when he has made no mention of the city by name. Thus the sinner woman was "in the city" where Jesus and Simon the Pharisee were dining. To the account of Barabbas as one imprisoned for a certain insurrection Luke adds that it "took

---

[6] *Die Apostelgeschichte*, pp. 62 ff; *cf.* Eng. trans., pp. 61 f.

place in the city." In parables also we hear of a judge
"in a certain city" and a widow "in the same city," of
"the streets and lanes of the city," not to mention the "city
folk" of the prodigal's wandering or of the nobleman's kingdom, if that is what "citizen" means. In the parable last
cited (the Pounds), the rewards of faithfulness were, according to Luke, not to "enter into the joy of thy Lord,"
but to be ruler over ten or five cities.

Luke associated the resurrection appearances with Jerusalem, and the whole beginning of the church is centered
there. There the apostles remained until endued with
power from on high, and even longer. If the appearances
of Jesus were originally in Galilee, or at least if Luke's
source Mark actually represented them there, Luke's transfer to Jerusalem is all the more striking. "Tarry ye in the
city," "depart not but wait," are the repeated and emphatic
commands of Jesus. The angels speak of an appearance of
Jesus promised when he was still in Galilee instead of an
appearance promised to occur in Galilee. Perhaps it is
noteworthy that the only measures of geographical distance in either volume occur in indicating the relative
nearness to Jerusalem of the two places outside of that
city where Jesus was seen, Emmaus, sixty stadia away, and
the Mount of Olives, only a sabbath day's journey.
The idea of metropolitan church organization is already
in the mind of Luke as he portrays Jerusalem as the place
where innovations are discussed, or sanctioned.[7] Less obviously Antioch is for him the capital of the Christian
mission.

He is not indifferent to the secular standing of other
cities: "Philippi, the first city of a district of Macedonia
and a Roman colony"; Tarsus, "a not insignificant city,"
whose citizens may be assumed to speak Greek and would
not like to be mistaken for Egyptians; Ephesus with its
honorific title "temple-warden of Artemis"; and of course

[7] Acts viii. 14; xi. 1-18, 22; xv. 2, 4, 6, etc.

he has due awe at the privileges involved in the citizenship of Rome.[8]

As in the Revelation of John, the "broad" street of the city appears in Luke's writings. There Jesus and his disciples taught and cured.[9] In the parable of the Marriage Feast, while in Matthew the dining hall was filled, after the refusal of those first invited, by sending out to the crossroads and highways, the impromptu guests in Luke are first collected from the "plazas and alleys of the city" and then from "the highways and hedges." It fits the urban viewpoint, though it may not be due to it, that Luke omits references to fields in the list of possessions surrendered, and the illustration of two men in the field at the *parousia*, as well as the detailed equipment of the vineyard. For Luke, the mustard seed is planted in a garden, not in a field, nor are the lilies lilies of the field.

In this connection it is worth while to mention Luke's attention to the matter of lodging. If city-bred perhaps he was sensitive to the unsheltered life of the country, the "lodging in the open" such as he assigns to Jesus and his disciples near Jerusalem before his death (at the Mount of Olives rather than at the village of Bethany), and perhaps after his resurrection.[10] He frequently mentions Jesus' prayer at night in the open. It was customary and it lasted all night. It is in this way that Luke alone comes to place the transfiguration at night, like the scene at Gethsemane.[11] It seems to me likely that Luke means the ascension also to be understood as taking place at night.

[8] Acts xvi. 37-39; xxii. 25-29; xxiii. 27.

[9] Rev. xi. 8; xxi. 21; xxii. 2; Luke x. 10 (*cf.* Matt. x. 14); xiii. 26 (*cf.* Matt. vii. 22); Acts v. 15 (*cf.* Mark vi. 56).

[10] Luke xxi. 37 ηὐλίζετο, with which Matt. xxi. 17 ηὐλίσθη now curiously agrees against Mark. I think the same verb lurks in the much-discussed συναλιζόμενος of Acts i. 4. See *Journal of Biblical Literature*, xlv, 1926, pp. 310 ff.

[11] Note Luke's references to prayer, to sleep and to "the next day."

For Luke the angel vision at the tomb was "at early dawn,"
and other theophanies, though not all, occur at night,[12] as
do the angelic prison deliveries. For the *parousia* Luke
can say "in that night" as well as "on that day." Compare also, "This night is thy soul required of thee." In
the Christmas story Luke notes that the shepherds were
camping in the fields at night when the angel visitation
came upon them. It is his same concern in the matter of
lodging which explains the detail of the birth of Jesus in
the open, "because there was no room in the inn." This
detail was partly obscured for the ancients because they
thought of the scene as a cave on account of the prophecy
of Isaiah xxxiii. 16 (LXX). It is obscured for modern
readers who think of a barn or stable because φάτνη is
translated "stall" or "manger" rather than "pen" or
"trough." The same writer tells of the better luck with
inns which those other travelers had on the Jerusalem-
Jericho road. It is a striking fact that, when the disciples
urge Jesus to send away the multitude from the deserted
place in order to buy something to eat, Luke alone says
"to lodge" as well as "to get provisions." He tells us of
the disappointed fishermen who had "labored through the
whole night." It was not necessary for Luke himself to
have been washed ashore from a shipwreck off the island

---

[12] Acts xvi. 9; xviii. 9; xxiii. 11; xxvii. 23. Such habitual inferences of different sorts are absolutely natural to any writer.
H. Drüner, *Untersuchungen über Josephus,* 1896, pp. 45 f., shows
how Josephus tends to describe events that require concealment
or craft as carried out at night, and to supply for intervals of
time the number five days, though we can see in many cases
that his sources, e.g., the canonical books of the Old Testament
or Maccabees, said nothing to either effect. With the former we
may compare in Acts Paul's escape "by night" from Damascus
(*cf.* 2 Cor. xi. 33), Thessalonica and Jerusalem; with the latter,
the habit of our evangelist to represent messengers as two in
number (*Beginnings of Christianity,* Vol. II, p. 140 *note,* and Vol.
IV, on Acts ix. 38), and the habit of Matthew to represent Jesus'
patients as two of a kind.

of Malta for him to speak feelingly of the fire and the "no common kindness" of the hospitable barbarians on a cold and rainy winter morning.

Luke is constantly noting how persons are entertained— whether at night or at meals. Jesus is often described by him at the tables both of Pharisees and of publicans. Nearly all the fourteenth chapter of Luke deals with various questions of entertainment. It represents the discussion as table-talk. Other conversations in Luke are at table, e.g., that on, "Who is the greatest?" with the emphasis on serving at table now and dining at Jesus' table hereafter. In Luke, Jesus contrasts the welcome of his Pharisee host and of the scorned guest; he recognizes the superficiality of mere table companionship,[13] and discusses the types of hospitality illustrated by Mary and Martha. The parable of Dives and Lazarus seems to turn about the question of inhospitality, while in another parable the shrewd but unjust steward is chiefly concerned that when he is discharged there should be people to welcome him into their own houses. The moral is that the children of the light should be making friends who will receive them into everlasting tabernacles.

For the disciples Luke gives the most explicit and repetitious advice about how to deal with entertainment on their mission. In effect it is: "Stay in the same house; do not go from house to house; eat the people's own fare, eat what they offer." In Luke alone Jesus promises his disciples that they should eat and drink at his table in his kingdom. He greatly desired to eat the passover with them before he suffered and when he rose he dined with them. He was recognized, we are told, in his "breaking of bread." This last phrase is frequent in Acts of the life of the church. Possibly the community of goods is in part conceived there as providing a common meal, "serving tables." Of one of his verbs for joy, Harnack says:

[13] Luke xiii. 26; xxii. 21; *cf.* xiv. 15.

From these passages [Luke xv. 23, 24, 29, 32] and from xii.19 and xvi.19 one sees that Luke likes to connect, indeed almost exclusively connects, εὐφραίνεσθαι with the partaking of food. Just in the same way we read in Acts xiv.17 that God fills men's hearts with "food and gladness" (see also Acts vii. 41), and in Acts ii. 46, "they took their food with gladness and singleness of heart, praising God." Luke evidently had a feeling for the joy that springs from the common festal meal, and regarded it also in a religious light.[14]

In Acts the author is frequently concerned to mention the hospitality offered and received. Hosts are mentioned by name—at Joppa, Simon the tanner, whose house was by the seaside; at Damascus, Judas on Straight Street; at Philippi, Lydia the purple seller from Thyatira; at Thessalonica, Jason who, as it proved, exposed himself to considerable risk for harboring Paul; at Corinth, Aquila a Jew, a native of Pontus, formerly of Rome, with Priscilla his wife, tent-makers. Apparently the house of Titus Justus next to the synagogue at Corinth and the lecture hall of Tyrannus at Ephesus were lent to Paul for teaching, not for lodging. The names of these friends are noteworthy as well as the full descriptions (Lydia and Titus Justus are further described as "god-fearers," i.e., Gentile adherents to Judaism), since rarely do these hosts play any rôle in the principal narrative. This is what makes so enigmatic also the references to his hosts later en route to Jerusalem—Philip the evangelist who had "four virgin daughters that prophesied," and "one Mnason of Cyprus, an early disciple, with whom we should lodge" (at Caesarea? or at Jerusalem? or, as Codex Beza tells us, at a certain village between?).

Of course there are other references in Acts to the hospitality extended to Paul—at Philippi by the jailer, on

[14] *Acts of the Apostles,* p. 278 *note.*

Malta by the natives at the scene of the shipwreck and by Publius the *primus* of the island, and at Sidon by his friends. There are leave-takings and greetings, escorts of welcome and of farewell. There are two or three short and different references to his place of residence at Rome, a hired apartment of his own or the guest room [15] of an inn or of a friend where he "lived by himself together with the soldier who guarded him." At any rate he was not committed to the barracks, as perhaps the other prisoners were,[16] or as he himself had been imprisoned in Herod's praetorium at Caesarea. The cordiality of entertainment is emphasized by various expressive terms in the original.[17]

So in the Third Gospel reference is made to the "greetings" of Gabriel or Elisabeth, to Jesus' welcome by the multitude or by individuals, and to his rejection by a village of Samaritans. How vividly and in what detail Luke describes the care which the good Samaritan bestowed on the victim of banditry, or the warm welcome that awaited the prodigal son at his return! It is Luke alone who records Jesus' injunction to his disciples to "greet no one on the highway," and his stern reply to the man who wished to follow him but first to say farewell to his family. With the same verb, according to Luke, Jesus says, "So therefore whosoever he be of you that saith not farewell to all that he hath, he cannot be my disciple." Such instances show how individual interests shade off into mere preferences of individual vocabulary.

[15] Acts xxviii, 23 ξενία. If, on the other hand, this passage means that the leading Jews attended a reception at which Paul is the host (ἦλθον πρὸς αὐτὸν εἰς τὴν ξενίαν), it still fits Luke's interest in entertainment.

[16] So Acts xxviii. 16 in the "Western" text.

[17] See Luke xix. 6; xxiv. 29; Acts xvi. 15; xxvii. 3; xxviii. 2, 7, 14. On the whole subject see my article "Luke's Interest in Lodging" in the *Journal of Biblical Literature,* xlv, 1926, pp. 305-322.

I*

CHAPTER XVIII

SOCIAL AND RELIGIOUS ATTITUDES

There are other interests of Luke that are more significant and more familiar than those mentioned in the preceding chapter. He is thought not only to have shared the
secular viewpoints of the Greeks, but to have been like
Paul specially interested in their acceptance of Christianity. Acts shows a sympathetic understanding of the
gradual process by which God "opened a door of faith to the
Gentiles." Central to the book both in thought and in
position are the words, "God visited the Gentiles to take
out of them a people for his name." Paul's mission to
them is told in a way that quite matches Paul's own sense
of special call as revealed in the letters. Like Paul the
author is interested in Old Testament passages that point
this way, and inserts similar predictions into his own lyric
passages.[1]

An attempt has sometimes been made to show that his
gospel is more universal in this sense than the others, but
the illustrations are often far-fetched and the evidence not
all on one side. It is true that he alone quotes the *Vox
clamantis* prophecy from Isaiah far enough to include the
words, "All flesh shall see the salvation of God," but
"salvation of God" rather than "all flesh" may well be
the phrase he wanted. In quoting from another part of
the same roll, "My house shall be called a house of prayer,"
he stops short of the words "for all the nations" (found

[1] Acts xiii. 47; xv. 17; Luke ii. 31 f.; Acts ix. 15; xxii. 21;
xxvi. 17 f., 23.

now in Mark). If he wished to show the universality of
Jesus or the brotherhood of all mankind by tracing Jesus'
ancestry to Adam (rather than to Abraham, as Matthew
does), his motive is not clear, nor could any but the ini-
tiated realize that the mission of the Seventy symbolizes,
as some modern scholars maintain, "the gospel of the un-
circumcision" (the Gentiles popularly being reckoned as
seventy nations), as the mission of the Twelve symbolizes
the "apostleship of the circumcision." To adduce from
the gospel such dubious proofs of Luke's catholicity is
quite unnecessary when we have in Acts the splendid
expression of universal religion and of human-divine kinship: "God is no respecter of persons: but in every nation
he that feareth him, and worketh righteousness, is acceptable to him." "He himself giveth to all life, and breath,
and all things; and he made of one every nation of men
. . . that they should seek God, if haply they might touch
him and find him, as he is not far from each of us. For
'In him we live, and move, and have our being.' . . . 'For
we are also his offspring.' "

Perhaps a more distinctive element in this connection is
Luke's emphasis upon God's rejection of the Jews while
accepting the Gentiles. Of course that appears in Paul's
letters also, especially in Romans ix-xi, and the phrase
in Luke "until the times of the Gentiles be fulfilled" reminds us of Paul's discussion there; but Paul's schematic
preaching "to the Jew first and also to the Greek" is represented in Acts both by narrative and by Paul's own words
as a regular process in which rejection of the gospel by
the Jews precedes its acceptance by Gentiles. Luke seems
to visualize more vividly the destruction of Jerusalem, and
while he omits in the apocalyptic chapter the prediction,
"and unto all the nations (Gentiles) the gospel must first
be preached" (if this is really what Mark said),[2] he speaks

[2] Mark xiii. 10. It is quite likely that in Mark as in Matthew
we should take "the Gentiles" with the preceding, "for a testimony

of Jerusalem as being trampled down by the Gentiles and
its people as carried captive throughout the Gentile world.

The wilful rejection of the prophets by Judaism is
most vigorously pressed in Stephen's speech and in its
concluding words:

> Ye stiffnecked and uncircumcised in heart and ears,
> ye do always resist the Holy Spirit: as your fathers
> did, so do ye. Which of the prophets did not your
> fathers persecute? and they killed them that showed
> before of the coming of the Righteous One; of whom
> ye have now become betrayers and murderers.

For us at least the work practically closes with the force-
ful statement of this twofold theme—rejection of Christianity by the Jews, acceptance by the Gentiles:

> Well spake the Holy Spirit through Isaiah the
> prophet unto your fathers, saying,
>> Go thou unto this people, and say,
>> By hearing ye shall hear and shall in no wise
> understand;
>> And seeing ye shall see and shall in no wise
> perceive:
>> For this people's heart is waxed gross,
>> And their ears are dull of hearing,
>> And their eyes they have closed;
>> Lest haply they should perceive with their eyes,
>> And hear with their ears,
>> And understand with their heart,
>> And should turn again,
>> And I should heal them
> Be it known therefore unto you, that this salvation
> of God is sent unto the Gentiles: they will also hear.

The rejection of God by the Jews carries for Luke as
its corollary the rejection of the Jews by God. This
unto them and to all the Gentiles," and it is possible that the
rest of the verse was not in Mark at all.

genuinely prophetic note changes the connotation of the proverb,"No prophet is acceptable in his own country." As Luke's illustrations show, he understood this to mean decisively that God sent the prophets to foreigners— enemy aliens of Syria and Phœnicia—even when there were many lepers and widows in Israel that were in need. Similarly in Stephen's speech stress is apparently laid on the fact that divine revelation and favor were found outside of Palestine. The particularly unpatriotic slant of such an attitude Luke well understood. It stung the Jews. "They were all filled with wrath," "They were cut to the heart, and they gnashed on him with their teeth." Paul's mere mention of a divine mission to Gentiles fanned the quieted mob in Jerusalem into a like murderous rage.

Possibly just because "Jews have no dealings with Samaritans," Acts relates how "Samaria had received the word of God" and makes other references to Samaritan Christianity. Quite as much to rebuke Jewish narrowness as to portray the benignity of God, the hero in Luke's narrative is twice pointedly made to turn out a hated Samaritan, in contrast to nine ungrateful (Jewish?) lepers or to a priest and Levite who pass by on the other side. Even when the Samaritans were inhospitable, Jesus rebuked the animosity of James and John against them.

Yet even here Luke's representation is not extreme. He is no doctrinaire internationalist. The Jewish viewpoint appears in some of his incidents. After all, the Samaritan was "this foreigner." Not all Samaritans were friendly to Jesus. When he violates Pharisaic prejudices he justifies his conduct by appeal to Jewish prerogative; for Zacchæus the chief publican is also a son of Abraham and the crippled woman is a daughter of Abraham. Peter is presented as no renegade Jew when he declares to his countrymen: "Ye are the sons of the prophets, and of the covenant which God made with your fathers, saying unto Abraham, 'And in thy seed shall all the families of the earth be blessed.' Unto you first God, having raised up his Servant, sent him to bless you."

Luke understood how hard it was for Peter and James to appreciate that God was no respecter of persons. Gentiles had their faults; they had to be cleansed and to avoid the grosser kinds of defilement. They appear in a favorable light partly because of the persistent wickedness of the Jews. Herein the author of Jonah finds a worthy successor in the third evangelist. In comparison with Matthew we shall have to admit that the absence from Luke of such phrases as "I was not sent but unto the lost sheep of the house of Israel," "Ye shall not have gone through the cities of Israel, till the Son of man be come," "Go not into any way of the Gentiles, and enter not into any city of the Samaritans: but go rather to the lost sheep of the house of Israel," frees his gospel from the most particularistic limitations.

Luke's gospel illustrates also Jesus' care for the "delinquent" classes. That oldest contemporary sobriquet, "the friend of publicans and sinners," is most fully exemplified in his pages. Without laboring this point, we may be content to note that he uses the word "sinners" more often than the other evangelists do all together, and that the detached gospel story of Jesus and the woman taken in adultery judged by its style and subject has most claim to come from his pen of any of the canonical writers.[3] But what is the animus behind Luke's repeated scenes of Jesus in the company of the moral outcasts? Is he defending their moral or their social situation?

There is much in the Gospel of Luke intended to rebuke Pharisaic pride, and the association of Jesus with publicans and sinners has that same negative meaning that Luke presents in his so-called sympathy with Gentiles.

[3] See my article "A Possible Case of Lukan Authorship" in the *Harvard Theological Review*, x, 1917, pp. 237-244.

It is not that Luke loves the publicans and sinners more, but the self-righteous Pharisees less, as the parable of the Pharisee and the Publican, the story of Simon and the sinful woman, and other passages show. For him the climax and perhaps the chief point of what is often miscalled, by omitting half of it, the parable of the Prodigal Son is the rebuke by contrast of the respectable but unsympathetic older brother. The joy in heaven over one repentant sinner is something which the impeccable and long-standing observer of commandments can never understand. Probably Luke's motive here is to demonstrate not so much God's love and forgiveness for the outcast, as Jesus' rebuke of self-righteous pride.

It should be observed that the evangelist's own view was that these parables were addressed not to the publicans and sinners, but to Pharisees and scribes, who "murmured, saying, this man receiveth sinners and eateth with them," or "unto certain who trusted in themselves that they were righteous, and set all others at nought." So also in connection with other parables, in which the established representatives of God are rejected for unfaithfulness, Luke adds characteristic comments on the false self-justification of the Jewish rulers. "And the Pharisees, who were lovers of money, heard all these things [the Unjust Steward and other references to untrustworthy servants]; and they scoffed at him. And he said unto them, Ye are they that justify yourselves in the sight of men; but God knoweth your hearts: for that which is exalted among men is an abomination in the sight of God." "They perceived that he spake this parable [of the Wicked Husbandmen] against them. And they watched him and sent forth spies who feigned themselves to be righteous." Even the parable of the Good Samaritan is elicited according to Luke by a lawyer who was not only "tempting" Jesus but "wishing to justify himself." Luke might have attributed to Jesus as he did to Paul at Pisidian Antioch the warning of Habakkuk to the "despisers" who after all cannot be justified by the law of Moses.

Probably the same kind of motive enters into his treatment of the question of wealth. It has often been thought that Luke had a special interest in the problems of money, and above all a sympathy with the poor. He has been called the socialist among the evangelists, and his gospel the Ebionite gospel. It must be admitted that he often represents Jesus as deriving his illustrations from finance, as in the parables of the Two Debtors, the Rich Fool, the Tower Builder, the Lost Coin, the Unjust Steward, Dives and Lazarus, and the Pounds. In many other passages, too numerous to repeat in full, Luke refers to money matters.[4] It is characteristic of Luke that, though the narratives in Acts do not make clear exactly what was Ananias and Sapphira's lie against the holy Spirit, or what was the "simony" of Simon Magus, these two startling condemnations were evidently intended to illustrate abuses in early Christianity precisely in the realm of finance. From Luke particularly come the proof-texts for the modern idea of the stewardship of wealth.[5]

His chief interest seems to be in the special question of

[4] See Luke iii. 13, 14; x. 35, 41 (?); xii. 13-15; xvi. 14 (lovers of money); xvii. 28 (bought and sold, not in Matthew); Acts iii. 6; viii. 27 (over all her treasure); xvi. 19; xix. 19, 25; xx. 33; xxiv. 26. Among phrases in his gospel where his difference from his parallels may suggest financial connotations are his word "purse" (βαλλάντιον x. 4; xii. 33), "store room" (xii. 24), the "cares" or "pleasures of property" (βίου, βιωτικός viii. 14; xxi. 34) and especially the use with "life" or "soul" of verbs implying acquisition as property, or purchase (xxi. 19; xvii. 33; *cf.* also xvii. 2 "it pays," and contrast all the parallels) or loss as a fine or refund (ix. 25; xii. 20 *v. l.*). It is Luke alone who at the call both of the four fishermen and of Levi reports that they "left all" as well as "followed him" (v. 11, 28).

[5] xii. 42 "steward" for Matthew's "servant"; xii. 48b; xvi. 1 ff.; xvi. 8-12.

poverty and wealth and the generosity of the rich toward the poor. It is this feature of the "communism" of the early church which interests him.[6] He alone notes that the women who ministered to Jesus (and to the twelve?) did so "out of their own substance." Like Barnabas and others later, they are probably to be thought of as having sold their real estate and as using the proceeds for the common good. It should be remembered that property was usually invested in such non-transferable forms and that the sale of it was necessary before it could be given to the poor or used for "ministration." Luke commends the chief publican who gives half his property to the poor, and quotes the advice of John the Baptist to share food or clothing with him who has none, of Jesus to lend money or offer entertainment without thought of repayment, and of Paul to work with the hands so as to be able to help the weak.

Several sayings of Jesus are quoted in encouragement of almsgiving, besides the advice to a certain rich man "to sell all and give to the poor," which is found in all the synoptic gospels:

> Give for alms those things which are (? within the cup) (Luke xi. 41; *cf.* Matt. xxiii. 26).
> Sell that which ye have and give alms (Luke xii. 33; *cf.* Matt. vi. 19).
> Give and it shall be given to you (Luke vi. 38; *cf.* Matt. vii. 1).
> It is more blessed to give than to receive (Acts xx. 35).

It might be inferred from all this, and indeed has often been said, that Luke felt special sympathy with the poor. He at least has not spiritualized the beatitudes as Matthew has done; he says simply, "Blessed are ye poor . . . blessed are ye that hunger now."

[6] Acts ii. 44 f.; iv. 34 f., 36 f.; v. 1 ff.; vi. 1.

But again, as in the other cases just considered, his interest is not mere sympathy with the unfortunate or ill-esteemed. The self-satisfaction of Jews in contrast to Gentiles, of Pharisees in contrast to publicans and sinners, has its corresponding danger in the complacency of the rich who fare sumptuously, take their ease and invite rich neighbors to dine. Luke's words are warnings to the rich quite as much as "good tidings to the poor":

> The hungry he hath filled with good things;
> And the rich he hath sent empty away (Luke i. 53).

To the Beatitudes he adds the woes: "Woe unto you that are rich! . . . Woe unto you, ye that are full now!" Dives and the Rich Fool are examples of the wrong use of wealth, as Zacchæus (and the Unjust Steward?) are of its right use. It is to possessors, not to the dispossessed, that Jesus speaks on alms and on the cares and pleasures of property. To them also he says: "Keep yourselves from all covetousness, for a man's life consisteth not in the abundance of the things which he possesseth"; "Whosoever he be of you that renounceth not all that he hath, he cannot be my disciple." This attitude of Luke toward wealth is similar to that of Old Testament piety and of early Christian ethics (as in the Epistle of James), and quite likely similar to the view of Jesus himself, only emphasized and perhaps exaggerated. Its roots lie deep in the social ideals and apocalyptic hopes which the evangelist inherited.[7] But the rebuke of wealth, as of Pharisaic pride (Luke

---

[7] The "text" of Jesus' sermon at Nazareth in Luke is taken from the prophets and begins with the proclaiming of good news to the poor. In the somewhat similar passage from Q (Matt. xi. 5 = Luke vii. 22), where Jesus gives a summary of his mission in reply to John the Baptist's question, there is some good evidence from the old versions that the concluding words "the poor have good news proclaimed" once belonged in Luke only, not Matthew (or Q). See F. C. Burkitt, *Evangelion da-Mepharreshe*, 1904, Vol. II, p. 238 f.

says "the Pharisees were lovers of money") and of Jewish national conceit, betokens a concern for the oppressor rather than pity for the oppressed, and, as a technique for social betterment, the appeal to conscience and sense of duty in the privileged classes rather than the appeal to the discontent and to the rights (or wrongs!) of the un-privileged.

Were Luke really interested in foreigners, Samaritans, publicans, sinners and the poor as despised classes, we might expect him perhaps to extend his sympathy to two other groups under like social disability in ancient Judaism —slaves and women. The injustice of their subjection, however, was rarely felt by either Jews or Christians. Luke like others takes slavery for granted and he records its illustration of abject obedience. "We are unprofitable servants; we have done that which it was our duty to do." With women, on the other hand, Luke apparently shows a keen sympathy and understanding, though by no means in the way of any feminist revolt. His interest may be described rather as artistic or domestic or sentimental. In connection with his fondness for contrasts we have already noted some cases where women are introduced parallel to men. In connection with his pathos, reference has been made to the lament over the daughters of Jeru-salem and to the scene by the bier of Dorcas. There may be a touch of humor in the last scene, Peter a mere man being asked to admire the needlework of the deceased. At least there would be in it something ludicrous for many a modern pastor, in spite of the pathos. There is certainly humor and feminine absent-mindedness in another scene when, at the house of Mary, mother of John Mark, Rhoda (note even the maid's name is given as well as her mis-tress') is too excited at Peter's return to open the door of the vestibule. Feminine, too, is the scene at the home of Martha and Mary in Luke. One can almost recognize

the characteristic temperamental differences of the two
spinster ladies and the consequent mutual impatience.
Luke alone records the beatitude on childlessness addressed
to the daughters of Jerusalem in the days of coming
disaster and the admiring cry of the woman from the
crowd, "Blessed is the womb that bare thee, and the
breasts which thou didst suck." Feminine and intimate,
too, is the mutual congratulation at the meeting of the two
expectant mothers, Elisabeth and Mary. It is the standpoint of Jesus' mother (contrast Matthew) from which
the birth stories of Jesus are told. In Luke his parents
are "thy father and I." This evangelist felt how Mary
would keep the sayings about the child and his own sayings
in her heart pondering them, and how a sword would
pierce through her own soul that thoughts out of many
hearts might be revealed.

Whatever their origin, such passages suggest a rare
delicacy of sympathy in their author. It is curious that
Luke has, besides, so many passages in which women are
the principal figures. Note their prominence for a time
in Paul's work [8] and the converts Lydia and Damaris.
The Pauline letters agree with Acts in naming Priscilla
(Prisca) before her husband two times out of three. Luke
thrice adds "wife" to the list of rival interests which a
man must forego:

> If any man cometh unto me, and hateth not his
> own father, and mother, and wife, and children, and
> brethren, and sisters, . . . he cannot be my disciple
> (Luke xiv. 26; contrast Matt. x. 37: father or mother
> . . . son or daughter).

> There is no man that hath left house, or wife, or
> brethren, or parents or children . . . who shall not
> receive, etc. (Luke xviii. 29; contrast Mark x. 29 =

[8] Acts xiii. 50; xvi. 13; xvii. 4, 12.

Matt. xix. 29: house or brethren or sisters or mother or father or children or fields).[9]

And they all with one consent began to make excuse. . . . I have bought a field . . . I have bought five yoke of oxen . . . I have married a wife (Luke xiv. 18-20; contrast Matt. xxii. 5: but they made light of it, and went their ways, one to his own field, another to his merchandise).

Luke remembered Lot's wife as well as Lot.[9a]

Even though Luke cannot be classed as the champion of the oppressed, his gospel contains a cheerfulness and kindliness that won for him from Dante the title *scriba mansuetudinis Christi*. There is really good news in his gospel, as the opening chapters show with their emphasis upon "God's mercy." And the passages from Isaiah which he quotes as descriptive of the ministry of John and of Jesus and of Paul have the same evangelical note.[10]

Surely Luke thinks of Jesus and God as kindly and as interested in seeking and saving the lost, persistent in doing good, like the shepherd who seeks the lost sheep "until he find it." A God who is "moved with compassion" like the Good Samaritan and the prodigal's father, a God who is "kind" and "merciful" (the adjectives are not

[9] For Luke's omission of fields see p. 249. The word "brothers" here and in viii. 21 probably includes sisters, as "parents" here and in viii. 56 means father and mother.

[9a] Luke xvii. 28 f. (Lot, *cf.* p. 233), 32 (Remember Lot's wife) are not in Matt. xxiv as are the adjacent verses.

[10] Luke iii. 4 ff. = Isaiah xl. 3 ff.; Luke iv. 18 f. = Isaiah lxi. 1 f.; Acts xiii. 47 = Isaiah xlix. 6. For Luke's extension of the first text, see above, p. 254. That in the second he stops short of the words "the day of vengeance of our God" has often been mentioned as a further proof of the benignity of Luke (or Jesus), but in the LXX version which Luke employed that phrase is perhaps as compassionate as any, "the day of recompense," and the sequel is even more comforting.

in Matthew's parallel), who "does good and gives from heaven rains and fruitful seasons, filling men's hearts with food and gladness"; a Jesus "who went about doing good," "who graciously bestowed sight on many blind," who rebuked the violent tendencies of his disciples at Gethsemane or in Samaria, but from whose portrait Luke omits so much [11] that might seem too stern or violent—such are some of the expressive elements which make Luke the primary exponent of the divine good will to men.

Especially in contrast with Matthew, Luke's cheerfulness is evident. Matthew dwells on the seriousness of future punishment, repeating over and over such phrases as "eternal fire," "outer darkness," "there shall be weeping and gnashing of teeth," "many are called but few are chosen." [12] It is perhaps characteristic of the two later writers that Mark's stern passage about cutting off the offending hand or foot and casting out the offending eye is omitted entirely by Luke, while Matthew actually uses it twice. In view of our ignorance of the original text of their source (Q) it is hard for us to tell which evangelist is responsible for differences between them, but the following parallels in Luke to Matthew's Sermon on the Mount are instructive because of the different taste they leave in the reader's mouth, whether the difference be due to the pessimism of Matthew or to the optimism of Luke:

[11] *Style and Literary Method of Luke,* pp. 91 ff.

[12] On the comparative pessimism of Matthew see H. G. Wood in *The Parting of the Roads,* 1912, pp. 160 ff. Other examples could be added. While Luke has both the sayings, "He that is not with me is against me" (from Q) and "Whosoever is not against you is for you" (from Mark), Matthew has only the former. Matthew unlike Mark arranges the productivity of the seed in good ground in the order of anticlimax, saying (twice), "some a hundredfold, some sixty, some thirty." Luke says simply "a hundredfold." See also the somber verses Matt. vii. 6, 19; xviii. 7: "Woe unto the world because of occasions of stumbling"; xxvi. 52: "All they that take the sword shall perish by the sword."

Matthew	Luke
vi. 22 f. The lamp of the body is the eye: if therefore thine eye be single thy whole body shall be full of light. But if thine eye be evil thy whole body shall be full of darkness. If therefore the light that is in thee be darkness, how great is that darkness!	xi. 34 ff. The lamp of thy body is thine eye: when thine eye is single, thy whole body also is full of light; but when it is evil, thy body also is full of darkness. . . . If therefore thy whole body be full of light, having no part dark, it shall be wholly full of light, as when the lamp with its bright shining doth give thee light.
vi. 33 f. Seek ye first his kingdom and his righteousness; and all these things shall be added unto you. Be not therefore anxious for the morrow: for the morrow will be anxious for itself. Sufficient unto the day the evil thereof!	xii. 31 f. Seek ye his kingdom, and these things shall be added unto you. Fear not, little flock; for it is your Father's good pleasure to give you the kingdom.
vii. 1 f. Judge not, that ye be not judged. For with what judgment ye judge, ye shall be judged: and with what measure ye mete, it shall be measured unto you.	vi. 37 f. Judge not, and ye shall not be judged: and condemn not, and ye shall not be condemned: release and ye shall be released: give and it shall be given unto you; good measure, pressed down, shaken together, running over shall they give into your bosom. For with what measure ye mete it shall be measured to you again.

There is a triumphant joy about Luke's story. "Great joy" is his phrase on several occasions, from the "good tidings of great joy" with which the angels hail Jesus' birth to the "great joy" with which the first volume closes, and throughout Acts. How characteristic of Luke is the simple sentence, "And there was great joy in that city"! Joy appears on some curious occasions and with some curious results. The unborn John "leaps for joy" in

Elisabeth's womb. One would not expect the disciples to rejoice when their Lord left them.[13] It was "for joy" that they failed to believe that Jesus was really risen and that Rhoda forgot to open the door to Peter escaped from prison. The mere statistics of the concordance show that the Greek words for "joy" or "rejoice" occur much more frequently in Luke's writings than in all the other evangelists put together.

So the word "grace" or "gratitude," which is allied in Greek to the word "joy," while it strangely enough is found in the other gospels only in the prologue of John, occurs, noun and verb, frequently in Luke and Acts in the sense of human grace and gratitude as well as of the favor of God to men. So it is almost exclusively in this author that we read that Jesus' patients glorified God and that men praised, blessed, magnified and glorified him. It is not needful to quote all the instances, but one recalls how in Luke's gospel the grace of Jesus is emphasized, as a child and again as a man at Nazareth, how he refers to the mercy of God (not his perfection as in Matthew), "for he is kind toward the ungrateful and evil," how in this gospel one finds the discussion of gratitude in the stories of the Ten Lepers, of the Obedient Servant, of the Two Debtors, and elsewhere. One recalls also the tone of gladness in which reference is made before and after to the career of Jesus. It is for Luke good tidings of great joy, or good tidings of peace, a visitation of the dayspring from on high, a career of doing kindnesses or of gracious curing, the fulfilment of God's promise to bless all men, to give them his salvation and to bring light to illumine the Gentiles, and his mercy and consolation to Israel.

---

[13] It was *post hoc* but not *ergo propter hoc.* Neither were the disciples at Pisidian Antioch "filled with joy" because Paul shook off its dust for Iconium, nor "had the churches rest throughout Judaea and Galilee and Samaria" because Paul had left for Tarsus!

Akin to praise and rejoicing is prayer, and Luke's gospel
shows an interest in Jesus' teaching and practice of prayer.
We are indebted to Luke for the parables illustrating
humility (Pharisee and Publican) and persistence (Importunate Neighbor, Unjust Judge) in prayer. He it is
who states that the prayer of Jesus in the open was on his
knees and that it was customary, repeated, prolonged and
passionate.[14] Luke mentions Jesus as praying on several
occasions when the other gospels do not do so, as at his
baptism, at the choice of the twelve, at the transfiguration,
at the teaching of the Lord's prayer, and elsewhere.[15]
Prayer appears in the Book of Acts in corresponding situations, as when the holy Spirit is conferred, when visions
or messages are received from heaven, when officers are
selected and when men are in danger or facing martyrdom.
It is in Luke's writings only that we get the frequent
combination of fasting and prayer.[16]

It is well known also that Luke has much to say about
the holy Spirit. The Book of Acts is particularly full of
references to its activity, and Luke reads something of the
same standpoint back into the gospel, especially into its
early chapters. Zacharias, Elisabeth, Mary, Simeon, John
and Jesus are represented as filled with the Spirit or led
in the Spirit or having the holy Spirit upon them. These
phrases and similar ones in Acts at once remind us of the
problems which this term raises. Men are indifferently

[14] Luke xxii. 41; xxii. 39; v. 16 (note tense and number:
"used to withdraw in desert places"); vi. 12; xxii. 44 (if genuine).
In Acts also Stephen, Peter, Paul and others kneel at prayer.

[15] Luke xxii. 32; xxiii (34), 46; *cf.* xxi. 36. The references to
Jesus' praying in Luke v. 16 and ix. 18, often instanced as not in
Mark's parallels, appear to be derived from Mark i. 35 and vi. 46
respectively. Luke's gospel refers twice quite incidentally (v. 33;
xi. 1) to the prayers of the disciples of John.

[16] Luke ii. 37; v. 33; Acts xiii. 3; xiv. 23; *cf.* ix. 11 with 9; x. 9 f.
The combination is omitted in the best texts of Matt. xvii. 21 and
Mark ix. 29 and of Acts i. 14; x. 30; 1 Cor. vii. 5.

spoken of as in it, under it, filled with it, baptized or anointed with it, instructed by it. They speak through it or it speaks through them. It is often indistinguishable from the Spirit of the Lord or the Spirit of Jesus or from God or Jesus. Without "holy" we are often doubtful whether it means the divine or human spirit; without "the" we are doubtful which article if either to supply.

These difficulties of expression are not peculiar to Luke, nor is the emphasis upon the Spirit unusual, as Paul's letters also testify. Luke's individuality in dealing with it is perhaps shown, first, in the clearness with which he notes its materiality (at Jesus' baptism he adds "in a bodily form" to the phrase "the Spirit descended as a dove," and at the baptism of Pentecost there were literal sound as of wind and tongues as of fire); second, in the definiteness with which he marks, its arrival (not until Jesus rose and received it from his Father, and the disciples had waited for it a brief but definite number of days, not until the gospel was heard, and hands were laid on, or baptism applied); third, in his repetition of the contrast with the baptism of John; fourth, in his association with it of a gift of tongues which he understood apparently to be a speaking in foreign languages.

Whether such phenomena imply a personal or an impersonal spirit it is hard to determine. When Luke says "the holy Spirit and we," it sounds personal, but when he combines it or exchanges it with such words as wisdom, faith, power, joy, and fire, and deals with it as an objective experience, it seems more impersonal. Evidently Luke was aware of the Sadducean skepticism about angels and spirits and was as fully convinced of their existence as he was of the resurrection.

When one speaks of Luke's emphasis upon the holy Spirit it is well to recall that he was equally convinced of the evil influences like the unclean spirits in the diseased, the python in the slave girl at Philippi and the evil spirit which attacked Scaeva's seven sons at Ephesus. Satan, the arch demon, is real to Luke, fully as real as to the other evangelists and to Paul, if not more so. According to Luke, Jesus "continued in temptations" throughout his ministry, and Satan left Jesus only "for a season" after his initial temptation. "Satan entered into Judas" and "asked to have" all the disciples, "that he might sift them as wheat." It was Satan himself who "bound" Jesus' patients with a "bond," like "the woman with a spirit of weakness who was bent double and could not unbend herself at all," or "oppressed" them like a tyrant, but who "fell like lightning" when at Jesus' name even the demons proved subject to the Seventy. For it is "the power of darkness" or "the power of Satan" that opposes the gospel, a "son of the devil," or one whose heart Satan has filled.

Doubtless this list of Luke's interests could be enlarged or slightly changed. The material from which they must be determined is limited and capable of different interpretation. In some cases his sources are responsible for his matter, and even when he appears to change his sources the changes are slight and can be variously explained. It is easy to attach too much meaning to them. Perhaps we should substitute for Luke's interest in lodging, in entertainment and in women the category "domestic tone" as Plummer does.[17] Perhaps we are justified in suggesting that in his gospel Luke has emphasized Jesus' appeal to common sense, for men to "know of yourselves by looking," to "judge of yourselves what is right," to "test the time" as they test the signs of weather in earth and sky, to exercise a "prudence of the just" comparable to the prudence of the unjust steward, since "the sons of this world are more prudent than the sons of light," and to calculate chances of success in advance, like a man projecting a

[17] A. Plummer, *International Critical Commentary, St. Luke,* 1895, p. xlviii.

tower, or a king considering war, and having put one's
hand to the plow not to turn back.

We could further suggest that Luke betrays himself
a seafaring man by his substitution of "lake" for "sea of
Galilee," and of "seaboard of" for "about" Tyre and Sidon,
by his reference in the last calamity to "the roaring of the
sea and the billows," not to mention the storm and shipwreck and other nautical details in Acts. It is difficult
not to believe that this author shows in Luke and in Acts
"fondness for the notion of repentance." [18]   It has been
suggested that he thrice makes Jesus rebuke sentimental-
ity.[19] He has been called both a democrat and a hater of
crowds. His interest in women and his "asceticism" about
wealth have suggested that he was also in favor of celibacy.
An ancient prologue to his gospel says he lived "eighty-
four years without wife or children," but better argument
could be found in his re-wording of Mark's saying about
marriage and resurrection and in the three cases already
cited where he refers to the renunciation of marital
claims. At least the prophetic women whom he mentions
were, he tells us, in the unmarried state,—"Anna, a proph-
etess, the daughter of Phanuel, . . . a widow even unto
fourscore and four years," and Philip the evangelist's
"four virgin daughters who prophesied." But many of
the traits ascribed to him may be quite fanciful.

The Acts has so much to say about the "God-fearers"
or Gentiles who, without becoming full proselytes, had
attached themselves to Judaism that some have naturally
conjectured that the author himself had followed this path
out of paganism into Christianity. If he was a born Jew
he was certainly of the Hellenistic rather than of the
Palestinian type, since his outlook like his Old Testament

[18] A. C. McGiffert, *The God of the Early Christians*, 1924, p. 8
and *note*. See below, pp. 288 f.

[19] Luke xi. 27; xiv. 15; xxiii. 28. See S. C. Carpenter, *Christianity
According to St. Luke*, 1919, p. 198.

is Greek rather than Hebrew. Other students, influenced by the traditional ascription of the books to "Luke the physician," have thought they detected in language and subject matter at least, even if not in technical terms of vocabulary, the training and interests of a doctor. Like the other evangelists he has many references to healing, but they are scarcely more numerous proportionately or more circumstantial. Perhaps they are told with especial tenderness. That suits what we have learned elsewhere of the author's gentleness and sympathy, but hardly proves him a physician. It seems easier to ascertain something of the author's social and religious attitudes than to detect in his writings clear evidence of his professional or religious status. The suggestions already made sufficiently illustrate the subtle manner in which the interests of the author affect the ultimate form of his work. By this influence his personality becomes a significant factor in the making of Luke and Acts.

CHAPTER XIX

THEOLOGICAL ATTITUDES

We have already had occasion to mention some of the practical aspects of the author's religion—his interest in prayer and in the holy Spirit and his sympathy with that form of Christianity which accepted Gentile converts, "making no distinction" from the Jews. It is natural to inquire further into the theoretical aspects of his religion and to see whether we can discover and classify the expression of his beliefs.

We are not in a position to know all the varieties of religious formulation current in the early church, nor do the works of Luke aim to present a systematic statement of doctrine. We must depend on phrases and allusions rather than on expositions. But the data available give the impression that the evangelist held, indeed took for granted, quite a considerable series of theological tenets and that these tenets were in the main the common property of large sections of the church. English scholars as different as Plummer, Rackham and Lake seem to discover independently that Luke's writings, one or both, supply proof-texts for most articles in the Creeds.

His works naturally show many points of contact with the next most voluminous New Testament writer, the apostle Paul. The tradition that the author was a companion of Paul has made it customary to think of him as affected by Paul's teaching. Not infrequently there are coincidences of thought and even of language as each writer deals in his own way with one or another of the subjects that fell within the round of Christian teaching. The speeches of Paul contain as we might expect much matter consonant with the tenor of his epistles, though it is doubtful whether the historian knew the epistles or had any certain memory or record of what the apostle said on the specific occasions. But the so-called Paulinism of the evangelist is the kind that suggests rather a common viewpoint or merely the acceptance of the Pauline terminology than a sympathetic insight into Paul's more mystical and deeper thoughts acquired under the spell of personal association.

The interests or characteristics which Luke has in common with Paul, as his emphasis on the gospel to the Gentiles and on the holy Spirit, joy and prayer, are too general to be significant, and among the more striking agreements of phrase there is no certain case of literary dependence. The Pauline words "justify," "faith," "salvation" and "grace" are for the author not new categories freshly coined, but the common change of his accepted religious currency. Such passages as the following illustrate how he introduces them:

> Then comes the devil, and takes away the seed from their heart, that they may not believe and be saved (Luke viii. 12; contrast Mark iv. 15).

> In him everyone who believes is justified from all things from which ye could not be justified in the law of Moses (Acts xiii. 39).

> Ye should turn from these vain things unto a living God. . . . He hath appointed a day in which he will judge the world in righteousness by the man whom he hath ordained; whereof he hath given assurance unto all men in that he hath raised him from the dead (Acts xiv. 15; xvii. 31; *cf.* 1 Thess i. 9 f.).

> That I may accomplish my course (*cf.* 2 Tim. iv. 7), and the ministry which I received from the Lord Jesus, to testify the gospel of the grace of God . . . the word

of his grace, which is able to build you up (Acts
xx. 24, 32).

Behind such phrases, as behind the other Jewish or Christian terminology of the author, must lie not some special
contacts or fresh theological thinking, but the usual circle
of ideas of a Christian group.

There are two elements in the earliest Christianity which
at this distance, and with the differences the centuries
·have wrought, we are liable to overlook.   The adjectives
technically applied to them are Messianic and apocalyptic,
but the elements themselves are more familiar than their
names.   They are closely associated historically: both of
them were thoroughly Jewish and constituted part of the
Jewish inheritance of the church; both of them gradually
sank into insignificance or rather were transformed.   But
at the start they provided the terminology and perhaps the
principal content of the gospel.   The two were almost
inseparable for Christians; for Jews they had been identical.   Yet the greatest variety existed among both Jews
and Christians concerning the details of these two lines
of thinking, and it is therefore interesting to inquire how
the *autor ad Theophilum* regarded them.

By Messianism is meant the Jewish national hope.   The
name is from Messiah, the anointed agent of God who
figured in some of the Jewish imaginative programs of reconstruction, but it is often applied more widely, especially
since in many cases the program made no mention of a personal Messiah. It is not possible here to summarize the information about this expectation available from surviving
Jewish writings or to discuss the problem of how Jesus related himself to this rôle and how the church understood it
and transformed it. We are in search of the standpoint of a
single and somewhat extensive writer of the early age
and we find that he clearly accepts the rôle for Jesus.

There is no doubt that for him Jesus is the Messiah.

Three times he pointedly explains *christos,* the rather peculiar Greek translation of the Hebrew *Messiah* (anointed), by using the Greek verb "anoint." It appears in the "keynote speech" of Jesus at Nazareth in the passage read from the Book of Isaiah, and when the Old Testament passage speaks of the attack of kings of the earth and rulers against the Lord and against his Christ, the evangelist identifies the term with Jesus by asserting that God "anointed" him—with the holy Spirit and with power, he adds elsewhere. Evidently for Luke the stories of Jesus' baptism by John and of his notable anointing by a woman were not, when they reached him, understood as literal etymological explanations of the term anointed. But without such explanations he was assured that "the Messiah is Jesus."

For Luke, Jesus is also a Jewish king. His birth at Bethlehem, the repeated assertion of Davidic descent, the promise of the throne of his father David, the fulfilment of promised lordship to David's seed—all emphasize this fact perhaps as much as the mere title, which Luke, like Mark, uses quite sparingly—"son of David." The opponents of Christianity are represented as taking this claim seriously [1] as a challenge to Caesar's kingship, and not merely as a taunt as in the other gospels. The *hosanna* at the triumphal entry becomes praise for "the coming king" (in Mark, "the coming one," or "the coming kingdom of our father David").

In a similarly Messianic sense must be understood the frequent reference to Jesus as redeemer, savior and Lord. The message of the angels contains two if not three titles —"Unto you is born . . . Savior, . . . Christ, Lord." The early chapters of Luke speak of Christ's mission as

[1] Luke xxiii. 2; Acts xvii. 7. But since the accusers in both Jerusalem and Thessalonica are Jews, Luke doubtless regarded their charge as based on malice rather than on loyal concern for the "tribute" and "decrees of Caesar."

K

salvation or redemption; the speeches of Acts suggest the association of Lord and Christ.

How clearly Luke understood the national element, and even the political element in this Messianic position of Jesus, is shown by his repeated association of his kingship or Messiahship with the Jewish people ("Israel," or "God's people," or merely "the people" as he often calls it), not to mention the comparisons with David and Caesar already noted. We are inclined to forget that phase of Messiahship. Luke did not overlook it, and since he can scarcely have ever held this political view of the matter himself, its presence in his work betrays either accurate information or accurate imagination. That the words peace, redemption, salvation and kingdom have for us spiritual meanings should not blind our eyes to their fitness to a more material and even military hope. Luke refers to the contemporaries of Jesus as awaiting the consolation of Israel, the redemption of Jerusalem, the Kingdom of God, the redemption of Israel or the restoration of the kingdom to Israel; as hoping for rescue from enemies, dethroning of tyrants, permanent sovereignty and international peace. More than any other New Testament writer Luke brings to our sight the current Messianic hope of Judaism.

On what grounds Luke identified Jesus with this Messiah it is not hard to discover. His main evidence is Jesus' resurrection from the dead, and he makes central in his theology a theme expressed at the beginning of Romans, which in Paul's letters is almost unique: "He was declared Son of God . . . .by the resurrection from the dead." Luke regards this event as the thing to which the first disciples and Paul were set apart to bear witness. It is plain that for this writer the resurrection of Jesus is the distinguishing article of faith for the Christian over against the Jew. Not only the Athenian philosophers found it a stumblingblock, but also the Jews. In his gospel the

author seems to sum up his verdict on the apostolic age
in the words of Abraham to Dives, that the Jews will not
be persuaded if one rose from the dead, just as they have
not really believed Moses and the prophets.

Indeed the resurrection is precisely what is written in
the law and the prophets, the hope of Israel, the promise
to the fathers. The speeches of Paul in his defense harp
on this theme. "Why is it judged incredible with you, if
God doth raise the dead?" The procurator can summarize
the matter as being "certain controversies . . . concerning
a certain deceased Jesus, whom Paul affirmed to be alive."
No New Testament writer more often refers to the resurrection as predicted in Scripture or cites more texts in its
support than does Luke. Paul, to be sure, says once, "He
hath been raised on the third day according to the scriptures," but we cannot tell what passages he had in view.
Luke, on the other hand, uses in the single speech of Paul
at Pisidian Antioch not only the words "Thou wilt not give
thy holy One to see corruption" (attributed also to Peter
at Pentecost), and "I will give you the holy and sure
blessings of David," but he also in the same passage apparently applies to the resurrection the Messianic proof-
text, which was a favorite in other connections, "Thou art
my Son, this day have I begotten thee." He identifies
with the resurrection and the incredulity with which the
Jews heard of it the words spoken in the prophets:

> Behold, ye despisers, and wonder, and perish;
> For I work a work in your days,
> A work which ye shall in no wise believe, if one declare it
> unto you.

Even his quotation from Isaiah liii,

> In his humiliation his judgment was taken away:
> His generation who shall declare?
> For his life is taken from the earth.

is perhaps understood by the evangelist as a prediction of

Christ's conquest over death (as Wendt, for example, thinks) rather than of the violence and injustice of his crucifixion.

In comparison with his resurrection the death of Jesus has little evidential value in Luke-Acts. The contrast between this fate and the Jewish program for the career of the Messiah is very obvious to a reader of these writings, but is apparently not a matter of moment to the writer. The cross of Jesus is for him no stumblingblock as it was to Paul the Jew, and it is no ground of hope and glorying, as it was to Paul the Christian. It is curious how it is treated in the speeches of Acts. The death of Jesus was an act of ignorant wickedness and rejection on the part of the Jews. God, however, thwarted its effect by raising Jesus from the dead. The resurrection is therefore the significant thing about Jesus. His death is only the prelude. The resurrection is the great fulfilment of prophecy, the demonstration of Messiahship, the occasion for repentance in view of a coming judgment and resurrection for all mankind.

In the gospels the death of Jesus is told rather than explained. But Luke strikingly omits passages in Mark which might seem to suggest a doctrine of atonement, as modern theology would name it. Mark's "to give his life a ransom for many" is not in Luke's parallel, and at least the shorter account of the Last Supper found in the "Western text" of Luke (which many scholars prefer as independent of Paul) omits the words "which is given for you," "which is poured out for you" (as well as all the words between), and thus all reference to vicarious death. That elsewhere Luke uses part of Isaiah liii as a proof-text for Jesus' death does not prove that he adopted from it the special theological explanation which later Christians have found in the unquoted parts of the same passage.[2]

[2] The chapter is quoted in Luke xxii. 37; Acts viii. 32 f. Also the term "servant" for Jesus (Acts iii. 13, etc.) is usually thought

While therefore Luke does not indicate how the death of Jesus fitted with the Messianic rôle, it is evident that in his mind the two were somehow adjusted or that an earlier adjustment was assumed. Such a death was at least necessary according to Scripture and is associated by the risen Jesus with his "entering into his glory" and with the "preaching in his name of repentance and remissions of sins to all nations." It is easy to guess that the Pauline theology lies behind such connections, e.g., that God highly exalted Jesus because he humbled himself to death, and that the remission of sins is based upon faith in him that died and rose again. "Through him," we read in Acts, "remission of sins is preached to you; and in him everyone who believes is justified from all things from which ye could not be justified in the law of Moses." Superficially this sounds Pauline enough, and no doubt Paul's work lies behind such a mode of expression, and yet one hesitates to assume that Paul's rather unique theology is shared understandingly by his biographer. Possibly the latter had no special penchant for such things; certainly he has no occasion in this work to elaborate such matters. As his Jewish background seems accurate in its Messianism, so his Christian background seems accurate in the simplicity of its theology. The speeches in Acts have been called "at least a triumph in archæology." They suit what we may assume of the primitive Christian thought about Jesus. It is possible of course that they are due to Luke's accurate information and were not composed by him out of his own imagination, but it is also possible that Luke himself had a very similar viewpoint, even though

to be ultimately derived from it. It is noticeable how out of the middle of a passage with a dozen "vicarious" phrases (Is. liii. 4-12), Acts quotes vss. 7*bcd*, 8*abc*, which have none. A striking expression in Acts xx. 28, "the church of God which he acquired through blood of his own," may refer to the crucifixion, but it is doubtful both in text and in interpretation.

he lived long after. And there are reasons for thinking that his emphasis on repentance and remission of sins should be connected not with the death of Jesus, but with his future coming. To this phase of his thought we must accordingly turn.

The eschatological or apocalyptic element, like the Messianic, is part of Christianity's inheritance from Judaism. Indeed, in Judaism itself the two were, as we have said, inseparable. Before Jesus came both were exclusively future; it was only Christianity that divided them. Yet Christianity still retained a large part of the futuristic element in the Jewish scheme. Put simply, the change was this. The Jewish plan for the future was still to be fulfilled. There would come a Messiah who would inaugurate the kingdom of God, the resurrection and the judgment. But the Christians claimed that this Messiah had already appeared in Jesus. He had lived and died, but he would come again, since he had not been holden of death but God had raised him. What the Jews expected of the coming of the Messiah the Christians now referred to what Matthew and Paul call his *parousia* or a second coming. The fact that his identity had been revealed in a period of life on earth and that his future position had been guaranteed by the resurrection and the session at God's right hand only made the expectation more certain, more concrete and more urgent. Evidently the Christians expected this event or series of events to come soon upon the stage. Not a single New Testament writer fails to voice this universal anticipation.

There has been much debate whether Jesus himself shared this expectation. Modern scholarship has succeeded in challenging the easy habit by which the eschatological passages in the synoptic gospels were overlooked or explained away. As the records stand, Jesus predicted the coming of the Kingdom of God with power, of the Son

of man upon the clouds of heaven in glory, together with
certain premonitory signs and associated events of the
judgment and the resurrection. Further, Jesus said that
this would happen before his generation passed away,
before some of his listeners tasted of death, before his
disciples had finished the cities of Israel in their itinerant
preaching. To be sure, he said also that no one but God
knew the exact hour and day, and that the gospel must be
first preached to all nations, and that certain disasters
must first befall Jerusalem, his followers and the whole
world. Sometimes he seems to identify himself with the
Son of man, but sometimes also he seems to make a distinction. Much uncertainty besets this and other detailed
questions. Nevertheless the gospels contain in general
abundant evidence of an apocalyptic outlook.

The reasons for denying to Jesus the apocalyptic viewpoint which his words seem to imply are several. If taken
literally his prophecies of a near catastrophe were not
completely fulfilled, and for some people the thought is
abhorrent that Jesus was mistaken, which is what they
understand unfulfilled prophecy to mean. For this rejection of apocalypticism on dogmatic grounds support is
claimed from two other considerations: the first is the incompatibility of apocalyptic with Jesus' ethics; the second,
the possibility of assigning the apocalyptic element to
Jesus' reporters. On the one hand it is urged that Jesus'
ethical teaching is sound and permanent, showing no trace
of an early expectation of a miraculous new world order,
but rather the ambition to bring in God's kingdom gradually
and spiritually through the transformation of human characters. It is assumed that this could not be combined
in the same person with a vivid certainty of impending
crisis—an assumption of logical consistency which human
experience will promptly deny. On the other hand it is
alleged that the followers of Jesus overlaid his ethical
teaching with their own apocalyptic notions, and that

evidences of this process are discoverable in the successive
layers of tradition represented by our synoptic gospels.
Their sequence is thought to agree with an ever heightening
emphasis on apocalyptic, for example in the series Q-
Mark-Matthew.[3]

Both these arguments can be met here only most briefly.
In the first place, incompatibility of eschatology and ethics
is probably a difficulty that only moderns would feel. The
prophets and the rabbis, Jesus and the apostles, not merely
were able to accept into the same mind the idea of a near
catastrophe and the demand for normal moral perfection;
they even used the eschatology to enforce the ethics. So
far are we from the dilemma of being compelled to choose
between the ethical and the apocalyptic teaching of Jesus.
In the second place, our records of Christian development
do not show an unvarying line of change in the direction
merely of increased eschatology. There was rather both
ebb and flow of tension in such matters, and beside a
tendency in some quarters to antedate the *parousia* there
was also a tendency away from literal and imminent apocalypticism. The Fourth Gospel, for example, says very
little of an outward return of Jesus, but much of the sending of the Paraclete. It has been thought that it represents,
instead of an enhanced apocalyptic, a kind of spiritualizing
of apocalyptic. It is at this point in the discussion that
the determination of Luke's attitude becomes important.

That the third evangelist shared in general the apocalyptic outlook of his age cannot be gainsaid. The collections
of the words of Jesus about the coming events which he
found in his sources he does not omit, but retains merely

---

[3] As one among many advocates of this view compare Streeter
in *Oxford Studies in the Synoptic Problem*, 1911, pp. 423-436.
But see now his *The Four Gospels*, where he gives, I think, more
just recognition to the opposite tendency, as illustrated in the
series Mark-Luke-John (p. 425), and to the effect of delayed
apocalyptic on the writing of at least its first and last members.

with changes of detail.[4] Even in the speeches in Acts, where he may be supposed to have had more freedom to express his own interests, there are repeated references to the return of Jesus, the judgment and the resurrection:

> This Jesus, who was received up from you into heaven, shall so come in like manner as ye beheld him going into heaven (i. 11).
>
> Repent ye therefore . . . that so there may come seasons of refreshing from the presence of the Lord; and that he may send the Christ who hath been appointed for you, Jesus: whom the heaven must receive until the times of restoration of all things, whereof God spake by the mouth of his holy prophets that have been from of old (iii. 19).
>
> This is he who is ordained of God the judge of the living and the dead (x. 42).
>
> He hath appointed a day, in which he will judge the world in righteousness by the man whom he hath ordained; whereof he hath given assurance unto all men, in that he hath raised him from the dead (xvii. 31).
>
> There shall be a resurrection both of the just and unjust (xxiv. 15).

The "kingdom of God" was not a new term for Luke but he uses it constantly with this sense of forecast. Sometimes it is added to his source to make the sense clear:

Mark	Luke
i. 38 I may preach	iv. 43 I must tell the good news of the kingdom of God
vi. 34 he began to teach them many things	ix. 11 he spoke to them about the kingdom of God
x. 29 for my sake and for the gospel's sake	xviii. 29 for the sake of the kingdom of God
xiii. 29 know that he (or it) is nigh at the doors	xxi. 31 know that the kingdom of God is near

[4] Luke xvii. 20-xviii. 8 and xxi. 5-36 are in the main from Q and Mark respectively.

K*

Thrice Luke refers to the kingdom of God in the message of those whom Jesus sent forth; Matthew once;
Mark not at all. The phrase occurs also as part of the
message of the apostles in Acts. It might seem that it
was identical with "the things concerning Jesus" which
also entered the apostles' message, but the latter looks
rather to the past—to the death and resurrection of Jesus
according to the Scriptures, as several contexts show,
while "the things concerning the kingdom of God" seems
to look forward to the future. Twice at the end of Acts
both are named together. The verbs with which Luke
connects the kingdom—"tell the good news" and "testify"
—suit this futuristic sense, whether of promise or of
warning.

It is important to bear in mind these two parts of the
Christian message—the first and the second coming of
Jesus as we now call them. There are certain likenesses
between them in the mind of Luke and certain differences. The word he used for them both is not the semi-
technical *parousia* but "sending." Each is prepared for
by a process of witnessing or testifying. The law and the
prophets heralded the first, the Christian missionaries the
second. "If they hear not Moses and the prophets, neither
will they be persuaded if one [like Jesus] rise from the
dead." "The law and the prophets were until John:
from that time the gospel of the kingdom of God is
preached." In some respects John is the counterpart of
the apostles, one preparing for the coming of Jesus, the
other for the Kingdom of God. Each has a baptism to
confer, and Luke repeatedly emphasizes the distinction.

Attention has already been called to Luke's interest in
the holy Spirit. It is important here to notice its association with eschatology. Luke makes plain that it belongs
not to the message of the past, but to that of the future.
As the Fourth Gospel says, "the spirit was not yet"
when Jesus died, rose or ascended. It was still to come,

and come it did "not many days" afterwards at Pentecost. It was promised to Jesus by the Father and was poured forth only when Jesus was exalted to God's right hand. It is one of the evidences of Jesus' exaltation and therefore an earnest of his return. It shares in the predictive work of the apostles. As its classical function in Old Testament times was pointing forward to the coming of Christ, so in Jesus and the apostles it appears to inspire their message of expectation. Even Zacharias is filled with the holy Spirit and prophesies; John the Baptist is filled with the holy Spirit and makes ready for the Lord a people prepared; Simeon looking for the consolation of Israel is filled with the Spirit as he anticipates and recognizes the salvation which God has prepared. Jesus is filled with the Spirit. He quotes as his program of announcement the predictive message of the Book of Isaiah. The Spirit of the Lord is upon him because he is "anointed" and "sent" to preach good news and to proclaim a good time coming—even "the acceptable year of the Lord." Q's famous thanksgiving of Jesus, "I thank thee, Father," etc., is prefaced in Luke by the words, "he rejoiced in the holy Spirit." The day of the Lord is according to Joel marked by pouring forth of the Spirit on all flesh. In Acts Peter is represented as applying this message to the experience at Pentecost, adding quite gratuitously to the text the introductory apocalyptic formula, "in the last days." Harnack has suggested that the story of Pentecost was originally even more eschatological than it now appears,—a preaching of the gospel to all nations as the fulfilment of the last preliminary before the end. Evidently Jesus' reply, "Ye shall receive power, when the holy Spirit is come upon you," has in the view of the writer of Acts some relevance to the question, "Dost thou at this time restore the kingdom to Israel?" For Luke the petition, "May thy holy Spirit come upon us and cleanse us," would be a reasonable equivalent for "May

thy kingdom come"; and there is some textual evidence
that the former rather than the latter was actually written
by him in the Lord's Prayer. We may say that such associations of Spirit and kingdom tend to spiritualize eschatology, but they have also the tendency to eschatologize
the Spirit.

Another idea which Luke connected more closely with
the Lord's return than we and perhaps other early Christians would do is that of repentance and remission of
sins. They are among his favorite phrases. The frequency of the former marks a notable difference from the
emphasis of Paul. That this "Pharisee of the Pharisees"
has so little to say (the concordance gives the cases)
about repentance, a doctrine cardinal to Judaism and congenial to Christianity, has never been explained. Luke
uses the term freely, as if like other terms he took it for
granted. In one breath he combines it with a good
"Pauline" phrase: "repentance toward God and faith
toward our Lord Jesus Christ." From Mark, Luke takes
the description of John's rite as "the baptism of repentance unto remission of sins,"[5] but the same message is
evidently as appropriate for the apostolic preaching of
the kingdom of God. Repentance and the remission of
sins are repeatedly associated in Luke and Acts, and each
occurs separately. They are connected not so much with
the Lord's death as with his resurrection, exaltation and
return, and with the gift of the holy Spirit.[6] Men are
instigated to repent by the fact that "God has appointed
a day in which he will judge the world in righteousness."
Remission of sins is granted to belief on his name as of
one "who is ordained of God to be the judge of the living

[5] Luke iii. 3 = Mark i. 4; Acts xiii. 24; xix. 4; *cf.* Luke i. 77.
Luke does not, however, take over from Mark, as Matthew does
(for John as well as for Jesus), Jesus' slogan, "Repent ye" (Matt.
iii. 2; iv. 17 = Mark i. 15). He omits repent of Mark vi. 12.

[6] Acts ii. 38; iii. 19; v. 31; viii. 22; xiii. 38; xxvi. 18-20. *Cf.*
Luke xxiv. 47.

and the dead." Repentance is "unto life"; the alternative
is "destruction." It is to "save oneself from this crooked
generation" before the day of the Lord come. Though the
speeches in Acts are strikingly lacking in ethical details
defining the "works worthy of repentance," one may assume
that ethics is motivated eschatologically. This explains
why, as Paul "reasoned of righteousness and temperance
and judgment to come," Felix was "terrified."

The ethical implications of apocalyptic cannot be regarded as a peculiarity of Luke. Indeed all early Christian eschatology drew the moral inference attributed to
Jesus, "The kingdom of God is at hand. Repent ye."
The inferential particles vary, but in each case a moral
imperative follows an apocalyptic prediction: ". . . wrath
to come. Bring forth therefore fruits worthy of repentance." "Watch therefore"; "Wherefore be ye steadfast";
"So then let us not sleep"; "Therefore be sober"; "Wherefore give diligence that ye may be found without spot and
blameless"; "Wherefore let us have grace." [7] This regular course of transition is to be remembered whenever an
effort is made to divide ethic and apocalyptic. Luke's
apocalyptic chapter ends on the same note as Mark's,
though his wording is fresh and striking. He has a
different description of the danger of being weighed down
or choked and different terms for the terrors of the end,[8]
and for the consolations of the faithful.[9] But does he
represent any discoverable difference in his attitude?

There is some reason to believe that Luke's apocalyptic
passages are affected by his Gentile viewpoint or that of

[7] Jesus (Mark i. 15 asyndeton = Matt. iv. 17 γάρ); John the
Baptist in Q (Matt. iii. 8 = Luke iii. 8 οὖν); Jesus in Mark (xiii.
35 οὖν); Paul in 1 Cor. (xv. 58 ὥστε) and 1 Thess. (v. 6 ἄρα οὖν);
1 Peter (iv. 7 οὖν); 2 Peter (iii. 14 διό); Hebrews (xii. 28 διό).
See the context of each passage.

[8] Luke xix. 41 ff.; xx. 18; xxi. 20 ff., 25 f.; xxii. 35 ff.; xxiii. 27 ff.

[9] Luke xxi. 18 f., 28; Acts iii. 19.

his readers. If we are right in accounting as technical terms of Jewish apocalyptic "the *parousia,*" "the consummation of the age," which we find in Matthew repeatedly but not in Luke, and "the abomination of desolation," "the beginning of birth-pangs (of the Messiah)," and "the tribulation," which Luke omits from Mark xiii, we can see that Luke is more intelligible to those who are unschooled in the terminology of Jewish apocalyptic. To the same score perhaps should be put the fact that while Mark and Matthew discuss the detail of Messianic mythology which included the return of Elijah before the coming of the Messiah, Luke has no parallel to these passages.[10] It may be for similar reasons that for certain cryptic passages in Mark xiii and elsewhere Luke substitutes more concrete reference to the fall of Jerusalem, encircled by armies, hemmed by siegeworks, trampled by Gentiles, its women in tears and terror, its infants dashed to the ground, its adults slain by the sword or carried captive among all nations.

One of the phases of apocalyptic which caused difference and difficulty in early Christianity was its imminence. "How soon shall these things be?" Naturally the urgency of the message and its moral power seemed to many persons dependent on the nearness of the coming. On the other hand, if it were made too imminent the result would be too much excitement, and its date would have to be postponed as years went on. The variation of early Christians in this matter consisted not simply in a greater or less amount of apocalyptic interest; the interest was very widespread. The difference among New Testament writers is to be found in their skillful adjustment between these extremes as regards imminence rather than in their acceptance or rejection of apocalyptic as a whole.

The emphasis upon apocalyptic naturally found expres-

[10] Matt. xi. 14; xvii. 10-13 = Mark ix. 11-13. *Cf.,* however, Luke i. 17.

sion in warnings of the nearness of the end. The opposite position—the end is not so near as you suppose—represents a later standpoint, and yet one that is entirely confident of the apocalyptic program. While the former attitude is fully recognized by modern students of the New Testament, the latter deserves to be observed as equally significant. It is precisely the attitude of Paul as he writes Second Thessalonians. His readers had taken too literally his apocalyptic expectation, or rather they had supposed he meant that the day of the Lord was "just at hand." His answer is to explain that certain events must come "first," and he shows that his program is still in an early stage. It is to correct excessive expectancy that Paul gives his elaborate description of the sequence—the man or thing that restrains, the man of lawlessness or the mystery of lawlessness and the apostasy, the day of the Lord, the coming of the Lord and our gathering together unto him. The Book of Revelation may be due largely to the same sense that "hope deferred maketh the heart sick," which it meets by its spiral series of woes and its proleptic assurances of the ultimate triumph of God's saints.

In fact, even the indifference to the eschatological hope is a mark of excessive expectancy and consequent disillusionment. Ezekiel had found it necessary to meet such lethargy by the threat of more urgent disaster, replacing the proverbs, "The days are prolonged and every vision faileth," or "The vision that he seeth is for many days to come, and he prophesieth of times that are far off." In the sub-apostolic age there was likewise unstable equilibrium between too much and too little imminence of anticipation. Already circulated as "Scripture" in the first century, and repeatedly quoted by Christians with approval (1 Clement xxiii; 2 Clement xi), was the anonymous saying which condemned "the doubters who say, 'These things we have heard even in the days of our fathers, and behold we have grown old and none of these things has happened to

us (but we waiting from day to day have seen none of these
things)'." Second Peter represents at a later date the
same kind of disappointment, a disappointment which then
had turned to skepticism and ridicule, and the writer tries
to revive the "promise of his *parousia*" by a series of explanations and excuses for the fact that "all things continue
as they were from the beginning of the creation."

It is this delay in part which makes the need of patience so great. Patience is not merely endurance in suffering, but the "patience of hope" and the quiet resigna-
tion of "waiting for God's Son from Heaven" (Thessalonians). "If we hope for that which we see not, then do we
with patience wait for it" (Romans). "Ye have need of
patience, that, having done the will of God, ye may receive
the promise. 'For yet a very little while,' 'he that cometh
shall come, and shall not tarry'" (Hebrews). "Be patient, therefore, brethren, until the *parousia* of the Lord.
Behold the husbandman waiteth for the precious fruit of
the earth, being patient over it, until it receive the early
and latter rain. Be ye also patient: stablish your hearts;
for the *parousia* of the Lord is at hand" (James, using the
expression μακροθυμέω instead of ὑπομονή). Even the
early gospel material called Q provides moral warning for
men who, like the wicked servant in the parable, say in
their heart, "My lord tarrieth," or "My lord delayeth his
coming."

It is this attitude of delayed fulfilment which seems
to differentiate Luke from his parallels in the synoptic
gospels. He does not carry it through consistently or consciously. Some of the sayings with most vivid expectancy
are retained from his sources, and, as we have noted, there
is a dramatic suspense about his whole narrative and an
apocalyptic tone in his missionary addresses. But as indicating his probable deferred eschatology, the following details are worth noting:

In the "little apocalypse" of Mark xiii we meet at once

a significant change. "Take heed," begins Mark, "that no man lead you astray. Many shall come in my name saying, 'I am he'; and shall lead many astray." In Luke there is another false cry besides "I am he." It is significantly enough, "The time is at hand." "Take heed," writes Luke, "that ye be not led astray: for many shall come in my name, saying, 'I am he,' and, 'The time is at hand': go ye not after them."

In the following verses Mark says of wars and rumors of wars that they "must needs come to pass but the end is not yet"; Luke, "these things must needs come to pass first; but the end is not immediately." The "first" is typical of the "delayed apocalyptic." [11] So is the "not immediately." Evidently there was danger that some would expect the end "immediately."

This indeed is explicitly said in Luke's introduction to the parable of the Pounds. The evangelist explains that Jesus spoke it "because he was nigh to Jerusalem, and they supposed that the kingdom of God was immediately to appear." The analogy with the *parousia* is made unmistakable in Luke by his reference to the purpose of the nobleman's journey "to receive for himself a kingdom and to return." [12] In the other gospels such a man is merely sojourning abroad, that is, away from home. Luke says "into a far country." Evidently the return cannot be soon. [13] In the parable of the Wicked Husbandmen we

---

[11] *Cf.* 2 Thess. ii. 3; Mark ix. 11 f.; xiii. 10; Luke xvii. 25; xxi. 12.

[12] A later Christian parable says expressly, "The sojourning abroad of the master is the time that remains until his *parousia*" (Hermas *Simil.* v. 5, 4). Indeed, the technical apocalyptic word *parousia* was probably itself a standing metaphor from just such a parable of a non-resident master. It was used in contemporary Greek of the official visit paid by a ruler to his subjects in any locality or by an absentee landlord to his estate. Luke, however, does not use the noun. He used rather the simple "come," and once the derivative noun "coming" (ἔλευσις).

[13] *Cf.* Matt. xxv. 19.

have another master sojourning abroad, but Luke alone adds the phrase, "for a long time."

The need of patience is urged in other parables. In the explanation of the parable of the sower it is Luke alone who says of those comparable to the good seed that they "hold fast" the word of God and bring forth fruit "in patience," while those comparable to the seed in thorns are choked "as they go their way" and they "bring no fruit to perfection." Again, it is the evangelist himself who gives the motive of the parable of the Unjust Judge. It was spoken, he says, "in view of the necessity for men always to pray and not to faint," i.e., not to lose heart. The trouble with the judge is merely that he procrastinates; he would not give the woman her due "for a time."

This parable is placed by Luke right after an apocalyptic discourse which he appears to derive in the main from Q, but his introduction to that discourse is noteworthy. He begins thus:

> And being asked by the Pharisees when the kingdom of God cometh, he answered them and said, The kingdom of God cometh not with observation: neither shall they say Lo, here! or There! for lo, the kingdom of God is within you. And he said unto the disciples, The days will come when ye shall desire to see one of the days of Son of man and ye shall not see it.

At this point Luke is joined by Matthew, but the words just quoted have been either added by Luke or omitted by Matthew. Although the answer which follows deals with the circumstances of the *parousia,* Luke suggests that the question which was asked was its time, "When?" As in the parallel to Mark first quoted, so here he warns against false alarms. He asserts that its time is not a matter of calculation on the basis of observation, for this is what the word παρατήρησις seems to mean, and he definitely predicts the days when men shall long and wait to see one

of the days of the Son of man.   No, "ye shall not see it." [14]
It is not yet, perhaps not in this generation.   Luke continues with one of those warning "first's": "But first must
he [the Son of man] suffer many things and be rejected of
this generation."   While we may not be sure of the origin
and meaning of all this passage, it seems in general to suit
Luke's perspective of hope deferred.

Evidently for Luke the interval was not consistently
thought of as limited to a single generation.   The opening
chapters in his gospel speak in the tone of Old Testament
prophecy, which with all its Messianic hope looks forward
to "all generations henceforth," "unto generations and generations," and ages to come.   As the audiences in Acts are
told that the promises are for them and their children or
simply for their children, so Jesus tells the daughters of
Jerusalem that the disasters shall come upon them and their
children.   Perhaps the same perspective of continued suffering is found in his statement that "Jerusalem shall be
trodden down of the Gentiles until the times of the Gentiles be fulfilled."   This is not from Mark; on the contrary, in Mark Jesus declares that God will shorten those
days of tribulation for the sake of his elect, a verse which
Luke significantly omits.   "Until the times of the Gentiles
be fulfilled" suggests a longer interval.

How, then, would Luke account for this delay?   Perhaps he would attribute it to the loving kindness of God, of
which as we have seen Luke is a most gracious exponent.
Two stories frequently noted for their likeness provide here
an interesting contrast.   Mark's incident of the fruitless
fig tree is apparently a parable of speedy destruction for

---

[14] In Mark, Jesus says to the high priest at his trial, "Ye shall
see the Son of man sitting at the right hand of Power and coming
with the clouds of heaven"; in Luke the parallel is, "From henceforth shall the Son of man be seated at the right hand of the
power of God." In Luke's version Jesus does not speak of his
coming, still less does he say his hearers will see it.

the fruitless nation. Luke omits this, but the parable of
the fruitless fig tree which he records has as its chief point
the vinedresser's delay. God intervenes not to shorten the
days, but to give the unrepentant still another chance.
Of course, Luke is not unmindful that the elect have an
interest in hastening the coming of the judgment. They
cry unto God day and night for vengeance. "I say unto
you, that he will avenge them speedily." Perhaps their
prayers will bring the *parousia.* "Nevertheless," adds
Luke with a wistful query, "when the Son of man cometh,
shall he find faith on the earth?" Better God's delay than
the unreadiness of men.

Once at least Luke suggests that the sending of the
Christ and of seasons of refreshing is contingent upon the
repentance of men. It is for this that God is graciously
waiting. The same deity "who in generations gone by
suffered all the nations to walk in their own ways" and
who "overlooked the times of ignorance" "now commandeth
men that they should all everywhere repent." It is in
accord with his past kindness that he should still give men
adequate warning, assurance and evidence. For Luke as
for the Jewish apocalyptists of his time (4 Ezra, Baruch)
and for the Christians of the second century, as indeed for
their pagan contemporary Plutarch (*De sera numinis vin-
dicta*), the delay is no carelessness nor slackness of God
"concerning his promise, as some count slackness." Rather,
as one of them argues, "God is longsuffering to you-ward,
not wishing that any should perish, but that all should come
to repentance." Finally the Christians themselves, for
whom in the earliest days "Thy kingdom come" and
"Maranatha" had been the watchwords, came in the time of
Tertullian actually to pray in sheer altruism for the post-
ponement of the end—*pro mora finis.*

PART IV

THE PURPOSE OF THE AUTHOR

CHAPTER XX

THE OBJECT OF LUKE-ACTS

The purpose of the writer is one of the constituent elements in any writing, though the effect of its influence varies and is not always easily determined. Much depends on the circumstances, and unfortunately the circumstances of the third evangelist are largely veiled from our knowledge. He might have written at a critical time when quite definite motives would have affected him, or for a special audience whose mind he knew and wished to change in one direction or another. More probably his circumstances were somewhat normal and did not lead to a violent or pronounced bias. In that case his motives were closely bound up with the three other factors that we have considered— the form and the sources of his writing and the personality of the writer.

The form of his work is narrative, and narrative carries with it the intention of supplying information. No matter how much Luke differs from the rhetorical historians of Greece and Rome and the pragmatic historians of Israel, his narrative shares with them the common intention of informing the reader concerning the past. Even were it plain that the story was intended to serve also as an argument, in any analysis of the writer's purpose this purely didactic motive would have to be accepted as significant. The Greek historians often describe their object as the entertainment ($\psi v \chi \alpha \gamma \omega \gamma \iota \alpha$) or the improvement of the reader. The Jewish historians increasingly used history for the inculcation of a religious philosophy of his-

299

tory. Josephus seems to have written in layers, so to speak, and his several versions of Jewish history were intended sometimes as an apologetic on behalf of his race for Gentile readers, at other times as a defense of himself and his cause against Jewish critics. But in all these the narrative form carries with it the motive, or at least the result, of conveying knowledge concerning the past. Artist or advocate, the historian is still historian, even if not in our modern sense. Luke's words about his own work and the work of his predecessors, a "narrative of the things fulfilled among us," "a treatise concerning all that Jesus began both to do and to teach," mean this, whatever else they may mean, or whatever other motives he had which he does not express.

Perhaps while speaking of literary form we should include the special type that we call gospel, if as has been suggested such a composition had already acquired certain generic characteristics at the time that Luke wrote. In that case Luke's purpose in writing the gospel conforms to the standard of purpose which Mark and others had set. The fullest expression of aim is in John: "that ye may believe that Jesus is the Christ, the Son of God; and that believing ye may have life in his name." Whether the motive is expressed or not, all the gospels appear to have been intended to create an admiration or something more than admiration for Jesus, their hero. Their ways of glorifying him naturally vary; their intention is similar. Luke aligns himself with his predecessors: "It seemed good to me also."

Luke, however, is indebted to his predecessors for more than form. His material is largely the contribution of others and it also supplies many features which can scarcely be distinguished from his own motives. Both in oral transmission and in writing, the things which Luke records had passed, as we have seen, through a medium of motivated succession. The very form in which each incident came

to him was far from being an objective narrative. It had
been told and retold for a purpose; its features had been
selected or suppressed to suit that purpose. It owed its
whole escape from oblivion in part because it suited a
purpose. Thus both in the gospel and in Acts the material
itself suggested and provided an intention. In so far as
the evangelist's aim agreed with this, his task was easy.
There is reason to believe that generally such agreement
existed. Here again, therefore, the scope or need for special
editorial purpose was slight. It is possible that at times
Luke's material came to him more colorless than he passes
it on, and that he had to revamp it to convey his own
intention. Some have supposed he even completely reversed its original tendency. That is conceivable although
evidence is lacking. There are parallels to such procedure
in writings like the Old Testament Book of Chronicles,
not to mention more recent examples. In the main, however, it is safe to assume that Luke was carrying forward
in his version of events the prevailing motives with which
they had been handed down. His own purposes must
have been minor and secondary. They are to be detected
rarely, if at all, and only in slight hints and details, or
in some elusive tone or spirit that pervades his whole
work.

Yet here again some discounting is necessary if we are to
limit our search to the author's conscious motives. Not all
changes or traits of his writings that he does not owe to
his sources are conscious to him. His personal interests
and characteristics inevitably appear in his work, some of
which we have tried to describe in earlier chapters, but
it is unlikely that many of them were introduced with a
purpose. It does not require special thought or deliberate
effort for any man to retell a story in his own style. He
cannot avoid making it agree more closely with the features of his own character. Modern experience should
warn us from supposing that because Luke's work creates

certain quite individual impressions, especially when compared with the other gospels, therefore those were just
the impressions he was most desirous of creating.

Though we recognize thus fully the difficulty of separat-
ing the author's conscious purpose from the other factors
contributing to his work, so much stress has been laid at
times on his dominating purpose that it is natural to inquire what effects the writing would convey and may have
been intended to convey to its original readers. Unfortunately we cannot tell now what that audience was.
Theophilus, to whom the work is addressed, is not otherwise known to us, and in any case he may have been the
formal rather than the typical recipient of the work. The
general readers may well have been Christians. If so, the
object naturally would be to confirm or correct their
Christian faith. Yet neither intention is obvious. No
passages seem worded as though the writer were removing
religious doubt with iteration of fact and presentation
of new evidence or were anxious to substitute one Christian
viewpoint for another. And, as we have already said, his
theology is something he takes for granted, it is not the
object of his writing.

A variety of motives is consistent both with what we
should expect of such a composition and with the phenomena of the text that we possess. The underlying material
with its quite variegated history carried with it a diversity
of aims which the author could well have made in turn his
own. Different parts of the whole work might suggest
or facilitate different objects, and the author's purpose
might change as his work progressed. His initial impetus
could have been due to a special need that he detected or
to his interest in a special person or community. Like
other authors he may have felt the need of self-expression,
the urge of some inner desire to turn to account the ideas
or materials at hand. In his preface he uses the very sim-

ple phrase, "it seemed good to me," to which he adds a clause which perhaps expresses his reason, that he had "followed" the events for a long time. He wrote because it occurred to him that he was in a good position to write. His skill and ease as a composer are evident to the modern reader; they could scarcely be unknown to himself.

It is not certain that his reference to earlier writers is depreciatory. They may have impelled him to write by their example rather than by their defects. Nor because he refers, as is commonly said, to the accuracy (ἀκριβῶς ἀσφάλειαν), fulness (πᾶσιν, ἄνωθεν) and order (καθεξῆς) of his own work is there any real reason for supposing that he wrote because his predecessors seemed deficient in these respects. Nor is that supposition warranted because he differs in scope, order and details from the surviving gospels. Perhaps his position toward the many before him was as noncommittal as that of Arrian, who in the preface to his *Anabasis of Alexander* cryptically remarks, "If anyone wonders why after so many historians this work of history occurred also to me, when such an one has both read through all their works and perused also this of ours, so let him wonder." Once launched upon his undertaking he selected and presented his material in such form as the material itself suggested. His changes in Mark, for example, even if they are not unconscious, are compatible with such quite minor purposes as the improvement of style, while usually the principal point of Mark's passage remains in Luke undisturbed.

One feature of Luke's whole work that might be conscious intention, quite as well as traditional *motif* or subconscious conviction, is the evidence of divine guidance and control that pervades it. The divine intervention is one of the credentials of the Christian movement. Possibly this thought is already in his mind when he speaks of his subject as "the things *fulfilled* among us." Like others he

was sensitive to the detailed fulfilments of Scripture, but
his references to this trait of Christianity are more general
than in the other evangelists and convey a slightly different
meaning. In Matthew the life of Jesus is "that the Scripture might be fulfilled." The correspondence between prediction and fulfilment calls attention to the fulfilment.
In Luke the Scripture serves a more apologetic motive, being applied to that which is hard to understand, like the
general proposition that Christ must suffer, rather than
to the specific details. There is a necessity about the
course which Luke's story takes, a "must," to use Luke's
own favorite auxiliary, rather than a mere predictive
"shall," a necessity revealed by Old Testament prophecy or
by visions. There is an abundance of reference to the
Scriptures in general: "all things that were written of Jesus
successively by all the prophets," as well as "the law" and
"the psalms." The supernaturalness of this divine purpose
is intensified by the "ignorance" of the actors, "who fulfilled without knowing the voices of the prophets which are
read every sabbath," and the foresight of the predictors,
whose words are "first" fulfilled in Christianity rather than
in their own time or in their own persons, as might have
been expected. It is a promise kept after so long an interval. God has "fulfilled unto us their children the promise that he made to our forefathers."

Luke carries this idea beyond the death of Jesus. The
resurrection also was predicted; its witnesses were chosen
in advance. It is followed by the program of repentance
and forgiveness of sins and, after an interval, by "the
restoration of all things" and the "resurrection both of the
just and unjust" and the "judgment of the living and the
dead." To all these "the prophets testify." Thus the
apostolic age also lies under the guiding hand of God.
Peter and Paul are "chosen" to preach to the Gentiles.
Their conversion is not merely the present visitation but
the long-standing purpose of God, "who maketh these

things known from of old." Both by its analysis of the career of Jesus and by its emphasis upon the conformity to divine schedule of its own story of preaching in Jesus' name, with its divergent outcome of success and failure, the Book of Acts, especially in its speeches, probably reveals an integral part of the author's own philosophy of history which he intended his history to substantiate. The author's verbs are definite and striking. Many are compounds of πρό, "in advance": foreknow, foreordain, foredoom, fore-announce, fore-appoint, foresee. God has set a day, he has elected the witnesses, he has fixed upon the judge, he has appointed the way. Those who believed had already been "ordained to eternal life," the Lord had "opened their heart," or "called" them.

It is in this connection that we are to understand much of the miraculous in Luke and Acts. It is more than mere divine credential for use at the moment. It looks forward to a future destiny. That is its meaning in the birth of John and Jesus, and in the conversion of Paul. That is the meaning of the gift of the Spirit. It is an endowment for future witnessing. Jesus' signs and wonders and mighty works designate him "a man approved of God," and even his resurrection is an assurance that he is appointed the man by whom God will ultimately judge the world in righteousness, while his ascension is an earnest of his return "in like manner."

Of course, detailed and immediate guidance is not excluded. The most striking passage is the account of Paul's baffled and tentative journey that leads him out of Asia Minor into Europe—striking for its negative elements and for its variety of expressions for the guide in so few verses (holy Spirit, Spirit of Jesus, vision, God). We have noted elsewhere the prominence of the Spirit as divine guide, and we should not overlook the complicated sets of visions associated with the twice-told tales of Cornelius and of Ananias of Damascus, or forget the repeated visions to Paul, not merely on the Damascus road, but at Jerusalem, at Troas, at Corinth, at Jerusalem again, and in the storm at sea. A frequent phrase is "The hand (or favor) of the Lord was with him (them)" or the like.

From the favor of the Lord to the favor of the people is for the author no difficult transition. *Vox populi, vox dei;* and for this writer "having favor with all the people" is one of the credentials of his heroes. The wonder, praise and other expressions of the bystanders are notes which underscore the impressive character of the events. The opposition, on the other hand, is described as ill-tempered and ill-mannered, and when overcome by divine intervention, conversion, frustration, or subterfuge it merely enhances the success of the Christian movement. "Surely the wrath of man shall praise Thee." It is not necessary here to remind the reader how many difficulties are surmounted in the course of the narrative, how persecution merely spreads the word or brings down signal judgment on the persecutor. This, too, is the Lord's doing and is marvellous in the readers' eyes.

It may well be supposed that Luke intended especially to show the legitimacy of Christianity from both the Jewish and the Gentile standpoint. For the former we can quote not merely the fulfilments of Scripture, but the conformity of the protagonists' conduct in both volumes to the Jewish law and practices. The circumcision of John, of Jesus, and of Timothy, the attendance at the temple by Jesus' parents and admirers and by the early Christians, and the regular participation in the synagogue services of Jesus, Paul and others, the ritual observances of shearing or shaving which Paul made in connection with vows— these are some of the points which would indicate that Christianity is not anti-Jewish. At the close of Acts Paul is represented as appealing to his early strict Jewish training and observance, his alms to his own nation, and his conformity, even in his Christian faith in a resurrection, to what the prophets predicted and what the twelve tribes earnestly hoped to attain by their devout worship day and night. It was a mistake, James implies, to suppose that Paul "taught all the Jews who are among the Gentiles to forsake Moses, telling them not to circumcise their children, neither to walk after the customs," or that he, Paul himself, did not "walk orderly, keeping the law." That he brought Greeks into the temple and defiled the holy place, as the Jews from Asia assumed, was simply untrue. He had done nothing against the Jewish people and the ancestral law. He had nothing of which to accuse his nation. The difference between them was one in which he had taken no initiative and felt no guilt. It was the Jews who rejected their own salvation at Pisidian Antioch, Corinth, Jerusalem, Rome, and elsewhere, as they had rejected their own Savior at Jerusalem. These historical circumstances as Luke portrays them, constantly attested by the divine sanction, showed the course of Christian development from a Jewish sect to an ecumenical religion.

The close conformity to Old Testament prediction of this transition combined to give the story a good apologetic value in meeting Jewish criticism. How consciously the author was using his material for this end we cannot know. He is at least aware of serious charges of apostasy from Moses,[1] but he is at pains to show that his characters have been good Jews. His work begins with Zacharias and Elisabeth, models of Jewish piety. Joseph of Arimathea, he tells us, was a "good and righteous man." Dorcas of Joppa was "full of good works and almsdeeds which she did." Ananias of Damascus had a good reputation among the Jews. So probably had the Seven, and of course Paul himself. The only reason mentioned anywhere in Acts for Paul's dangerous persistence in going to Jerusalem for his last visit is "to be at Jerusalem the day of Pentecost,"

[1] Acts vi. 11, 13, 14; xxi. 21, 28; xxviii. 17, 22.

"to worship at Jerusalem," and "to bring alms and offer-
ings to my nation." The last references are in one of
his speeches of defense, where of course he insists throughout that his beliefs as well as his conduct are orthodox for
Jews.

Even the Gentiles are represented as being before their
contact with Christianity on good terms with the Jews.
It is Luke who tells us that the centurion at Capernaum
was cordially recommended by the elders of the Jews as
one who "loveth our nation and himself built us a synagogue." Another centurion, Cornelius, "had a good reputation with the whole nation of the Jews," "gave much
alms to the people [i.e., the Jews] and prayed to God
alway." "He was righteous and God-fearing" and "devout" (so was even "a devout soldier that waited on him
continually") and "feared God with all his house." This
last phrase shows that Luke's frequent "God-fearers" as
a term applied to Gentiles who became Christians is not
used as a colorless technical phrase or to explain the transition from paganism, but to invite sympathy and respect
from the Jewish standpoint for these Gentile Christians.

Still more patent is Luke's defense of Christianity from
charges brought against it as breaking Roman law. It
may even be conjectured that his Jewish apologetic had
as its aim the satisfaction of Rome's demand that foreign
religions must be licensed to be permitted. If Judaism
was a *religio licita* and Christianity was not, it was important to show that Christianity was only a legitimate form
of Judaism and could shelter under the Jewish name. Our
knowledge of Roman law on these points and of Rome's
treatment of the Christians in the first century is too uncertain for any assurance. We might quote the complaint,
"These men, being Jews, . . . set forth customs which
it is not lawful for us to receive, or to observe, being
Romans," as indicating that Paul and Silas were criticized

for trying to convert the Roman citizens of the Roman
colony of Philippi to accept a forbidden religion. But
the context acknowledges that Paul and Silas were themselves both Jews and Romans and hence in an entirely
legitimate status. The charge at Thessalonica is quite
different (disturbance of the peace and lèse majesté),
agreeing quite nearly with Luke's formulation of the charge
against Jesus at Jerusalem. This explicit recitation of the
accusations against Jesus in terms which might seem to
incriminate him under the Roman law, "perverting our nation, and forbidding to give tribute to Caesar, and saying
that he himself is Christ a king," in reality only makes
more explicit the acquittal of later Christianity from all
such political guilt. Luke appears to be interested in the
charges, but he is more interested in the verdict. The
Romans find no fault in Jesus or in his followers. Pilate's
acquittal and his desire to release Jesus are repeated in
Luke's gospel even oftener than in the others, though
Luke's general tendency is apparently to avoid such repetitions:

xxiii. 4   I find no fault in this man.

xxiii.14   Ye brought unto me this man, as one that
            perverteth the people; and behold, I, having
            examined him before you, found no fault in
            this man touching those things whereof ye
            accuse him; no, nor yet Herod: for he sent
            him back unto us; and behold, nothing
            worthy of death hath been done by him. I
            will therefore chastise him, and release him.

xxiii.20   And Pilate spake unto them again, desiring to
            release Jesus.

xxiii.22   And he said unto them the third time, Why,
            what evil hath this man done? I have found
            no cause of death in him: I will therefore
            chastise him and release him.

L

In Luke alone we have the testimony of the penitent thief,
"This man hath done nothing amiss," while the words
of the centurion at the cross are turned from a religious
or superstitious confession, "Truly this man was (a) son
of (a) god," to the judicial remark, "Certainly this was
an innocent man." Even Joseph of Arimathea is explicitly characterized by this writer as one who had not
consented to the crucifixion.

The final hearings of Paul are in close resemblance to
those of Jesus. In both cases Herodian prince and Roman
procurator agree in their verdict of "not guilty." The
language is much the same. Luke again formulates the
charges against Paul in intelligible political terms, "a
pestilent fellow, and a mover of insurrections among all
the Jews throughout the world, and a ringleader of the
sect of the Nazarenes, who moreover assayed to profane
the temple"; or earlier at Thessalonica, "These that have
turned the world upside down are come hither also . . .
and these all act contrary to the decrees of Caesar, saying
that there is another king, Jesus." Of course Paul repeatedly denies all charges, and those who examine him dismiss them. Claudius Lysias writes that nothing was laid
to his charge worthy of death or of bonds; Festus declares,
"I found that he had committed nothing worthy of death";
and the verdict is shared by Agrippa after he had heard
Paul: "They spake one to another, saying, 'This man
doeth nothing worthy of death or of bonds.' And Agrippa
said unto Festus, 'This man might have been set at liberty,
if he had not appealed unto Caesar.' "

It is perhaps an evidence of the author's own interest in
using these Roman acquittals as precedents that he makes
his heroes refer to them in their speeches:

> iii.13 Peter to the Jews in Solomon's Porch:
> "Whom [Jesus] ye delivered up, and denied
> before the face of Pilate, when he had
> determined to release him."

xiii.28 Paul to the Jews at Antioch: "And though they [the inhabitants of Jerusalem and their rulers] found no cause of death in him, yet asked they of Pilate that he should be slain."

xxviii.18 Paul to the Jews at Rome: "Who [the Romans], when they had examined me, desired to set me at liberty, because there was no cause of death in me."

The story of Jesus and Paul, whether told by the author or by his characters, certainly needed some explanation if it was to carry the impression of innocence in the sight of Rome. The cross of Jesus and the chain on Paul were unmistakable evidence of Roman legal intervention. If the writer had the slightest reason to be sensitive to the verdict of Romans, if either he himself or his readers were inclined to regard Rome's judgment as significant, especially if the Christian movement were itself at the very time of writing suspect or worse in the eyes of the law, it would be natural to attempt to avert the superficial impression which the experiences of Jesus and Paul might make. Even the repeated statement that the Romans exonerated them was not enough. It must be explained why when innocent they were arrested, why when acquitted they were yet not freed. Several lines of explanation appear in Acts.

There is the constant explanation that the Jews took the initiative. This may be due in part to the Christians' own hostility to the Jews, possibly in part to a desire to "whitewash" the Romans. But it serves an apologetic purpose as well. In the last reported interview of Paul, already referred to more than once, it is plainly set forth: the Jews delivered Paul to the Romans, the Romans wished to release him, the Jews "spake against" his release, Paul consequently appealed to Caesar, but Paul himself had

nothing of which to accuse his nation. Throughout the
Book of Acts is emphasized the recurrent initiative of the
Jews. It is to suit this motive, as well as the precedent
of Jesus both predicted and fulfilled in Mark (not Luke),
that Agabus the prophet makes the prediction, not quite
literally fulfilled in the sequel, that the Jews should bind
Paul and deliver him into the hands of the Gentiles. If
"lawless" in Peter's speech at Pentecost is the technical
rabbinic term for Romans, we have the same combination
there, "him [Jesus] being delivered up through the hand
of men without the law ye [Jews] did kill and crucify."
It is not a federal lawsuit but a Jewish plot—"a plot of the
Jews" at Damascus, "plots of the Jews" at Ephesus, "a
plot laid against him by the Jews" at Corinth, and "a con-
spiracy of Jews who banded together and bound themselves under a curse" at Jerusalem, and a Jewish "plot to
kill him on the way" back from Caesarea. It is not spontaneous Gentile hostility, but persecution or riot provoked
through Jewish instigation at Pisidian Antioch, Iconium,
Lystra, Thessalonica, Beroea, Corinth, and Ephesus. The
Jews showed their malice by going out of their way in
raising trouble, as Paul himself had done when "he per-
secuted the saints . . . even to outside cities." At Lystra
it was Jews of Antioch and Iconium that persuaded the
multitudes and stoned Paul. At Antioch it was Judaizers
who came down from Judaea that troubled the converts,
subverting their souls. "When the Jews of Thessalonica
had knowledge that the word of God was proclaimed of
Paul at Beroea also, they came thither likewise, stirring
up and troubling the multitudes." At Jerusalem the local
Jews (and Jewish Christians) criticized Paul for his work
among the Gentiles, while it was "certain Jews from Asia"
who "saw him in the temple, stirred up all the multitude
and laid hands on him," and then later failed to appear
at Caesarea before Felix to substantiate their false charges.
Paul would be almost pleasantly surprised to hear the lead-

ing Jews in Rome say, "We neither received letters from Judaea concerning thee, nor did any of the brethren come hither and report or speak any harm of thee," though they added, "as concerning this sect, it is known to us that everywhere it is spoken against."

The Roman magistrates recognized that it was a Jewish controversy. The matters were not justiciable, or were so obscure that procurators and proconsuls could not fathom them. So Gallio drove Paul's Jewish accusers from the judgment seat while the procurators Felix and Festus tried to put them off with delays and alternatives much as Pilate had tried to do. The Romans felt they had no competence to settle questions about words and names and Jewish law which they could not understand. Paul came to their attention as a disturber of the peace, but the trouble was never an overt act of Paul, but either the malevolence of Jews, selfish financial considerations or mere misunderstanding, and so Paul suffered, though innocent. If the procurators did not promptly free Paul, it was merely in order "to do a favor to the Jews."

Not only did God protect him in such misfortunes, reviving him when stoned, releasing him when imprisoned, encouraging him when in danger, but the officials themselves were kind to him. The proconsul in Cyprus and the *primus* in Malta welcomed him, the Asiarchs in Ephesus became his friends and sheltered him, Roman soldiers repeatedly defended him from violence, treated him with kindness and respect, and stood in awe of his Roman citizenship when they discovered it. Even Jewish leaders were not all hostile to the movement, according to Luke. "A great company of the priests were obedient to the faith" and there were "certain of the sect of the Pharisees who believed." Of the Sanhedrin, Joseph of Arimathea, as we have noticed above, had not assented to the death of Jesus, and Gamaliel urged the policy of *laissez-faire,* and later some of its members who were "scribes of the Pharisees' part" defended Paul. It was quite conceivable to them that "an angel or spirit had spoken to him" and that Christianity was "the plan and work of God."

Christianity, the author asserts, is no innovation, no sacrilege. This is true even from the standpoint of Greek religion. The Christian reader triumphantly applauds when a municipal official like the town clerk at Ephesus reads the riot act: "These men are neither sacrilegious nor blasphemers of our goddess. If therefore Demetrius and the craftsmen that are with him have a matter against any man, the courts are open and there are proconsuls: let them accuse one another. But if ye seek anything about other matters, it shall be settled in the regular assembly."

For the biographer such details more than cancel the superficial impression that Paul suffered as a malefactor. His journey to Rome is recorded not as the commitment of a criminal, but as the appeal to the supreme court of an innocent man enjoying from Roman officials all the privileges of citizenship. The book closes with Paul living two whole years in his own quarters, accessible to his friends and preaching his gospel boldly and without hindrance. What was the sequel after two years we are not there told and we cannot learn elsewhere. But it is not likely that the author deliberately suppressed a final sentence, whether "not guilty" or "guilty." Perhaps the outcome was too well known to need telling; perhaps it was to be told in another volume; perhaps it was not known, or at least not yet known when the book or its principal source was written. Perhaps the outcome was indecisive—the case quashed, a natural death, or a jail delivery and a new régime. This we do not know, but since the author has made already a good case for Paul in the eyes of the Roman law one of his objects is already accomplished, whatever the sequel.

It has been sometimes thought and recently argued again in quite definite form that Acts was written as a brief for use in Paul's trial. Theophilus, we are told, must have been a Roman of rank and influence, in the highest society; Streeter suggests T. Flavius Clemens, a Roman aristocrat with Christian connections, very close to the emperor. The abrupt ending must imply that Paul is still on trial, and so we are brought to Rome in the days of Nero and to the eloquent and faithful Luke standing by his loving master and writing out of loyalty and anxiety this first Christian *apologia*. That Theophilus was a Roman of rank is unfortunately not proved by his name or by his title "most excellent." Even if we should accept the explicit reference to the *stratopedarch* or "prefect of the prætorian guard" which some MSS. read in Acts xxviii. 16, we cannot be sure that Paul's personal fate was still the author's concern when he wrote, or that he himself was so intimately associated with this critical moment in Paul's life. We shall have to admit, on the other hand, that several of the words in the address to Theophilus do permit, and when compared with the latter part of Acts positively possess, the connotation of *apologia,* and that the close of Acts itself is filled with that mood. It is quite probable that Luke's avowed purpose so far as his preface expresses it, "that thou mightest know the certainty concerning the things wherein thou wast instructed," is to correct misinformation about Christianity [2] rather than, as is so often supposed, to confirm the historical basis of Theophilus's religious faith. He or any unsympathetic reader is expected to agree with Gallio or Festus that "the Way" is not "a matter of wrong or of wicked villainy," that "there was no charge of such evil things as I had supposed," or with zealots for the law who find "that there is no truth in the things whereof they have been instructed concerning Paul," or who can say of him, "We find no evil in this man."

[2] See my article, "The Purpose Expressed in Luke's Preface," in *The Expositor,* June, 1921.

If one objects that the narrative method is not an effective form of defense and that the work as a whole contains
much material that cannot be construed as a mere series of
legal precedents applicable in the courts of Rome, one
must admit that on such matters of fitness opinions differ.
De gustibus non disputandum. To judge from the speeches
of defense which Luke himself invents or records, he
favored the narrative method more than we should.   In
Acts Peter defends himself by telling the story of Jesus;
Stephen, by a sketch of Old Testament history; Paul, by
relating his own conversion.   For such a writer narrative
was evidently counted a useful method, if not for a legal
brief, at least for persuading hostile or suspicious audiences
of the innocence of one's religion.

In conclusion we may say that, while Luke's motives
may have been varied and are now not easy to trace
throughout his work by the manifest influence which they
exerted, nevertheless some aims can here and there be conjectured.   When these are added to similar effects in prior
stages of the material, the element of motive must account
for much of the ultimate character of Luke-Acts.   We may
find our own purposes more or less satisfactorily fulfilled in
the evangelist's records, but our aims are not always like
his.   We may choose our own "golden texts" for these volumes—compendiums of theology or history—like the angels'
triad formula for Jesus, "a Savior, Christ, the Lord," and
the geographical scheme of Acts "in Jerusalem and in all
Judaea and Samaria, and unto the uttermost part of the
earth," but I suspect the author's motive is more faithfully
represented by such sentences as:

> God sent the word unto the children of Israel, preach-
> ing good tidings of peace by Jesus Christ.
> God visited the Gentiles, to take out of them a people
> for his name.
> Neither against the law of the Jews, nor against the
> temple, nor against Caesar, have I sinned at all.

CHAPTER XXI

PLAN AND SCOPE OF HIS TASK

The preceding chapter has discussed the effect which Luke wished to produce upon his readers. In the two following chapters I desire to summarize the design which he entertained with respect to his materials. The conscious purpose of a writer includes these two quite different phases or points of approach. In reflecting on his task he thinks partly of his audience and of the conviction or impression that he wishes to convey, and partly of his stuff and of the business of collecting, criticizing and presenting it. His attitude to his task in the latter sense is what now concerns us. What, we may ask, was the scope of his undertaking as he conceived it? What ideal of workmanship did he entertain? What responsibility did he feel for the matter and manner of his composition? What plan had he for the arrangement of his writings?

The answers to these questions have perhaps already been partly hinted. Their further consideration, even though some repetition is involved, is certainly relevant to our full visualization of this literary undertaking. As frequently, many suggestions must be offered that are merely probable, while others can be quite definitely rejected as improbable. Particularly certain modern standards of workmanship can be rejected for Luke. This merely negative distinction by correcting our excessive modernizing of the picture should be of value. To some extent his purpose can be compared with the intention that his contemporaries had in approaching their tasks. But in the main our answers must be inferences directly from his writings.

It is fascinating to try to transport ourselves into the soul of this ancient writer, to imagine ourselves with him in his *scriptorium* as he sat down to pen (or to dictate?) his influential volumes. Here was a man of parts, a gentleman and a scholar, launching upon the most ambitious literary undertaking of the early church. No wonder that the scribes and decorators who pored over the pages of the New Testament in later centuries often quite sympathetically portrayed the several evangelists at work. Also to modern men of books and writing, the author of this famous two-volume "Outline of Christianity" is a congenial figure. We know something of how books are made today and we would fain penetrate behind our ignorance of that ancient work in its making. It is of course only too easy to idealize this canonized Luke, or on the other hand to make him and his outlook too nearly in our own image. Already in the middle ages men painted him in their own landscape and in their own dress, as they did the other saints, and they supplied details about his writing which pious imagination thought inevitable. As the calf-faced figure of Ezekiel's cherubim or even the holy Spirit was represented hovering above him while he sat writing at his scroll, so a few scribes, finding the wording of his preface, "it seemed good to me to write," too plain and uninspired, followed Luke's own language in "the first ecumenical decree" of Acts and added a reference to his inspiration by substituting "it seemed good to me and the holy Spirit to write."

For safer clues to the authorial consciousness one would naturally turn to the expressions of the Greek and Roman historians. They have, first and last, a good deal to say about purpose and method in history, about the collection and criticism of materials, and kindred questions. Their actual practice sometimes throws further light on the conception or execution of their task. But the technique of classical historiography as thus disclosed can hardly be assumed as the standard of our evangelist. Among themselves the classical historians do not agree, nor do their words always correspond to their practice. They criticize one another for carelessness and invariably claim for themselves accuracy and concern for truth. They practice the tricks of the most florid rhetoric or decry the rhetorical excess of their colleagues. They express indifference to details, names, divine portents or antiquarian research, or they query the veracity of what others tell, whether because inherently incredible, biased in purpose, or merely carelessly compiled at second hand. The classical historians represent, therefore, no constant standard, and Luke cannot be understood by our appropriating to him a chance remark of Polybius or Tacitus. Of the tradition of their discussion—for even the technique of history seems to have had a tradition of quite theoretical discussion—Luke was probably wholly ignorant, even though at times he naturally conforms to it or falls within the wide range of the variation of ancient practice.

Contemporary custom illustrates, however, the ways of Luke's authorship in at least one respect, in that it is usually nearer to him than are our modern ways. It suggests what would seem to the modern viewpoint some limitations. We may doubt, for example, whether even the most theoretical men of the Hellenistic age ever arrived at our present standards of history, and in this respect Luke would be no exception. The ideals of verification or research that we count so important his contemporaries largely ignored. One of the most competent of modern students has written this warning: "We must always bear in mind that the ancients were even further from a genuine science of history than from a genuine science of nature. . . . The method of historical research which we regard as an imperative duty is scarcely a century old. Isolated individuals may have risen to its level before that in both ancient and modern times; but the general rule remains." [1] In the fiction of speeches, in indifference to dates and to other minor data, in objectivity and in many other traits besides the ones we have mentioned, Luke belongs to the ancient rather than to the modern standards.

As for the general scope of his work, Luke's limitations are often quite obvious to the modern reader. His omissions as they seem to us are a matter of frequent, if ungrateful, comment. How much he does not tell us that we should like to know! Though he gives us a birth story of Jesus such as Mark does not supply, and the summary of Jesus' childhood, he has but one concrete incident to record for "about thirty years" which preceded Jesus' ministry, and for the outcome of his history he tells us nothing of the later years of Peter or even of the result of Paul's trial. How many outward vicissitudes of Paul's earlier life the book of Acts omits is suggested by his own list of adventures in 2 Cor. xi. 23-27. The record in Acts up to this point (viz., about Acts xx. 1) mentions a stoning at Lystra and a beating at Philippi, and hints at other plots and dangers escaped. Otherwise it is silent on all "those things which are without," as well as on what Paul calls "that which presseth upon me daily, anxiety for all the churches," so fully revealed in his correspondence.

The reasons for these omissions are not always evident. Certainly they are not always part of the author's conscious purpose. Probably all four of the main factors that we have been considering help explain them. By exclusion as well as by inclusion those factors had determining effects. The sources certainly by their gaps limited the possibility of completeness. The conventions of the time did not encourage chronological paraphernalia for simple

[1] U. von Wilamowitz-Moellendorff, *Greek Historical Writing,* 1908, pp. 4 f.

history. The author may have lacked interest as well as knowledge in reference to the older outgrown controversies revealed to us by Paul's epistles. Psychological analysis, sociological development, and theological definition were as foreign to Luke's viewpoint as their modern names suggest. Further, his definite purpose may have led him consciously to exclude certain classes of details. He was under no compulsion to tell all that he knew of every sort of fact. His method of selection might not agree with our own, nor indeed with every ancient writer, but selection was doubtless necessary. We may compare and contrast with his procedure the expressed method of the historian Herodian when he declares that, since he is covering so much more ground than the mere reign of Commodus, he will not give as the more detailed historians do "the stations in the journey and the things said by him in each city and the signs which seemed to appear many times by divine providence and each locality and the formations of troops and the number of soldiers who fell on each side in the battles." [2] The story of Acts is not a campaign of war and its selection of details is not Herodian's. It gives only three times the total of Christian accessions. But it is not sparing of speeches, or of place names and stations of travel, or of the providential signs and interventions.

The omission caused by the abrupt end of Acts is the most conspicuous perhaps in the whole work. Some alternative explanations have already been mentioned, and they show how any one of several factors may explain an omission. Perhaps the author's information here came to an end. Then his source, whether his own information or the writings of others, must be credited with this abrupt silence. Perhaps he had no interest in going further because the outcome was indecisive, or was too well known to his readers. The Christian Fathers suggested quaint no-

[2] Herodian ii. 15, 6.

tions of their own, attributing this method of closing (and
indeed everything else that Scripture writers did) to conscious intention. According to the Canon of Muratori,
the author limited himself in Acts to things that were done
in his own presence—doubtless the "we" suggested this—
and so omits the passion of Peter, and Paul's journey from
Rome to Spain. Chrysostom, accepting the usual later
view that Luke was with Paul to the end, declares that the
sequel would have been no different in kind from what
has already been told, "bonds, tortures, fightings, imprison-
ments, plots, slanders, daily deaths," and implies that it
was an intentional, even a conventional, secular custom thus
to stop in mid course. He says:

> And why then did Luke not relate everything, seeing
> he was with Paul to the end? We may answer that
> what is here written was sufficient for those who would
> pay heed. . . . It was no object with the sacred
> writers to be writers of books: in fact, there are many
> things which they have delivered by unwritten tradi-
> tion. . . .
> At this point the historian stops his account and
> leaves the reader thirsting so that thereafter he guesses
> for himself. This also non-Christian writers (οἱ ἔξω)
> do. For to know everything makes one sluggish and
> dull.[3]

It would be possible to suggest ancient parallels to
Luke's closing before the death of his hero. Second Maccabees ends with the success of Judas, not with his defeat
and death. "Philostratus leaves his readers in uncertainty
as to the fate of Apollonius of Tyana on the ground that
his alleged source, the diary of Damis, broke off before
it could be known whether Apollonius died or was translated."[4] Luke himself omits a direct statement of the death

---

[3] *Homilies on Acts,* 1 and 55 (Migne, *Patrologia Græca,* Vol.
LX, coll. 15, 382.

[4] B. W. Bacon, *American Journal of Theology,* xxii, 1918, p. 15.

of John the Baptist, though he certainly knew it, and all reference to the end of Peter and of James the brother of Jesus. His first volume stops, whichever text we follow, with the barest substitute for a definitive closing scene or ascension such as is given in the beginning of Acts. Other histories are divided into books sometimes just before rather than just after a principal figure is disposed of. A modern editor would probably in each case divide between the four books of Samuel-Kings rather differently than was done, so that the lament of David over Saul (2 Samuel i), the death of David (1 Kings ii) and the assumption of Elijah (2 Kings ii) would stand at the close of a volume rather than near the beginning.

These parallels inevitably raise again to our minds the attractive possibility that after all Luke's plan did not terminate with the end of Acts, but that a third volume to Theophilus was to have carried Paul to his expected (Acts xx. 25) death, and continued with a still further installment of Christian history. It is not impossible that such a book was written and lost. It is more like the fate of more recent undertakings if it was planned but not finished.[5] Yet there is really no evidence for either form of the hypothesis, and we may be again arguing from our own tastes rather than from the author's own conception of his task. According to the latter, biographical completeness was perhaps no desideratum, and the arrival of Paul at Rome and his successful and unhindered preaching there may have seemed to the author not only to fulfill the scope of Jesus'

[5] The chief advocate of this hypothesis piously concludes: "How much foolish fable mongering even in the next century, how much laborious minute effort and how much strife of scholars should we have been spared, had it pleased God to permit the first Greek among the writers of Christian faith to attain the completion of his irreplaceable work!" (Zahn, *Kommentar zum Neuen Testament*, Vol. V, p. 862.) See his article, "Das dritte Buch des Lukas," in *Neue kirchliche Zeitschrift*, xxviii, 1917, pp. 373-395.

commission (Acts i. 8), but to make a true, triumphant and effective conclusion to his own narrative.

Certain quite physical limitations of ancient book-making distinguish Luke from the modern writer. It should be recalled that he wrote on rolls of papyrus and that his work, which was from the first intended to be multiplied for publication, would be copied on rolls. These rolls as used in his time were probably limited in size. Such limitation required that long works should be divided into two or more volumes and that each division should be within the standard length. Of course, different lengths may have been customary at different times and places, and a roll of standard length could contain varying amounts of text in accordance with the way in which the writing was done.[6] But it is probably no accident that the several volumes of ancient writers so often nearly agree in length. Luke and Acts are almost exactly the same size; so indeed is Matthew. This fact suggests at least one quite external measure that may have determined the scope of these three longest books in the New Testament.

With respect to the smaller units or paragraphs, the ancients conversely had more freedom than we do. In modern prose some paragraph division is always required and no sentence can be left ambiguous in its connection. The ancients, however, were under no such compulsion. Paragraphs did not have to be marked and a sentence that connected or divided two complete sections created no embarrassment, until modern editors attempted to assign its paragraph relation. While much of Luke's work easily falls into separate scenes as paragraphs, his summaries or

---

[6] The size of the letters, and the number of lines to the column, would vary in rolls of the same length. The width of the column would not always be just the standard commercial στίχος. Of course, a Greek translation would occupy more space than a Semitic original. This explains why the longer Old Testament volumes of history were divided in halves in the Septuagint.

other connective sentences remind us that all our elaborate analyses into sections and sub-sections were not conscious to him and are not quite in accord with the manner of one who thinks and writes continuously.

So, too, the modern efforts to detect a subtle plan in the author's arrangement are doubtless misplaced. The triplications which a recent discoverer finds in the gospel, and the six panels which Turner created for a chronological analysis of Acts,[7] are a discovery that would surprise no one more than the author of these volumes. Such plan as he had was largely suggested by the material available to him, and all he needed to do was to set it down in a simple and natural manner. In the Book of Acts, for example, it was possible for him to follow an outline which, beside being roughly chronological, at the same time could represent several forms of transition. There was a transfer from Jerusalem and Judaea to the Gentile world, from Aramaic-speaking disciples to the Gentile converts, from Christianity under the law to Christianity without law, from the apostleship of Peter to the work of Paul. It was possible for him to suggest certain intermediate stages, to note anticipations of the final results or to emphasize the turning-points in the history. But all this was largely inherent in the nature of his material and, instead of crediting the author with subtle schematization or a far-fetched plan such as delights the modern commentator who invents it, we may accept him as one who had the skill to recognize some of the significance of the development which he records.

"The conventions of every art," writes a modern student of the gospels, "are determined by what is mechanically possible." [8] We may add that they are restricted by what

[7] G. Mackinlay, *Recent Discoveries in St. Luke's Writings,* 1921; C. H. Turner in Hastings' *Dictionary of the Bible,* Vol. I, p. 421; B. W. Bacon in *Harvard Theological Review,* xiv, 1921, pp. 137 ff.

[8] Streeter, *The Four Gospels,* p. 156.

M

is, even if possible, mechanically difficult. Now ancient
writing of books lacked many of the conveniences of modern times. Especially the citation of other books would be
far more difficult in antiquity. A passage cannot be found
so easily in a roll as in a codex or book with leaves. So
without small numbered units like chapter and verse,
in addition to clearly named and numbered volumes (not
to mention the invaluable help of a concordance), it would
be less easy to find a second time a passage that had been
once discovered and only imperfectly noted. Even if
accuracy were desired, quotations from Scripture could
not be exact. Frequently quotation from memory would
be inevitable. That some early Christians had collections
of proof-texts we have already suggested. A work of
Melito in the second century was apparently just such a
convenient book of selections. Whether Luke had such a
book we do not know, but we do know that he did not
always copy out his quotations directly and verify them
by turning up the passage in the Old Testament text. Perhaps he had not access to what would have been even so
large a library as complete manuscripts of "the law of
Moses and the prophets and the psalms." For subdivisions
he had not of course our modern chapters and verses. Even
the minor prophets were for him less distinguished than
for us, since they were one roll, "the book of the prophets,"
rather than Amos, Habakkuk, etc.[9] It is only the first
(for us the first and second) psalm to which he refers by
number.[10]

Books other than Scripture Luke would have been still

[9] Acts. vii. 42; xiii. 40; *cf.* xv. 15, and contrast the reference to
Joel (ii. 16, though this name also ought very likely to be omitted),
and more frequently to Isaiah.

[10] Acts xiii. 33. This is probably the earliest known citation of
the kind. It does not show that all the psalms in the Psalter
were already numbered. See J. H. Ropes in *Beginnings of
Christianity,* Vol. III, pp. 263-5, where the reading is also
discussed.

less likely to use or refer to. In matters of chronology, geography or contemporary government there would be available no public library, nor even a small collection of handbooks. His immediate sources would be his main authority, and he would be unlikely to attempt to verify them. To be sure, he may have deliberately omitted Mark's reference to David as receiving shewbread "in the days of Abiathar," because the narrative in Samuel actually places this incident under Ahimelech his father. But we may doubt whether he verified allusions to Quirinius, Lysanias, Pilate, Festus and Roman officials elsewhere by reference to works of general or local history. He had neither the facilities nor the desire to make the laborious calculations such as would verify synchronism or detect anachronism. I think he did not use the works of Josephus if he knew them, and the same may be said for the letters of Paul.

In other respects Luke's simple narrative differs from the modern methods of composition. It was not to make his book readable and popular that Luke avoided footnotes and bibliographical references. These devices, which are demanded in some modern forms of composition, were in his day unused or quite unknown. In place of footnotes that are merely asides, parentheses could be used. Luke has a strange way of introducing into a speech what we should put in a footnote, or at least in a parenthesis. Thus the death of Judas Iscariot is related as part of Peter's speech on the choice of his successor; the crime of Barabbas is described in a relative clause attached to the cry for his release. We should not know from him that the risen Jesus appeared to Peter on Easter Day or to Paul on his first visit to Jerusalem, that Herod Antipas beheaded John the Baptist, or that Paul brought alms to Jerusalem on his last visit, were it not for references to these facts included in the words of the actors.[11]

[11] Cross references as well as other explanations occur in the speeches. There is for example the following series: John the

These are not the only abrupt or brief references. We
may compare the passing statement that Herod Agrippa
"killed James the brother of John with the sword." Aris-
tarchus is introduced three times—as a Thessalonian, a
Macedonian, or both. Likewise there is given a second
reference to Agabus as though he had never been mentioned
before, instead of such cross reference as we find in the
adjacent allusion to "Philip the evangelist, who was one
of the Seven," or in that to "Judas who was called Iscari-
otes, being of the number of the Twelve." Proper names
are given or omitted where we should expect the opposite
course. Details are brought in too soon or too late. Explanations are repeated or are strangely lacking. These
like the many minor obscurities, discrepancies and gram-
matical inconsistencies [12] may be due to the way in which
the author edits his sources. Not every modern writer

Baptist predicts the baptism with the Spirit and that prediction
is recalled by the risen Jesus when he promises the Spirit. The
prediction of Jesus (and of Joel) is recalled by Peter at Pentecost.
The prediction of Jesus and the experience at Pentecost ("at the
beginning") is recalled by Peter in reporting the conversion of
Cornelius. Subsequently Peter again at Jerusalem harks back
to the conversion of Cornelius ("from early days") and James
at the same council refers both to that event, "how first God did
visit the Gentiles," and to the words of the prophets, "known
from of old." The decrees drawn up on that occasion are rehearsed
to Paul (as though he had never heard them?) when the latter
makes his last visit to Jerusalem. As C. W. Emmet says (*Beginnings of Christianity*, Vol. II, p. 277 *note*): "A modern writer
would have simply added a footnote, 'See above for the arrangement already made with respect to Gentiles.'" Besides all this,
Paul twice independently quotes the Baptist's prediction of the
coming of Jesus (at Antioch of Pisidia and Ephesus).

[12] Harnack, *Acts of the Apostles*, Chap. VI, gives a full list
for the second volume. The instances are perhaps not so numerous in the gospel, but we can see how those which occur there
are often due to the way in which the sources were used. Thus
omissions from Mark leave unexplained the mention of the Baptist
as dead and of the stone at the tomb. For other examples see
Style and Literary Method, pp. 101 ff.

would be more careful or consistent. Had Luke been a little more meticulous in such matters he doubtless would have avoided these things.

We can have no doubt that he used books that dealt with his own subjects—what we call his written sources—though we may despair of identifying all these older documents. But his method of using them differed from our modern method in many ways. We have already touched on these problems in earlier chapters. If several sources dealt with the same event, selection and combination might seem a necessity, but would be a laborious task, *onerosa collatio*, as Pliny calls it. The "one-source theory" has therefore *a priori* much in its favor for many ancient texts. Much easier than an attempt to follow in one's reading and composition three or four different rolls, turning from one to another without losing one's place in any, would be the method of following one source at a time. There is evidence that in the case of Mark this is just what Luke mostly did. For long stretches he either followed him continuously or abandoned him altogether, perhaps for another source. It is quite likely that in the gospel material, except for the continuous and extensive chain of events at the passion, the units were so small and the events so simple that parallel accounts if recognized as such could be more easily ignored by Luke. In secular history or in such attempted continuous history as Acts represents, parallel accounts, if they existed, would have to be regarded; but it is probable that in Acts the author was more troubled with gaps than with overlappings in his sources. For these gaps his favorite filler is the summary, as it is less obviously in the life of Jesus: "Jesus increased in wisdom and stature," "they remained there many days," "the word of God increased and multiplied," "and it came to pass thereafter that he went about through cities and villages, preaching and bringing the good tidings of the kingdom." These summaries and a frequent accompanying confusion in the context are quite rightly said to mark the panels of his work, but they are the seams in his piecing together of his sources rather than parts of his own plan. The intervening sections are, if not original with him, doubtless copied from his source *en bloc*.

As has been already said, a Hellenistic writer was wont to paraphrase his source into his own style, but no matter how closely he followed either text or subject matter he would not mention his source or indicate what he was doing. Where the divergences of another account came to his attention or were mentioned in his source, he might refer to the difference, though often quite indefinitely. There if anywhere the main source was mentioned by name.[13] Luke has no such citations of his authors, and not even in his preface does he say who his predecessors were or explain that he used or even had read their writings.

It has been observed that writers who began with the more complicated comparison and revision of sources often succumbed to the temptation to easier methods as they continued. Zeal at the beginning of the task droops as time goes on, and fewer sources are used and they are less worked over. So Livy and Diodorus Siculus used more sources in their first books and worked them in together more than in later books where verbatim use is found.[14] A somewhat similar phenomenon appears in Matthew's treatment of Mark's order: at first he selects and re-arranges Mark's material quite freely, but before long he goes back and picks up in order the passages that he has omitted, and then all the remainder of Mark from chapter six to the end he transcribes, with some omissions and additions, but without a single alteration of sequence. I am not sure that Luke illustrates this principle at all, but evidently we would do well to think of his sources

---

[13] *Cf.* Tacitus *Ann.* xiii. 20: *nos, consensum auctorum secuturi, si qui diversa prodiderint, sub nominibus ipsorum trademus.*

[14] A. von Gutschmid, *Kleine Schriften*, 1889, Vol. I, p. 22.

as decreasing rather than as increasing in number, for example, in Acts. Again, if the Biblical style of his first two chapters really is artificial and imitative, may it not be in part the remitting of the author's effort that makes the Biblical idiom less conspicuous and more sporadic in the later parts of the gospel and in Acts?

In using these sources the ancient writer evidently had no fear of being charged with plagiarism. He did not anticipate that his readers would ever compare his work with its predecessors. I think it is quite wrong to suppose that Luke or even John in writing assumed in the readers a knowledge of earlier gospels. The new work was in each case intended to stand by itself. It is we moderns who make the comparison, and only too often we suppose that the author anticipated such comparison, as though John were correcting or supplementing Mark and the other Synoptics, or that Luke were producing a different version to serve for a different community alongside of established and well-known predecessors like Mark and Q.[15] Each wrote a work to serve its own purpose independently and without regard to others. At most an ancient author could hope to be a supplanter.

There is one custom of ancient historical writing with

[15] One of the defects of Streeter's valuable work is, I think, his impression that the several gospels and their variant forms of text acquired so early a kind of ecclesiastical authority and acquired it each in a special locality. For the view expressed above I may claim the suffrage of Professor Harnack in *The Origin of the New Testament*, 1925, pp. 72 f. *note. Cf.* Easton, *The Gospel according to St. Luke*, 1926, p. ix: "He presupposed no acquaintance with Palestinian conditions on the part of his readers and he knew that they would interpret much that he had to tell in terms of their own surroundings; above all, he knew that they would interpret much of his story in terms of their own developed theology,—and he was content that it should be so. And, in addition, he meant his Gospel to be interpreted on its own merits, not after comparison or harmonizing with other documents."

which I think quite likely Luke's work agrees. I mean
the custom of carrying forward the work of one's predecessors. Such historians combined in their labors two quite
different tasks. For the older history they depended on
the works of others, the later history they themselves
were the first to compose, or at least they first compiled
and edited the older rough materials. We have already
referred to this difference in the first and last part of
Polybius; the same difference applies to the Latin historians. Sometimes, to be sure, the new historian began
just at the point where the older one broke off. At other
times he went back further over the last part of the work
of his predecessors or possibly over the whole of it before
adding the newer contributions which he could make out of
his own research and knowledge of his times, and occasionally from his own participation in the recent events.
Herodian after referring to the fact that the life of Marcus
Aurelius had been recorded by many wise men continues:
"But I have recorded what after the death of Marcus
through the course of my own whole life I have seen and
heard—in some of them I have participated by actual
experience while employed in services of the emperor or
the state." Yet when next he refers to his own knowledge
of the acts of the emperors that he is recording he makes
plain that for Severus, an earlier one of them, he has full
if not unprejudiced predecessors.[16] Josephus in telling
the story of the Jewish War reviews at length on the basis
of other men's works the period that preceded. Hardy
has shown that Tacitus, though his aim is to continue the
work of Pliny from the accession of Domitian, really goes
further back, to the beginning of the Flavian period, just
as Aufidius Bassus the continuator of Livy began not at

---

[16] Herodian i. 2, 5; ii. 15, 6. It would not be unparalleled if
after this assertion of personal knowledge Herodian relied on
previous historians throughout. See E. Baaz, *De Herodiani
fontibus et auctoritate,* 1909.

9 B. C., where Livy left off, but apparently at the beginning of Augustus's principate.[17] It is altogether probable that Luke's work begins as a revision of his predecessors, but continues after his sources cease and he himself for the first time sets the narrative in writing. In that case the last part of Acts with its less Semitic style and its emphasis upon the innocence of Paul before the bar of Roman law, not to mention the possibly autobiographic "we," may reveal the free hand of the final editor writing without alien influence in a style and with a purpose congenial to himself.

The methods of procedure for these two ways of writing history would naturally be somewhat different. The composition of older history would be the easier, as according to ancient standards it required no new search for materials, but the comparison and rewriting of the work of others. Pliny the Younger discusses the contrast between the two subjects of history—*vetera et scripta aliis* or *intacta et nova*. In the case of the former the labor is one of collation; all research has been done.[18] Certainly neither Luke nor his non-Christian contemporaries would expect to make fresh research into the remoter past when one or more written accounts already lay before them. Antiquarianism was not unknown in Hellenistic history, but it was not much practiced.[19] Indeed, the opportunities for fresh research and verification would be rather limited.

Aside from the comparison of variant versions, the succeeding editor would be limited to conjecture and inference, and in some cases he could pick up floating oral tradition if he cared to bother with it. The use of inference and imaginative elaboration is almost inevitable

---

[17] E. G. Hardy, *Studies in Roman History,* First Series, 1906, pp. 323 f.

[18] *Epp.* v. 8 *parata inquisitio, sed onerosa collatio.*

[19] J. B. Bury, *The Ancient Greek Historians,* 1909, pp. 188 ff. It was called πολυπραγμοσύνη or *curiositas.*

M*

when older sources are freely paraphrased, as we have seen
by some examples (Chapter XIII), but it lacks authority
and is often dangerous, as modern historians know to
their sorrow. If for example Luke assumed that the darkness at the crucifixion was an eclipse of the sun, he was
probably mistaken; but he was not the last reader of
Mark's narrative of the passion who did not stop to calculate that Jesus was killed near the passover, and that
the passover occurred near the full moon when eclipses of
the sun are impossible. Early enemies of Christianity
offering naturalistic explanations fell into this trap only
to be exposed with ridicule by the delighted believers.
A modern historian with modern sources of verification
might possibly have taken the trouble to find out whether
contemporary astronomical records mentioned such an event.
If he did not, he would be as likely as ancient writers to
jump to conclusions without thinking of all that the story
itself implied.

Indeed, Luke's narratives often suggest just such failure
to think the situation through. This natural and almost
inevitable defect only the most rigid self-criticism can
avoid. Imagination rarely is aware of minor inconsistencies, and we need not be surprised if a writer like Luke
sometimes made such slips, though we may distrust our own
power of detecting them. Often we are only sure that he
has failed to make his stories perfectly clear *to us*. With
some diffidence we may suggest that the situation at Pentecost is not quite consistent as it is told. If the apostles
spoke in foreign tongues, how did the polyglot audience
communicate with each other? Paul's discussion in 1 Corinthians of *glossolalia* adds to our suspicion that Luke has
understood the "tongues" of the early disciples a little too
literally as foreign languages. Of course some obscurity
may be intentional, or at least suitable to complex occasions. Mob scenes at Nazareth, Corinth and Ephesus are
not explained as logical performances. The author leaves

us in doubt whether Stephen's death was an execution or a lynching, a doubt which the victim himself may well have shared. We have spoken of Luke's condemnation of wealth and covetousness. Is it unfair to suggest that he has so taken this for granted that he has not quite made clear why the rich men in two parables in Luke and why Ananias and Sapphira and Simon Magus are all so severely punished? It is obvious, too, that our author delights to recount how the disciples were protected by divine intervention on one hand, or by the natural workings of Roman justice on the other. At Philippi these are so combined, or the circumstances are so imperfectly reproduced, that either the earthquake or the *lex Porcia* was unnecessary for the vindication and release of Paul and Silas.

This scene, with the triumphant Christian prisoners demanding to have the magistrates eat humble pie, suggests with many like details what to the taste of later generations might seem a kind of naïveté on Luke's part. Indeed, no modern critic has more unerringly picked out this feature of the Book of Acts than did Chrysostom, though in his *Homilies* he is of course concerned either to deny it in each case or to justify it. He says that Paul pressed the matter of his innocence at Philippi for the sake of protecting the converts whom he was leaving there. On a similar occasion, when Peter escapes from prison and the disappointed Herod has the soldiers who guarded him killed, Chrysostom justifying the ways of God incidentally defends the historian. If the latter lays stress on the eminence of Cornelius, of the Ethiopian eunuch and other Christian inquirers, the commentator warns against our supposing that Luke glories in their dignity. When Peter asked Sapphira whether she and Ananias sold the land for so much, it was not to trap her into lying, but because he wished to save her.

Chrysostom found such things distasteful without some edifying explanation. We should regard Luke as more than human if he had not indulged in a certain partisanship, satisfaction or pride in those turns of his tale that marked the triumph of Christianity. And even Chrysostom did not hesitate to accept those proofs of the miraculous, or divine "economy" as he calls it, as when the cured lame men carry their beds or leap, which Luke had inserted for just that purpose, or to admire how Luke makes the unbelievers wax eloquent in defense of Christianity.

CHAPTER XXII

APPROACH TO HIS SUBJECT

We may certainly set down as one of the attitudes of Luke to his subject a personal sympathy and interest. Harnack refers to him as "an enthusiast for Christ." His own Christianity is undisguised. Without this even the most extraordinary literary talents would never have enabled him to write the gospel that Renan called the most beautiful book in the world. Dispassionate writing of history is hardly to be expected of any ancient author. No more than Tacitus himself did Luke fulfill the Roman's description of the ideal historian as *sine ira et studio*. We have suggested that particularly in Acts he wrote with the intention of defending Christianity. This would affect his attitude to his subject as well as his attitude toward his hearers (or readers, as we now call them).

For example, Luke believed in miracles. Few in his day did not believe in such miracles as he did. As another evangelist says, they would not believe except they saw signs and wonders. Luke accepted the stories as they came in his sources because as a Christian he believed they were true. If his change in Mark's first reference to Jairus' daughter represented her as dying or even dead (like Matthew's "just deceased") rather than as *in extremis,* and if he later explains the common synoptic statement, "they laughed him to scorn," by adding, "knowing that she was dead," the exaggeration is really slight. The other resuscitations at Nain, at Joppa and at Troas are told with similar restraint. If Luke is his own source **for**

the "we" passages, we shall have to admit that the miracles
are not due solely to others.   He himself and probably
the actors themselves, like Paul, were not slow to accept
supernatural explanations.   Throughout his work the influence of the holy Spirit is portrayed as more than natural.
The other miraculous elements are numerous and include
the prediction of the future, the visitation of angels, visions,
immediate divine intervention protecting the heroes or pun-
ishing the villains, and of course many cures or exorcisms.
It is commonly said that as a physician Luke was especially
interested in these "cases" and accurate in describing their
diagnosis and therapy.   But even were the author's medical
training assured, we may suppose that it would not produce
in his day a more skeptical or scientific caution about
miracles than if he had been a layman.

In this and in our whole attitude to the miraculous we
must free ourselves from the presuppositions of our own
times.   Our very definition of miracle as the violation of
known natural laws was impossible for an age in which the
concept of natural law was hardly scientifically postulated.
Ancient writers would neither affirm nor deny the abstract
possibility of the miraculous under these terms.   Reason,
experience or common sense might make a man incredulous
when such tales were told.   Like the writers of *paradoxa*
or *incredibilia* they might entertain their readers by narrating extravagances, or by suggesting aetiological bases of
myths; like Herodian the historian they might regard it
superfluous to substantiate their histories by listing the
omens and miracles which accompanied the events recorded,
or they might regard as superstition or imposture the claims
of wonder workers and prophets in religions to which they
did not belong.   But every sincere believer—and as such
our author must be regarded—would assume for his own
religion the probability of "mighty works and signs and
wonders" and would take for granted their evidential
value.

This is hardly the place to carry further the discussion of this most controversial subject. It is important, however, to recall here above everywhere else that Luke was a child of his time. The excesses of credulity and extravagant miracle-mongering that prevailed among some of his contemporaries he did not share, but he accepted without skepticism and recorded in good faith as proofs the mighty works, signs and wonders,[1] and the supernatural events or explanations that tradition, written record, experience or inference provided him. He would not share the modern prejudice against them of the natural scientist, nor appreciate the demand for well-sifted and first-hand evidence of the scientific historian.

It is this good faith of the writer which explains the complete fitness of the miraculous element in the narrative. It is not for the author extraneous intercalation, or special pleading that he has forcibly introduced, but is an inherent and natural part of his work. The naïve motifs which must often have showed more crassly in the older tradition have become less obvious as what were once primarily wonder-tales have become incorporated in sober tradition. It is often noted how unobtrusive and congenial to its setting is the virgin-birth motif in Luke. It is barely mentioned. It has none of the earmarks of Gentile polytheism or of ascetic aversion to the marriage relation. I do not mean to deny that here and often elsewhere the miraculous element is left hanging. But this is due more to the author's brevity and his failure, already noted, to work his description out to the last detail than to any injection of deliberate

---

[1] The Greek words are δυνάμεις and σημεῖα καὶ τέρατα a standing combination, and in Acts i. 3 the word τεκμήρια. Translators do well to drop the adjective "infallible" in the last case and to avoid altogether the word "miracle," which though etymologically suitable carries anachronistic modern connotations into the ancient text. Paul (2 Cor. xii. 12) like Luke (Acts ii. 22) uses the first three words all together and apparently claims to have wrought them himself.

fiction into the alien context of actual history.   Arising
spontaneously and growing in a favorable environment, the
miraculous element enjoys a kind of "protective coloration"
which has enabled the apologists quite justly to claim for
its context a remarkable degree of verisimilitude.

It would be possible to illustrate extensively this twofold
naturalness of the miracles of Luke, their complete accordance with the kind of thing that his contemporaries believed,
and their firm rooting within the fabric of historical tradition as both he and other writers record it.   The student
of the secular historians of his age will recognize readily
his place among them in this regard.   We have already frequently compared him with Josephus.   An illuminating
parallel is the latter's account of the death of Herod
Agrippa I.[2]   Both writers agree that the king was miracu-
lously punished because he permitted his adulators to call
him a god.   They describe the occasion of the blasphemy
and the character of the disease.   They differ in many
details, but their differences in what we may call the supernatural elements or the religious interpretation are no
greater than their differences in matters which belong by
right to the realm of sober history.   Luke describes the
occasion as a conference with the Sidonians and Tyrians,
Josephus as a festival in honor of Caesar (Claudius).
Both locate the event at Caesarea, both mention the gorge-
ous apparel, and both cite the blasphemous adulation, though
in one case it is said to have been called forth by his words,
and in the other by his appearance.   Luke evidently regards the punishment as divine retribution for Herod's
offenses against Christianity,—*mors persecutoris,* and he
describes his disease in terms which in the Greek or Hellenistic Jewish world had since Herodotus become the regular fate of the impious or blasphemer, being eaten with
worms.   Josephus, on the other hand, who describes his

[2] *Ant.* xix. 8, 2 §§ 343-351 compared with Acts xii. 20-23.

disease as abdominal pain, supplies the plainly supernatural element of portent and fulfilled prophecy. The king saw an owl sitting on a rope above his head and died five days after, in accordance with the prediction made years before by a German fellow prisoner, who had not only successfully foretold Agrippa's rise to power when he once before saw an owl, but had warned him, "Remember when you see this bird again you will have but five days to live." [3] Josephus just like Luke, therefore, interweaves edifying interpretation, superstition, tradition and accurate political history without any obvious incongruity. Only the modern critical reader would attempt to disentangle the elements.

It would be difficult to find a scene more full of the viewpoint of antiquity than this at Malta:

> The barbarians showed us no common kindness: for they kindled a fire and received us all because of the present rain, and because of the cold. But when Paul had gathered a bundle of sticks and laid them on the fire, a viper came out by reason of the heat and fastened on his hand. And when the barbarians saw the creature hanging from his hand, they said one to another, Probably this man is a murderer, whom, though he hath escaped from the sea, yet Justice hath not suffered to live. Howbeit he shook off the creature into the fire, and took no harm. But they expected that he would have swollen, or fallen down dead suddenly: but when they were long in expectation and beheld nothing amiss come to him, they changed their minds and said that he was a god.

The ancient Greek writer shows his own background in every line. Not only is the language idiomatic,[4] but if

---

[3] *Ant.* xviii. 6, 7 § 200. On the five days see p. 250 *note*.

[4] Note the two genitives absolute and the two cases of litotes. The latter are characteristic not only in themselves (see above, pp. 120 f.), but in their connections. For example, οὐχ ὁ τυχών is often used with just the verb παρέχω as here; τὰς τυχούσας φιλανθρωπίας occurs in Dion. Hal. xiv. *frag.* 6, 1.

one may say so, the ideas are idiomatic too. The natives, whatever their non-Hellenic tongue, are barbarians. Their alien speech foreboded to any Greek unfriendly treatment, especially to shipwrecked strangers. Their kindness is therefore merely one of the series of providential escapes of this charmed hero, not only from Jewish plots and the soldiers' plan to kill the prisoners as a last resort, but from the *inhospita Syrtis,* from shipwreck, from the savages, dreaded as pillagers of shipwrecks, and from serpent bite. The ideas he attributes to these barbarians are not, however, alien to the author himself. Any ancient would believe, were he "Greek, Jew, barbarian, Scythian," that an escaped criminal could not evade his nemesis, though perhaps only a Greek or Roman would speak of Justice personified. The fear of serpents and the typical test of religion that it can tread upon the adder and serpent, handle snakes and defy poison—this, too, is well known to every religion; and all these points could be illustrated profusely from ancient literature. To the examples collected in the commentaries others could be added.

The fickleness of the savages the author himself has illustrated in the reverse direction at Lystra. Unfortunately for Paul, on that occasion his deity was the first, not the last, guess of the changing Lycaonians. Luke also says that Jesus promised the Seventy "the authority to tread upon serpents and scorpions." As the treachery of American savages to every white man was assumed by our ancestors, so the inherent hostility of barbarians to Greeks was assumed quite as casually by Diodorus Siculus, when in describing the gold mines of Egypt he says that the prisoners were guarded by barbarians who could not be bribed through conversation or any friendly entreaty.[5] In similar manner it was taken for granted by Andocides when he speaks of his own escape from shipwreck near

<hr/>

[5] Diod. Sic. iii. 12, 3 φιλανθρώπου τινὸς ἐντεύξεως; *cf.* φιλανθρωπίαν in Acts.

"a barbarian country where many who had come ashore after suffering the most cruel tortures had been killed."[6] To a contemporary like Dion of Prusa such unexpected hospitality would suggest by contrast the well-advertised barbarity of those ghouls who lived on dangerous leeward coasts battening on the loot of helpless human driftwood, or even like Nauplius luring mariners to their ruin.[7] The murderer bitten in the hand would suggest to many readers the widespread idea of poetic justice that the member which sins is the part to receive punishment.

If the fear of barbarians is distinctively Hellenic, the same cannot be said of the superstitions about serpents. Here, for example, are just two passages from part of the literature of unadulterated Judaism, the Tosefta:

> They say concerning R. Chanina ben Dosa [*c.* 80 A. D.] that he was standing and praying and a serpent bit him and he made no pause. His disciples went and found it dead on the mouth of its hole (*Berachoth* iii. 20).
>
> R. Simeon ben Shatah [*c.* 80 B. C.] said, "May I not see the consolation if I once did not see a man with a sword in his hand running after his fellow; the latter thereupon went into a deserted building followed by the other; I entered after him and found the one slain and a sword in the hand of the murderer dripping blood. . . . But he who knows the thoughts, he exacts vengeance from the guilty; for the murderer did not stir from that place before a serpent bit him so that he died" (*Sanhedrin* viii. 3).

Of course, the evangelist does not spoil his story by inquiring just what language these Maltese spoke. In

---

[6] *De mysteriis* 138. Andocides accused of sacrilege is arguing that if he had been guilty the gods would not have saved him from the sea. Lucian regards escape from shipwreck as a kind of *deus ex machina* (*Merc. Cond.* 1; *Herm.* 86). Contrast our "He that is born to be hanged shall never be drowned."

[7] Dio Chrys. vii (*The Hunter*) 31 f., p. 105 Morellus.

spite of his evident interest in language, that would be a too modern *curiositas*. Nor does he stop to ask how the visitors knew their inner thoughts even if they spoke them aloud (in Punic?), nor whether then or later any poisonous serpents were to be found on that island. It was not even necessary for him to assure the reader that actual *mirabilia* occurred. Here and elsewhere in Luke-Acts the positive flavor of the antique and the supernatural is as conspicuous as is the absence of the modern rationalism.

That Luke thought of himself as writing literature has already been suggested. Matthew's gospel was from the first well adapted to ecclesiastical use, whether for public reading or catechetical instruction. Luke's work bears more of the evidence of a literary self-consciousness. It is true that his materials lent themselves no more easily to the ancient demands of literary revision than to modern demands for historical arrangement, and Luke's literary ambition remained satisfied with rather superficial results. But that he made the effort is one evidence of his conception of his task. Even his language is book language. Professor Moffatt has said: "Luke's style is a written style rather than a spoken style. The distinction between these two styles in literature is hard to find, but it is real. In Matthew's version of the sayings of Jesus, for example, we frequently hear the true teacher, who writes to have his hearers catch and recollect what he is saying; there are places where this tendency comes out distinctly in the arrangement and the style. Whereas Luke writes to be read; the bookman appears as well as the reporter or the catechist." [8]

The preface of Luke's gospel, which is also I believe the general preface to his whole work, is one of these marks of literature. Its mere presence in this work is significant, while its contents come as near as we get to

[8] *The Expositor*, July, 1922, p. 1.

an expression of the author's own self-consciousness. As a recent writer says, it shows "that personal note, which indicates a certain freedom and plasticity of thought on the part of an individual writer in relation to the traditional material, which achieves its finest result in the Fourth Gospel." [9] It is important, therefore, to know just how much that preface claims. Many too modern and too definite claims have been read into it. Some of them are exactly opposite to the limitations that I have proposed as restricting Luke's own plan for the undertaking. I may then be permitted once again to suggest what I believe is the meaning and, further than that, the connotation of several of its expressions.[10]

In the first place, it is an idea congenial to modern scholars that Luke here is representing himself as a man of research. He has "traced the course of events." But whatever the meanings possible here to $\pi\alpha\rho\eta\kappa\delta\lambda\delta\upsilon\theta\eta\kappa\acute{o}\tau\iota$, "research," "investigation" or "inquiry" is not a probable one. What I have said above or shall add presently is against the theory that Luke's work entailed much that might be called *Erforschung*.

In the second place, against my somewhat negative judgment about the arrangement of Luke's episodes the word "in order" will be cited as voicing Luke's assertion of chronological order. But $\kappa\alpha\theta\epsilon\xi\tilde{\eta}s$, while it refers to arrangement, does not imply concordance between the order of events and the order of their narration. It means rather a narrative orderly and continuous in itself. I think the first part of the word implies that events will be told one at a time "in succession," and the use of the simple word

[9] R. H. Strachan, *The Fourth Evangelist: Dramatist or Historian?* 1925, p. 68.

[10] See my earlier discussions cited above, p. 9 *note*, with the endorsement of J. H. Ropes, *Journal of Theological Studies*, xxv, 1923-4, pp. 67 ff., and the dissenting criticism of A. T. Robertson, *Expository Times*, xxxv, 1924, pp. 319 ff.

ἑξῆς in prefaces and elsewhere merely means that the narrative is to follow at once, like our "hereinafter" or "as follows."

In the third place, the two words "accurately" and "certainty" will be appealed to as implying a claim of veracity that only the most modern kind of research and verification, testing of authorities, acquaintance with the origin of tradition, and the like, could justify. With all their modern sound the words are not quite so broad. I do not mean to imply that the author is less confident of himself than the well-documented modern writer. His grounds for assurance are different and he is not setting this over against scientific skepticism, but rather against ignorance or prejudice. ἀκριβῶς implies exact detail. Hence it may be used with verbs of inquiry (usually (mis)translated "diligently") and with verbs of knowing or telling (usually translated "accurately"). Its opposite is not falsehood but meagerness of circumstantial information. Whether we take it with "followed" or "write," in this sentence it claims explicitness of information more than tested certitude. ἀσφάλεια for this author in this place has to do, I believe, with meeting unfavorable judgments of Christianity. It appeals to "the facts." Its opposite is rumor and prejudice.

That Luke aimed at and claimed completeness is proved for many by his words " all things" and "from the first." When further "traced the course" is applied to research, and "taken in hand" is understood as a criticism of his predecessors, Luke's ambition for scholarly thoroughness seems even more articulate. The infancy narratives are regarded as the first fulfilment of his claim to superior inclusiveness. The real meaning of this clause seems to me quite different. What the author wishes to say is that he personally for the later part of his narrative has been in intimate touch with or even an eyewitness of all things. Thus παρηκολουθηκότι claims something better than research, namely, first-hand or contemporary knowledge, and ἄνωθεν carries back not from the ministry of John to Luke's birth stories, but from the time of writing back over a considerable period of the author's own association with the movement that he is describing. The sequel rather than the prelude to the gospel constitutes Luke's own special contribution. It distinguishes his work from the earlier records based on the tradition of "those who had been from the first eyewitnesses and ministers of the word." As already suggested, Luke like other writers of his time is·the *continuator* of older evangelists, adding to his revision of their records later chapters out of his own more recent and intimate experience. It is to this phase of his work that I believe the general preface refers, as we should expect it to do.

While, therefore, no translation can fully represent the precise connotations of the original, we shall be on the safe side if we read into Luke's preface no more than the following English paraphrase, with all its imitated obscurity and verbal irregularity, implies.

> WHEREAS many have ventured to recompose a narrative about the matters consummated among us, as those who had been at the start witnesses and helpers in the mission handed down to us, I also, gentle Theophilus, decided to write for you seriatim since I had been now for a long time back in immediate touch with everything circumstantially, in order that you may gather the correctness as regards the accounts that you have been given to understand.

Only in the preface does the composer step in front of the curtain. Except in this quite usual way the author nowhere explicitly discloses his self-consciousness. He does not, like many other writers, repeatedly obtrude on the reader his own labeled judgments or feelings. His character no doubt affects his objective record in many ways, but his own personality, even if included in the "we" of Acts, is not conspicuous. That he intended to be anonymous is unlikely. His name was probably known to Theophilus and to others of his early readers. But characteristic of the objectivity of his work is the fact that in the earliest known canon of the New Testament Marcion could include Luke's gospel without any author's name. To do so required no mutilation of the text.[11] Perhaps already the facts of authorship were unknown. Of course the heretical Marcion was later soundly berated for this omission of "full title and due declaration of authorship" by Tertullian and other exponents of a fourfold gospel canon with the orthodox traditions of authorship. Doubtless it will be again accounted heresy if I propose in the next chapter that for us these works are still practically anonymous. Yet we really lose little by the obscurity into which first the writer's own reticence and then the vicissitudes of time have cast him. Especially as literature the work of this unidentified author can be appreciated. A modern novelist says:

> Literature wants not to be signed. Creation comes from the depths—the mystic will tell you, from God. The signature, the name, belongs to the surface personality, and pertains to the world of information; it is a ticket, not the spirit of life. While the author wrote, he forgot his name; while we read him, we forget both his name and our own. When we have

[11] The lack of signature in the preface and in the body of the work, and the absence of any identifying tag or pasted label led to the addition in orthodox circles of the sub-title, "According to Luke," and in the text of Acts to such sporadic scribal readings as "Lucius of Cyrene who remains until now" (xiii. 1, *Prophetiæ ex omnibus libris collectæ; cf.* 1 Cor. xv. 6), or "Luke and those with me" (xx. 13 for "we," Ephrem Syrus) "and Luke of Cyrene" (added at xii. 25 to "John whose surname was Mark" by Ephrem Syrus). The simple "we" also creeps in at xi. 28 (D, Aug., etc.) and xvi. 8 (Iren.).

finished reading we begin to ask questions. . . . Then a book changes its nature, and we can ask ourselves questions about it such as, "What is the author's name?" "Where did he live?" "Was he married?" "Which was his favorite flower?" We are no longer reading the book, we are studying it and making it subserve our desire for information.[12]

Our study of Luke's conception of his task may seem to have resolved itself into a prolonged list of limitations. We have spoken of his omissions and abrupt conclusion, his inconcinnity in the separate episodes and his obscurity of general plan, the absence of certain kinds of details and of footnotes and citation of sources, his want of research and verification, his reliance on conjecture and imagination and his unscientific credulity and naïveté. These are mentioned, however, with no desire to find fault with his accomplishment, but rather to defend him from unfair criticism. Our verdict on his work depends on the standard that we propose to judge him by, and it would be unfair to judge him by modern standards for history or literature. His success must be estimated in the light of his own conception of success. Even so it is possible to be enthusiastic over the author's courage in attempting such a task, and over his signal success in fulfilling it. The admiration which Harnack expresses for the achievement involved in the composition of Acts we can share, even if we do not agree in all details.[13] Essential for any judgment of Luke's work is the perspective that compares him with his own time rather than our own. Both praise and blame may

[12] E. M. Forster, "Anonymity, an Inquiry," in *The Atlantic Monthly*, cxxxvi, 1925, pp. 593 ff.

[13] See the introduction to his *Acts of the Apostles*. Fortunately for the present writer it is unnecessary here to attempt to rival that masterly appreciation of Harnack's or to venture criticisms of some of his positions. See also J. Weiss, *Ueber die Absicht und den literarischen Charakter der Apostelgeschichte*, 1897.

fail of this safeguard. In the matter of accuracy, for example, we ought not to judge Luke more severely than we judge the Greek historians. His own interest was not merely plain history, but edification.

There are some sound words on this point by Percy Gardner:

> The Gospels are works of perfect candour, good sense, and truth. Yet they are, to use a Jewish expression, "Haggadah," or edifying religious narrative rather than history proper. . . . In saying this, we of course imply no kind of blame on the Evangelists. They worked according to the best lights of their time. It is not their fault that the way of regarding history has since changed. It is treating them most unfairly if we judge them by the canons of our own time, or expect them to conform to notions as to the writing of history which in their day were nowhere accepted.[14]

Of Acts Deissmann says:

> Being a pious record for popular reading [it] does not speak of the first church in the dry tone that might be adopted by an ecclesiastical bureaucracy publishing its tables of statistics, but with the pious earnestness which we are accustomed to associate with missionary gatherings. The writer of the first missionary history becomes enthusiastic, and makes his readers enthusiastic, over the church of the saints, which is viewed of course only in a transfigured light. But the historic lines are unmistakable.[15]

This question of the historical value of Luke's work, and the other question raised just before it of the author's identity, must receive some further consideration in the next and concluding chapter.

[14] *Exploratio Evangelica*, 1899, p. 166. *Cf.* V. O. Janssen, *Der literarische Charakter des Lukas-Evangeliums*, 1917.

[15] *St. Paul, a Study in Social and Religious History*, 1912, p. 117.

CHAPTER XXIII

AUTHORSHIP AND ACCURACY

We have now completed the task which we set before ourselves of examining four principal factors in the making of Luke-Acts. We have inquired in turn into the material which was used in that construction (Chapters III-VIII), into the prevailing ways of thought, expression and composition with which the author complied (Chapters IX-XV), into the author's individuality as it affected his work (Chapters XVI-XIX) and finally into the purpose of writing (Chapters XX-XXII). We have followed the method of analysis, but our object has been to study what historically considered was a synthesis. In other words, we have been pursuing a reversed process. We have taken the finished product to discover how it was produced instead of beginning with the factors and arriving at the product. We differ from the original author as the student differs from the manufacturer. The manufacturer makes and assembles the component parts and builds his machine; the student or inquisitive boy takes the machine apart in order that he may see how it was put together.

The analysis thus enables us to imagine the original process. Beginning with the author's personality, some of whose traits and interests we have been able provisionally to recover from his writing, we can place him in the milieu of antiquity, the characteristics of which and differences from our own in literary methods, in language and in outlook on life we endeavor to learn from a wider study of its varied writings. To these two factors we add a third—

the author's objective or purposes. This also in part reveals itself from his writings, and we begin to see a real, concrete situation behind the personal pronoun and the simple and definite historic tense, "it seemed good to me also to write." Finally we must add to this picture not merely papyrus and ink, but the whole supply of available information, oral and written, reliable or unreliable, which comprised the materials out of which Luke-Acts was made. To omit this last is to describe of a factory its "head" and its "hands" and its machines, to supply it with motive power, but to overlook the raw materials. The sources of Luke-Acts carry us behind the author and behind his own time to his predecessors, and to the things that were successively done and said, seen and heard, reported and written by them. Luke's preface seems to acknowledge these prior processes, and they are perhaps more mystically expressed by another evangelist: "That which was from the beginning, that which we have heard, that which we have seen with our eyes, that which we beheld, and our hands handled . . . that which we have seen and heard, declare we unto you also."

If we have enabled our reader to understand these four factors so that he can again reconstruct from them the two familiar books that they once produced, we have completed our task. No further summary is needed, since our purpose has been description and not argument. Yet it is scarcely possible to leave this subject without some reference to certain questions which even the casual reader of Luke-Acts only with difficulty can keep out of his mind. They are also the questions which scholars have so insistently raised and debated. They are roughly two: first, "When, where and by whom were these volumes composed?" and second, "Is their story historically true?" It is fitting that the relation of our preceding analysis to these questions should be discussed, even though the discussion must be brief and the conclusions largely negative.

It may seem strange that a volume like this, which purports to consider the origin of a writing, should postpone to such a secondary place the specific questions of date, provenience and author. Such indeed is not the usual procedure. The common method is to begin with these questions and to lay emphasis on their solution. Yet it is doubtful whether for an understanding of the writing these problems are really so significant as those that we have more fully considered. The general analysis that we have made holds true, however these questions are answered, and it tells us really more about the book's genesis. It is far more important to know the personality of the author than his name, to know his purpose in writing than his profession, to know the technique of his age than the exact year, to know his position in the transmission of history than his habitat. Even Paul's very personal letters are not much illumined by our knowledge of such questions —that he was named Saul or Paul, that he was a tentmaker, that he wrote in the sixth decade of the first century and that he was born in Tarsus and wrote from Ephesus or Corinth. Much less significant are such personalia in the writers of history. The biographical emphasis is often made prominent in the study of literature, but every sound scholar and teacher must know how really subordinate such things are and how often they either obscure the more significant facts derived from literature itself or put them in a wrong perspective. It is no doubt interesting to trace the references to the English men of letters in parish registers of births and deaths. It would be attractive if we could discover just what Shakespeare did for a living or who were the personal friends of the author of Beowulf. It would be convenient if we could date with certainty all the Apostolic Fathers. Yet even if we could know that the Epistle to Diognetus was written precisely in a given year of the second century, or if we found out that Dionysius of Halicarnassus did not write the history attributed to him, but a man of a different name and place, the contents, value and interpretation of those works would still remain about the same.

Curiosity about literary men is natural and innocent in later generations, but the supply of information does not always meet the demand—witness the scanty lives of the Greek tragedians which later grammarians composed and treasured. In Christian circles also such interest was not awanting, at least from the middle or end of the second century onward. As concerning other writings of the New Testament, the church came to have its tradition also concerning the Third Gospel and Acts. Typical statements and perhaps the earliest ones extant are in the Canon of Muratori, usually dated near 175 A. D. The following translation, though it does not reflect the obscurity of the original Latin text, represents with some conjectures its main tenor.

> The third book of the Gospel, according to Luke, Luke that physician, who after the ascension of Christ, when Paul had taken him with him as companion of his journey, composed in his own name on the basis of report. However, he did not himself see the Lord in the flesh and therefore as he could "trace the course of events" he set them down. So also he began his story with the birth of John.
>
> But the Acts of all the apostles were written in one volume. Luke compiled for "most excellent Theophilus" what things were done in detail in his presence, as he plainly shows by omitting both the death of Peter and also the departure of Paul from the city, when he departed for Spain.

Now the characteristic of these and other early Christian statements is that they are so obviously dependent on the internal evidence of the writings in question, and on combination and inference from the New Testament text. It is difficult to decide whether any external evidence was really available, or whether the appeal they made to the internal evidence for confirmation was not merely a repetition of the data from which the conjecture had in the first place been drawn. The following are some of the internal data they used:

1. Both volumes are addressed to Theophilus and are written by the same author.

2. In the Acts the pronoun "we" appears in places, and this is understood to imply that the author was an eye-witness of what is related in those parts of Acts (and some adjacent ones), including several journeys of Paul and the two years at Rome with which the volume closes.

3. As a corollary to this understanding of the "we" passages it was consistently inferred that when the author does not use "we" in Acts and in Luke he was not an eyewitness of what is related. There is no "we" in the narratives of the gospel, and the preface which circulated with that book appears to distinguish the author and his contemporaries ("us") from those who "had been from the first eyewitnesses and ministers of the word." Identification of the author with an apostle was, in spite of all tendency in that direction, in these writings perforce excluded as *ex hypothesi* impossible.

4. According to 2 Timothy (iv. 11), which the ancients believed a genuine letter of Paul from prison in Rome, at one time (the time of writing) Luke was the only Christian companion with Paul. Other passages which they assigned to Paul's Roman imprisonment mention the presence of Luke and call him "the beloved physician" or Paul's "fellow-worker." [1]

There are other data or passages which the Fathers used occasionally for further details, in which, however, the tradition was never quite uniform. In Luke's preface Theophilus was understood allegorically in accord with etymology as every "lover of God," "informed" (κατηχήθης)

[1] Col. iv. 14; Philemon 24.

was interpreted as "indoctrinated," πεπληροφορημένων as "fully believed," παρηκολουθηκότι πᾶσιν, as "having been a follower of all the apostles"—all of which explanations were probably wrong. Emphasis was laid on the opening sentences of each of the gospel narratives, and the personal differences of the evangelists were deduced therefrom with the help (not always consonant) of the four faces of the living creatures in Ezekiel. Luke was variously identified with the Lucius of Acts xiii. 1, the Lucius of Romans xvi. 21, the companion of Cleopas in Luke xxiv. 13, the unnamed brother of 2 Corinthians viii. 18 "whose praise is in the gospel," etc. Other theories arose and became fixed about his birthplace, place of missionary work, etc.[2]

But for our main questions, Who? When? Where? the principal data above listed probably supplied a sufficient basis for answer. If the author was with Paul throughout his imprisonment, Luke alone fulfilled the requirement, and the abrupt ending of Acts after two years at Rome suggested precisely that as the time and place of writing. Such a process of inference could have been the origin of the uniform tradition. Of course, if any real knowledge as to who wrote these books was still extant when this tradition crystallized, that was either used if it agreed or ignored. It is possible that in the second century it was really known that Luke had been the author, but probably the tradition would have come into existence quite as early and as definitely if it were not known, on the basis above suggested. Unfortunately we cannot now determine which mode of origination was the actual one. There is much about the tradition and the circumstances of its origin to lead us to suspect that it was derived solely from the New Testament text. But the uniform testimony of early Christian writers to the belief in Luke's authorship is no less compatible with some genuine tradition. It cannot be

[2] On the tradition of authorship see *Beginnings of Christianity*, Vol. II, pp. 209-250.

said that the data left us in their writings suit one origin much better than the other.

If, disregarding this tradition as being of doubtful value, we wish to form an independent guess about the origin of these books, we are driven to the same internal evidence that the Fathers used for our answer. If we follow the same method we shall come to the same conclusion as the early Christians did, and then we shall argue as they did on the same basis. We cannot now, however, feel quite confident about the links in their chain. It is not so clear that the references to Luke, and especially that which says, "Only Luke is with me," were written by Paul, and written at Rome, and written in the two years with which Acts closes. Nor are we quite certain what to do with the "we" passages. In fact, no theory about them is without grave difficulties. They may be derived by the evangelist from a diary source, but even if they are due to his own presence at the events it does not follow either that they represent the full extent of his participation, or that the close of the book marks the time and the place of its composition.

This is not the appropriate occasion for a full discussion of the tradition of Lucan authorship. The arguments on both sides may be read elsewhere. The debate seems to turn largely on two questions: (1) whether the literary phenomena of the "we" passages imply that the author of the whole work actually accompanied Paul; (2) whether the treatment of Paul's visits to Jerusalem, especially that of Acts xv with its decrees, is too unhistorical to have emanated from one who later was Paul's associate. The former seems to be at present an insoluble riddle; the latter carries us into realms where our information is quite insufficient for secure judgment. It is easy to sympathize with both points of view with regard to it and also with an unwillingness to leave the matter undecided. So to leave it may, however, be the wisest course.

N

To these very negative positions others equally negative but more assured should be added.

1. An argument against the derivation of the "we" passages from a written source in the first person is often drawn from the presence of the evangelist's own distinctive vocabulary throughout these sections. It is difficult to know why the author in using a source would retain the "we" and yet otherwise assimilate its style to his own. To this it may be replied that when the author does use a source he does more or less assimilate its style, as his treatment of Mark shows. That in the "we" passages he should have chosen to retain the "we" is admittedly peculiar. But the abrupt and unexplained "we" is as peculiar and unexplained under any alternative hypothesis. It need not be supposed that if for some unknown reason he chose to retain this striking characteristic of his source he would be less likely to follow, in other regards, his usual custom of paraphrasing his source so as to transform it into his own style.

2. An argument in favor of authorship by Luke the physician has been in recent years developed from the alleged medical interest displayed by the author and from his use of words which occur also in the medical writers. But, as we have already more than once argued, it is doubtful whether his interest in disease and healing exceeds that of his fellow evangelists or other contemporaries who were not doctors, while the words that he shares with the medical writers are found too widely in other kinds of Greek literature for us to suppose that they point to any professional vocabulary.

3. Against the author's personal association with Paul might be urged the fact that in his preface he seems to distinguish himself from eyewitnesses and ministers of the word. This difficulty was not felt by the Patristic writers, since they separated the gospel from Acts and applied the preface to the former only, and were willing to admit that

Luke was not an eyewitness of Jesus. In fact the preface was, as we have said, often understood to state elsewhere that the author had "accompanied all" the apostles. If, however, we apply the preface to Acts also, as we probably should do, the author's apparent denial of direct association would imply that in Acts also he was not an eyewitness and minister of the word. To this argument it may be replied that the preface does not plainly exclude the author from all participation in "the things fulfilled among us." The eyewitnesses and ministers are "from the first" and may mean merely the original oral sources for the earlier part of the work. Indeed, it is possible and perhaps probable that for a considerable later section of his narrative the author, so far from denying eyewitnessship, is positively claiming to "have been in immediate contact with everything since a good while ago." This interpretation of the words κἀμοὶ παρηκολουθηκότι ἄνωθεν πᾶσιν has the advantage not only of being a more accurate rendering of the Greek than many others, but of making less abrupt, and one may say less inexplicable, the insertion of the pronoun "we" in later passages.

While, therefore, modern scholarship cannot unanimously accept or reject the tradition of Luke's authorship, we do well to realize just what the alternatives are as regards the making of Luke-Acts. If we reject the tradition, or if we simply leave the matter open, we have then an anonymous early Christian writing in two books of great importance and interest, whose genesis can be partly traced in the manner that we have attempted to indicate in this volume. If we accept the attribution to Luke, to Epaphras,[3] or to some other named companion of Paul, we have really added very little to our knowledge of its origin. The same four factors enter in. We know very little more about the author than we did before. If he was a physician, the fact

[3] *Cf.* J. A. Blaisdell in *The Harvard Theological Review*, xiii, 1920, pp. 136 ff.

is interesting, but perhaps has very little bearing on either
the style or viewpoint of his writing. That his name was
Luke makes no difference to the traits of character, the
viewpoint, the literary methods of the time or the editorial
history of the work and of its sources. We might in this
case feel a little more confidence that in limited sections
of his work the author is using his own knowledge rather
than oral and written sources. Even here, however, the
alternative makes no very significant difference, since the
"we" passages, and indeed the rest of the outline of Paul's
itinerant labors, must be assumed for other reasons to be
based on detailed and reliable knowledge, though the author
may have acquired it at second hand. Our curiosity is not
satisfied by such well-justified suspension of judgment,
and many persons will prefer ill-founded dogmatic certainty to what they like to condemn as "negative" criticism. Honesty requires that we should not claim more than
we know. We do well also to realize how little our uncertainty about the author's identity interferes with our
effort to make clear and complete the story which we have
aimed to recover. The main lines in the picture are quite
independent of any assurance about such less important
matters as the author's name or occupation, or even about
his quondam association with Paul.

As to the exact date and place of writing the evidence is
equally indefinite, within certain obvious quite wide limits.
I refrain from the thankless process of confuting arguments
which purport to answer these questions more precisely.

The accuracy of Luke-Acts is another question that might
seem to demand rather earlier and more extensive consideration. "Is it true?" is not only the child's spontaneous query, but the question of many an adult reader of
Scripture. The debate of the critics has had this question at its center, and it is because the Lucan authorship
was regarded on both sides as assuring the accuracy of

the writing that this ancient tradition has been so vigorously attacked and defended. The apparent agreement by both parties to the debate that accuracy and Lucan authorship stand or fall together is somewhat curious. The opponents of the Lucan tradition have attempted to prove from definitely established inaccuracies or contradictions with the Epistles that a companion of Paul did not write these books. They have inferred that therefore inaccuracy pervades the work throughout. The defenders of tradition have assumed that Lucan authorship proved accuracy and that accuracy proved Lucan authorship. Evidence tending to establish either point was felt to strengthen the other. As the *reductio ad absurdum* of such a view I may quote the quite serious axiom with which Ramsay begins his latest *apologia:* "It may, of course, be taken for granted that, if Luke did not write the Acts, it could not possibly be accepted [as trustworthy]. The case for belief rests on his personality."

Anyone familiar with these two moot questions must have followed our discussion with some impatience because of our studied avoidance of these issues. Only a few occasional hints bearing on them have been thrown out at relevant points in our analysis. It is not intended that even here we should attempt to canvass fully the historical trustworthiness of these writings. It must suffice for us to indicate merely the general bearing of our analysis upon the matter.

Now it is obvious that no analysis of origin can change the actual value for history of a given writing. Its historical accuracies or inaccuracies were there when it was written, and we cannot now change it. What Pilate said of his superscription on the cross holds true of other writings. False or true, for better or for worse, what stands written stands written. The writing of Luke-Acts has passed into history as an historical event, and it is an unalterable fact like every other fact:

> The Moving Finger writes; and, having writ,
> Moves on; nor all your Piety nor Wit
>   Shall lure it back to cancel half a Line,
> Nor all your Tears wash out a Word of it.

The utmost, then, that either the analysis of a book's origin or the more direct discussion of its reliability can accomplish is to affect the opinion of its modern readers. Its own intrinsic value can neither appreciate nor depreciate at the hand of friend or foe.

The method we have here followed of viewing the writings of Luke as a work originating by a definite historical process in past time lays emphasis upon this finality of its creation. Prior to the question of its truth we have set the question of its genesis. It may be confidently claimed that this order of procedure often throws light on the question of historicity, and perhaps more often gives the question of historicity a less insistent place in our thoughts. It is desirable to approach historical records in this sequence and with this distinction. We should inquire what the author thought took place before we ask what took place. We should ask why the author narrates it as he does before we ask whether it is true as he narrates it. The study of the making of a book is a prerequisite to its evaluation.

All four factors in the making of Luke-Acts affected its historical trustworthiness. Of great significance was the material out of which it was created, the written sources, oral information or personal experience of the writer. The accuracy of this material settled in advance the maximum accuracy possible to the evangelist. He could decrease its accuracy by changes made in using it. Where the material was contradictory he could exercise his own judgment in selecting what he thought the preferable version. He could omit entirely what seemed to him untrue. He could not, however, without some evidence to rely on, present any fuller or more accurate account than the total available material contained. As we have said, the evange-

list could rise no higher than his source. In that respect
his material largely determines his accuracy. He can improve its literary or artistic or religious values, but not
its historical worth. He can check up one source by
another, but except for the most unusual and fortunate
conjecture he can never be more correct than the best
information that comes to him. He can be only as accurate as all that he read or heard or experienced permitted
him to be.

The second factor in the making of Luke-Acts also
affects its value—the methods and standards of the time.
Aside from the value of one's sources much depends on
the way one uses them. If they are reproduced verbatim
and in full, the copy has the same actual value as the
original. If they are unintentionally changed, or if they
are changed without superior knowledge, there is a loss.
This applies to both oral and written sources. Even when
an author is an eyewitness much depends on the habits
prevailing of interpreting phenomena, and of course all
through the history of the tradition prior to the evangelist
the motives, preconceptions and emphases prevalent in the
group of transmitters have had their effect.

The third factor in the making of Luke-Acts is the
author's personality. This, too, affects the accuracy of
his work. The individual coefficient is, as every expert in
legal evidence knows, a very variable element. It is not,
however, the author's identity that needs to be known,
his name or even his own part in the events, but his personal habits of mind as affecting the reliability of his work.
It is for this reason that even for the matter of accuracy
the tradition of authorship by Luke is, as we have said,
relatively unimportant. Authorship by a companion of
Paul is in itself no guarantee of trustworthiness. A reliable second-hand report sometimes excels the first-hand
impressions of eyewitnesses. Paul himself might not have
been able to write as objective a biography as is provided

by this obscure admirer. As a gospel writer, Paul might have proved less able to achieve a detached interest in the past or a faithful reproduction of what the eyewitnesses who had "known Christ according to the flesh" reported of him than many an unknown contemporary. So significant for the historical value of the gospels is the personal equation of those who undertook to write them. The real riddle, for example, that baffles us in the Gospel of John is not the name or personal history of the writer, or even the religious environment which influenced him, but a kind of inscrutable "Johannine" personal psychology and manner of authorship. If we should decide that he himself actually saw and bare witness, we have still to ask *how* he saw and bare witness. In like manner, though not so profoundly, the personality of his less mystical predecessor has operated on the tone, the character, and inevitably even the accuracy of the Third Gospel and the Acts.

Finally, the author's purposes affect in a greater or less degree the trustworthiness of his report. His major purpose may be accuracy itself, and such an object will assure the reader. That is why authors so often mention it. But aside from the difficulties which beset this aim, difficulties inherent in the accessible materials and in the limitations of current literary technique, no ancient writer, not to mention modern ones, aimed with singleness of mind at this exclusive goal. Other purposes more or less consciously were his collaborators. Without implying any intent to deceive or suppress on the author's part, we may say that every edifying, entertaining, interpreting, apologetic or polemic impulse gives the writing a corresponding limitation in the selection and presentation of the most colorless factual data.

In view of the complexity of the process of authorship, and the many factors on which historical accuracy depends, it becomes obvious that a uniform grade of reliability can hardly be expected in any writing. The author's own method may be careful throughout or careless throughout, but this does not mean uniformity in his result. It is obvious that inferences cannot be drawn from a few matters to the whole. A number of proved errors or a few proved facts in a work do not carry much presumption about the value of the rest. Even an eyewitness may be reliable in one type of information and unreliable in another. When an author's sources are of different merit, his product will differ accordingly. Further, this accuracy will be affected in quite varying degree at different parts of his work both by the prevailing standards of writing and by the conscious aims and motives of the evangelist as he arranges and narrates his story. A study of the origin of Luke and Acts will warn us against passing judgment for or against the work as a whole. Our alternatives are not to take it or leave it, to accept it "from cover to cover" or to reject it *in toto*. We shall prefer to form our verdict about its contents piece by piece.

Such a detailed testing of accuracy is not here possible, and in many points is never possible, since the criteria of historicity are not available. A few general observations bearing on the subject may be ventured where some data for forming a judgment exist. We have in the Gospel of Mark, for example, an actual source of Luke, and we can discover how accurately Luke's paraphrase represents the original. The comparison is reassuring for this stage in the process. Luke evidently reproduced his sources faithfully, in general purport though not in wording. He omits some things in his sources which seemed to him unimportant or perhaps untrue. He rephrases somewhat even the sayings of Jesus. Rarely, to judge from his use of Mark, does he alter violently either the sayings or the narrative. He retains, with slight exception, the order of Mark. He does not profess to know more than Mark about the time or place of his anecdotes, but rather less. Apparently he does not intend to exaggerate Mark's mira-

N*

cles. If we may draw any inference from this evidence, we shall feel some confidence that wherever Luke employed a written source that we cannot control he may have used the same method. This does not prove that Luke's version is complete and accurate; it proves only that it is not less accurate and that it does not attempt to be more complete than was the information he relied on. The earlier material may have left much to be desired. All we can say is that the last editor apparently did not further much impair its value because of his own way of handling what came to him.

In another section and in another way the accuracy of Luke's work permits of some testing. His outline of Paul's missionary career not only is confirmed constantly by striking coincidences in the Pauline letters—references to Paul's own life, like his escape over the wall of Damascus, and to his associates, most of whom if named in Acts are named also in the Epistles; there is further the testimony of archeology to the geographical and political setting of Acts. Here again we often feel assured; but it is reasonable to combine with our assurance a good deal of doubt in other sections of Acts where Luke and Paul do not so obviously agree, or where archeological confirmation is not forthcoming.

For this same latter half of Acts we have from non-Christian sources some chronological data also, which, while not confirming the evangelist exactly, suggest no limits of date into which the sequence of events and scanty references to officials, as found in Acts, cannot be fitted. But we may at the same time reasonably doubt whether the evangelist's information was as reliable for earlier Jewish history, when, for example, in contrast to Josephus he seems to place the census of Quirinius in the reign of Herod the Great (*pace* Sir William Ramsay), and Lysanias of Abilene under Tiberius, and Theudas prior to the time of Fadus the procurator and even prior to Judas of Galilee.

These and many other details both favorable and unfavorable to Luke's accuracy must of course be very carefully tested before a verdict is reached on them, but our present purpose is merely to suggest that the same work can be relatively more true in some parts than in others and not equally reliable in its various types of information.

Not only the author's sources, but also the various conventional usages to which we have referred cause variations in his trustworthiness. The prevailing conceptions of nature and miracle explain why he describes the marvelous as he does and why he emphasizes it. Even in modern times large groups of persons differ in their view of such things, but they deal with the material in accordance with the standpoint which they severally share. Luke is neither more credulous nor more scientific than might be expected of one in his circumstances. And if by our modern standards the ancient attitude toward miracle seems lacking in reality and accuracy, we shall expect less trustworthiness in passages that involve the miraculous than in those that do not. By an even more clearly recognized ancient convention Luke's speeches were, as we have said, probably written without intending strict historical accuracy.

While it is necessary, therefore, to avoid extreme claims for our historian, our study of the origin of his work will remind us that in our doubts we are casting no moral reflection upon him. In so far as his inaccuracy is due to his sources he is exempt from blame; indeed, in so far as his accuracy is due to his sources he is not deserving of special praise. In transmitting what information came to him he was merely a faithful scribe, subject to the limitations of his material, or sharing its merits. Our study of that material, its growth, selection and molding by tradition will help us to understand that it was not "cunningly devised fables," that it was not invented either by Luke or by his predecessors with any desire to mislead. It was the inevitable growth of given seed in given soil, the seed being the historical facts, the soil the environment of Christian faith and piety.

In like manner our study will deter us from complaining of Luke's methods of writing, since we realize that he is merely conforming to the standards of his time. We can demand of him nothing more. Other ages of historiography, including our own, have also had their standards, not always superior to those of antiquity. We today may not invent speeches, but we often invent psychological explanations; we may not overlook the social and the economic factors in history, but perhaps we overlook the personal and the spiritual elements. We lay stress on verbatim quotation and insist on well-documented footnotes, but our sources are not always infallible, our transcription not always accurate, our use of them not always ingenuous or unprejudiced.

The main effect of our method of study upon the question of historicity will be, however, neither to verify nor to correct the data recorded in these volumes, but to give reality, interest and attention to the later stage of history which the making of Luke-Acts represents. Instead of trying to conceal our real ignorance with plausible speculation, *obscurum per obscurius,* we shall turn our minds from the hidden underlying facts to the more accessible fact of the creation of this significant literary production. That fact itself—the making of Luke-Acts—by its concreteness, its verifiable fitness to its historical setting, and its irrefutable revelation of its author's mind, times and heart can lend to our study of Scripture an element of historical certainty and human interest, which the more controversial and debatable subjects of date, authorship, inspiration, orthodoxy and accuracy do not permit.

INDEX

369

names of places, in Mark, 77 f.,
84; in itineraries of Acts,
60 f., 144; omitted or retained,
53 f., 60; explained, 241 f.;
foreign, 123 f.; confusion of
spelling, 171; variation of
spelling, 227.
"native place," 167 (and *n*).
Nazareth, 38, 95, 188, 189, 242,
262 *n.*, 268, 277, 334.
Nepos, 132.
Nero, 7, 87, 315.
Nestle, E., 243.
Niese, B., 166, 169 *n.*
night, scenes at, 249 f.; in Josephus, 250 *n.*
Nineveh, 208 *n.*
Norden, Eduard, 6, 8, 125 *n.*,
142 *n.*, 145, 196 *n.*
Nunc Dimittis, 192.

objectivity, of Mark, 79 f., 83,
91 f.; of Luke-Acts, 320, 347.
Octateuch, 11.
officials, government, 240, 247,
313, 327.
Olympiodorus, 204.
omissions by Luke-Acts, 16 f.,
320 f., 349, 365; of Jesus' limitations, 92; of Mark vi. 47-
viii. 26, 95.
Onasander, 202 f.
optative, 115, 239.
optimism, 266 f.
order of Luke-Acts, 102, 104,
345.
Origen, 72.
Overbeck, Franz, 196 *n.*

pairs, of persons, 250 *n.*; of
illustrations 233 f.; of parables, 149, 233.
Palestine, knowledge of, 84, 170,
241, 242, 244; style appropriate to, 227, 242; Latin in,
89 *n.*
Papal   Biblical   Commission,
66 *n.*

Papias, 28 f., 50, 71, 72, 86, 87,
88, 105, 130.
papyri, 29, 116 f., 118, 119, 120,
141, 194, 205 f., 215.
parables, literary form of, 55;
purpose of, 80; in non-Marcan sources, 110; in Mark, 78,
80; in Jewish literature, 135,
149-152, 150 *n.*; pairs of, 149,
233; parables of Jesus, Dissimilar Guests, 234; Dives and
Lazarus, 234, 251, 262, 279;
Drag Net, 233; Fruitless Fig
Tree, 296; Good Samaritan,
119, 253, 259, 265; Hid Treasure, 233; Importunate Neighbor, 233, 269; Importunate
Widow, 233, 269, 294; Leaven,
149, 233; Lost Coin, 101, 149,
233, 260; Lost Sheep, 100, 101,
149, 233; Marriage Feast,
100; Mote and Beam, 100,
148 *n.;* Mustard Seed, 100,
149, 233; New Wine after
Old, 233; Obedient Servants,
150, 268; Pearl of Great
Price, 233; Pharisee and Publican, 259, 269; Pounds, 100,
249, 260, 293; Prodigal Son,
233, 237, 253, 259, 265; Prudent Builder, 149, 234, 260;
Prudent Warrior, 149, 234;
Rich Fool, 151, 260, 262;
Sower, 266 *n.*, 294; Talents,
100, 248; Two Builders, 102,
149, 151, 153 f., 233, 244; Two
Debtors, 234, 260, 268; Unjust
Judge, 233, 269, 294; Unjust
Steward, 151, 259, 260, 262;
Wicked   Husbandmen,   151,
269, 293 f.
Paraclete, 284.
paradox, 54, 148.
paragraphs, 324 f.
parallelism, Semitic, 54, **123,**
147, 152, 233; in biography,
231 f.; in illustrations, 233 f.
paraphrase, in use of sources,
67 f., 158, 160 f.; in repeating